JOURNAL OF APPLIED SPORT PSYCHOLOGY

Volume 11 Number 2, September 1999

The Official Journal of the Association for the Advancement of Applied Sport Psychology

Contents

JOURNAL OF APPLIED SPORT PSYCHOLOGY **11,** 171–180 (1999)

Exercise Imagery: Its Nature and Measurement

HEATHER A. HAUSENBLAS AND CRAIG R. HALL

The University of Western Ontario

WENDY M. RODGERS

University of Alberta

KRISTA J. MUNROE

The University of Western Ontario

The lack of research on imagery use by exercisers and the success of imagery use by athletes—for both motivational and cognitive functions—highlights the need to examine imagery use by exercisers. Thus, the general purpose of the present research was to (a) examine the nature of exercise imagery and (b) develop a questionnaire to assess exercise imagery. To this end three research phases were undertaken. Phase 1 examined the nature of imagery use by exercisers and Phases 2 and 3 involved the development and psychometric analysis of the Exercise Imagery Questionnaire-Aerobic Version (EIQ-AV). Results of Phase 1 revealed that 75.7% of the exercisers (N = 144) reported using exercise imagery for both motivational (e.g., goal attainment and psychological management) and cognitive (e.g., performance enhancement and learning) purposes. In Phases 2 and 3, the psychometric analysis of the EIQ-AV revealed three factors (i.e., Energy, Appearance, and Technique) with adequate internal consistency estimates. Suggestions for future research on exercise imagery and with the EIQ-AV are discussed.

There has been increased attention, interest, and research given to the role of imagery in physical activity, particularly sport. In the sport arena the value of mental imagery as a performance enhancing technique is well recognized by athletes, coaches, and sport psychologists (Hall, 1995). Athletes report using imagery for both motivational (e.g., imagining winning a medal) and cognitive functions (e.g., imagining strategies; Hall,

---

Please address correspondence to: Craig R. Hall, School of Kinesiology, The University of Western Ontario, London, ON, N6A 3K7, Phone: 519-661-2111, ext 8388, Fax: 519-661-2008, Email: chall@julian.uwo.ca

1041-3200/99/0171–0180$1.00/0

Mack, Paivio, & Hausenblas, 1998). Coaches often encourage athletes to use imagery to help facilitate the improvement and learning of skills (Hall & Rodgers, 1989). As well, imagery is often a central component in the mental training programs developed and implemented by sport psychologists (e.g., Daw & Burton, 1994). Given the recognized value and widespread use of imagery in sport, it is not surprising that researchers have been interested in investigating why imagery works and how athletes can use it effectively.

Sport, however, is only one form of physical activity. It is conceivable that imagery may be used in other forms of physical activity, in particular exercise. Hall (1995) was the first to propose that exercisers may use imagery by suggesting that imagery may be as powerful a motivator in exercise as it is in sport. He argued that regular exercisers may imagine themselves participating in exercise, enjoying their workouts, and achieving their desired exercise goals.

Unfortunately, research examining exercise imagery is lacking. Indeed, there is only anecdotal evidence supporting Hall's (1995) proposal that exercisers use imagery. For example, the following anecdote illustrates the motivational function of exercise imagery: "For weeks before actually starting to exercise, she visualized herself moving freely as she worked out. She enjoyed this image and later it helped her to do what she wanted to do" (Pipher, 1995, p. 102).

The lack of research on imagery use by exercisers and the success of imagery use by athletes—for both motivational and cognitive functions—highlights the need to examine imagery use by exercisers. An investigation of exercise imagery must start with a determination of how extensively, if at all, exercisers use imagery. It must then consider what functions exercise imagery may serve. A measure of exercise imagery becomes imperative if the relationships among exercise imagery and variables known to influence exercise intentions, attitudes, and behavior are to be examined. Thus, the general purpose of the present study was to (a) determine the nature of imagery use by exercisers and (b) develop a questionnaire to assess exercise imagery. To this end three phases were undertaken.

PHASE 1

The purpose of Phase 1 was to determine the nature of imagery use by exercisers. Based on research conducted on imagery use by athletes (Hall et al., 1998; Hall, Rodgers, & Barr, 1990; Salmon, Hall, & Haslam, 1994) three basic questions were investigated: *When* do exercisers use imagery?, *Why* do exercisers use imagery?, and *What* do exercisers image?

Method

Participants

Participants were 144 volunteer aerobic exercisers (*M* age = 23.08, *SD* = 7.46) from a university community. The majority of the participants were female (92.3%) and full-time university students (85.4%). The participants reported having exercised for an average of 7.63 years (SD = 6.24) with a frequency of 4.01 (SD = 1.51) times per week.

Procedure

An open-ended approach was utilized to examine the nature of imagery use in exercisers. This procedure ensured that the participants were active agents in identifying the meaning of the construct (i.e., the semantics and descriptors used), and thus eliminated the experimenter-demand characteristics of a pre-imposed list of imagery situations. To this end, participants read the following description of exercise imagery:

> Imagery involves mentally seeing yourself exercising. The image in your mind should approximate the actual physical activity as closely as possible. Imagery may include sensations like hearing the aerobic music and feeling yourself move through the exercises. Imagery can also be associated with emotions (e.g., getting psyched up or energized), staying focused (e.g., concentrating on aerobic class and not being distracted), setting exercise plans/goals (e.g., imagining achieving the goal of losing weigh), etc.

After reading this description, participants indicated if they ever used exercise imagery. Participants who reported using such imagery were then asked the frequency of imagery use on a 7-point scale ranging from 1 (*rarely*) to 7 (*often*). They were next asked the following questions: (a) "What do you imagine about exercising? List all the things you imagine," (b) "Why do you imagine exercising? List all your reasons," and (c) "When do you imagine exercising? List all the situations."

Participants were informed that the study was voluntary and that their responses would be confidential. Once informed consent was obtained, the questionnaire was completed either immediately before or after a regularly scheduled aerobic class. The questionnaire was returned directly to the experimenter or placed in a drop off box located in the aerobic room. Completion of the questionnaire took approximately 10 minutes. A response rate of 96.6% was obtained.

Results and Discussion

The majority of the participants reported using exercise imagery (75.7%). The frequency of imagery use by these participants was relatively high (M = 4.19, SD = 1.58). All participants that indicated using imagery responded to the open-ended questions.

Participants provided a total of 177 responses to the question "When do you imagine yourself exercising?" Participants imagined themselves exercising most frequently before going to bed/sleep (n = 36). Other times exercise imagery was reported was during class/studying (n = 32), when daydreaming (n = 30), before/after exercising (n = 20), while walking/driving (n = 13), while exercising (n = 10), waking up/morning (n = 10), after/while eating (n = 9), when feeling out of shape (n = 7), when listening to music ($n = 4$), watching TV ($n = 4$), and when stressed ($n = 2$).

Participants reported a total of 246 responses to the question "What do you imagine about exercising?" The responses were organized into representative categories, the content of the categories were labeled, and the percentage of total responses falling in each category were calculated. As a reliability check, this procedure was undertaken independently by two of the authors and an agreement rate of 91% was obtained. The following nine categories emerged: body image ($n = 48$), techniques/strategies ($n = 45$), feeling good about oneself ($n = 37$), motivation ($n = 35$), general exercise ($n = 22$), fitness/health ($n = 21$), music ($n = 20$), goals ($n = 14$), and maintaining focus ($n = 4$).

Participants provided a total of 159 responses to the question "Why do you imagine exercising?" Following the procedure above, two of the authors independently categorized the responses and an 86% agreement rate was obtained. The following 11 categories emerged: motivation ($n = 44$), feeling good about oneself ($n = 31$), body image ($n = 21$), strategies/techniques ($n = 16$), stress relief ($n = 12$), fitness/health ($n = 8$), goals ($n = 7$), habit/routine ($n = 6$), music ($n = 5$), getting energized ($n = 5$), and maintaining focus ($n = 4$).

The results of Phase 1 indicated that imagery use was frequent among exercisers, was employed at a variety of times, and was used for both motivational (e.g., feeling good about oneself, getting in shape), and to a lesser extent, cognitive purposes (e.g., rehearsing strategies and techniques). However, in order to further examine exercise imagery and how it relates to other psychological variables, a measure of exercise imagery is required.

PHASE 2

The purpose of Phase 2 was the construction and psychometric analysis of a questionnaire designed to assess imagery use by exercisers. First, construction of the questionnaire involved developing the individual items. The participants' open-ended responses from Phase 1 provided the basis for item development. This procedure reduced the possibility of exclusive investigator biases, and enabled item development using language and concepts that participants were familiar with and understood. Second, psychometric analysis (i.e., content, factorial, and concurrent validity) of the questionnaire was undertaken. Specifically, in regards to concurrent validity the relationship between imagery use and exercise frequency was examined. Commensurate with research in sport (e.g., Hall et al., 1990; Salmon et al., 1994), it was hypothesized that frequent exercisers would report more imagery use (as based on their scores on the questionnaire) than less frequent exercisers.

Method

Participants

Participants in Phase 2 were from two distinct samples. Sample 1 was 307 volunteer aerobic exercise participants (97.4% females; *M* age =

22.92, *SD* = 6.16) from a university community. The sample reported exercising for approximately 8 years (*M* = 8.04, *SD* = 6.10) for an average of 5.64 (*SD* = 2.76) hours per week. Sample 2 was 171 volunteer aerobic exercise participants (97.7% female; *M* age = 22.42, *SD* = 5.14) from a different university community. The sample reported exercising for approximately 8 years (*M* = 7.65, *SD* = 6.80) with an average frequency of 5.73 hours per week (*SD* = 2.98).

Measures

Based on the open-ended results from Phase 1, a questionnaire was developed. The questionnaire items represented the categories that were derived from the open-ended responses. Examples of items from the categories were: motivation ("When I imagine exercising, it keeps me going"), feeling good about oneself ("I imagine the good feeling associated with exercising"), fitness/health ("I imagine getting fit by exercising"), technique/strategies ("I imagine doing the patterns/steps"), body image ("I imagine toning up by exercising"), stress relief ("When I imagine exercising, it relieves my stress"), goals ("I imagine achieving my exercise goals"), music ("I imagine moving to the music in an exercise class"), getting energized ("When I imagine exercising, I get psyched up"), and maintaining focus ("When I imagine exercising, it helps me to stay focused").

To establish content validity, three exercise professionals and three exercise participants commented on the wording, phraseology, and scoring of the questionnaire items. Minor revisions were made to the questionnaire items based on their comments. This process resulted in a questionnaire containing 23 items with each item being rated on a 9-point scale ranging from 1 (*never engaging in this type of imagery*) to 9 (*always engaging in this type of imagery*).

Procedure

An identical protocol to that employed in Phase 1 was followed. Completion of the questionnaire took approximately 10 minutes and response rates of 96.5% and 97.7% were obtained from samples 1 and 2, respectively.

Results and Discussion

To reduce the items to a meaningful and manageable structure, a principal components factor analysis with varimax rotation was conducted for each sample. Criteria for retention of an item on a factor was set at .50. From this analysis a three-factor structure emerged accounting for 63.8% of the variance in sample 1 and 67.6% of the variance in sample 2. The first factor was labeled Energy (e.g., "When I imagine exercising, it relieves my stress"), the second factor was labeled Appearance (e.g., "I imagine losing weight by exercising"), the third factor was labeled Technique (e.g., "I imagine doing the patterns/steps"). The three factors il-

Table 1
Means and standard deviations of the EIQ—AV subscales for high and low frequency exercisers in sample 2

Subscale	High *M (SD)*	Low *M (SD)*	*F* Value *df* (1,70)
Appearance	7.82 (1.05)	7.16 (1.54)	3.85, $p < .05$
Technique	6.76 (1.17)	5.44 (1.98)	14.8, $p < .01$
Energy	6.73 (1.18)	5.55 (1.98)	8.81, $p < .01$

lustrate the multidimensional use of imagery by exercisers. Cronbach's alpha calculated for the three factors for both samples ranged from .81 to .90 (Nunnally, 1978).

To examine concurrent validity the relationship between imagery use and exercise frequency was examined. The exercisers in sample 2 were subdivided on the basis of number of hours they exercised per week. To obtain extreme groups, participants ($n = 38$) exercising three hours or less a week (which represented the lower 22.2% of the distribution) constituted the low frequency group, while participants ($n = 35$) exercising eight or more hours a week (which represented the upper 23.5% of the distribution) constituted the high frequency group. To determine if these two groups differed on the subscales (i.e., Appearance, Energy, and Technique), a multivariate analysis of variance was performed in which the group (i.e., low frequency versus high frequency exercisers) served as the independent variable and the subscale scores served as the dependent variables. There was a significant multivariate main effect for frequency of exercise, Wilks' lambda = .82, $F(3,68) = 4.84$, $p < .01$. Univariate ANOVA's revealed that the low frequency exercisers reported significantly less imagery use than high frequency exercisers on all three subscales (see Table 1). This result parallels those found for athletes; elite athletes use imagery more then novice and recreational level athletes (Barr & Hall, 1992; Hall et al., 1990; Salmon et al., 1994).

PHASE 3

The general purpose of Phase 3 was to further examine the psychometric properties of the instrument developed in Phase 2, now termed the Exercise Imagery Questionnaire—Aerobic Version (EIQ—AV). First, confirmatory factor analysis was undertaken to determine if exercise imagery was a multidimensional construct consisting of three factors (i.e., Appearance, Energy, and Technique). In this case we were testing the fit of the overall model to data collected for this purpose (Byrne, 1989). Second, five day test-retest reliability of the EIQ—AV was undertaken.

Method

Participants

To conduct the confirmatory factor analysis. Two distinct samples were collected. Sample 1 were 144 volunteer exercisers (89.0% female; *M* age

Table 2
Results of the confirmatory factor analysis

	χ^2	χ^2/df	RMSR	Standard-ized RMSR	GFI	Ad-justed GFI	NFI	NNFI	CFI
Sample 1	40.5	1.69	.05	.05	.94	.89	.92	.95	.97
Sample 2	49.6	2.06	.05	.05	.96	.93	.95	.96	.97

= 22.01, *SD* = 5.50) from a university community. Sample 2 were 267 volunteer exercisers (97.6% female; *M* age = 22.39, *SD* = 5.12) from a different university community. To examine the test-retest reliability of the EIQ—AV, data was collected on 18 university students (*M* age = 21.55, *SD* = 1.49) who reported exercising an average of 9.32 hours per week (*SD* = 6.48).

Procedure

First, to conduct the confirmatory factor analysis the EIQ—AV was administered to the two samples of exercise participants. An identical protocol to the previous two phases was employed and response rates of 96.3% and 94.7% were obtained for samples 1 and 2, respectively. Second, to examine test-retest reliability, the EIQ—AV was administered on two occasions (five days apart) and an overall response rate of 90.0% was obtained.

Results and Discussion

A confirmatory factor analysis was conducted for each sample using the LISREL 8 computer program. As suggested by Gauvin and Rejeski (1993), various fit indices were used to determine the adequacy of the fit of the model. These were the chi-square statistic (χ^2), the ratio of chi-square to degrees of freedom (χ^2/df), the root mean square residual (RMSR) and the standardized root mean square residual (Standardized RMSR), the goodness of fit index (GFI) and the adjusted goodness of fit index (AGFI), the normed fit index (NFI) and the non-normed fit index (NNFI), as well as the comparative fit index (CFI). A nonsignificant χ^2 index indicates a good fit, but is rarely obtained in practice. A χ^2/df index that is smaller than 2.0 suggests a good fit. An RMSR index of .1 indicates a reasonably good fit, whereas an RMSR of .05 represents an excellent fit. It is desirable to have non-normed fit indices and comparative fit indices that are .9 or higher (Gauvin & Rejeski, 1993).

The model for both samples did not initially meet the criteria for 5 of the 9 indices which would suggest a poor model fit. The modification indices suggested that specific items from all three factors be removed. This revised model was tested and yielded a good fit as reported in Table 2. The model for each sample now met 7 of the 9 criterion indices. For

Table 3
Items comprising the Exercise Imagery Questionnaire—Aerobics Version

Item	Factor
1. When I imagine exercising, it keeps me going during the day.	Energy
2. I imagine toning up by exercising.	Appearance
3. When I imagine exercising, it relieves my stress.	Energy
4. When learning a new routine, I imagine doing the moves perfectly.	Technique
5. I imagine form/body position.	Technique
6. I imagine becoming healthy by exercising.	Appearance
7. When I imagine exercising, it takes my mind off my work.	Energy
8. I imagine losing weight by exercising.	Appearance
9. When I imagine exercising, it gets me energized.	Energy/Technique

sample 1, the AGFI was just under .90, and for sample 2 the χ^2/df was slightly larger than 2.0. The other criterion not met in both samples was χ^2. Stevens (1996) and Byrne (1989) have both indicated that χ^2 is better used as a descriptive statistic than a criterion of model fit because, although it can indicate a fundamental problem with the model, it is also sensitive to sample size and can remain significant due to this factor alone, regardless of the model fit. Furthermore, one item loaded on two factors, Energy and Technique, so it is clear these two factors are not orthogonal, thus increasing the likelihood of a significant χ^2 (Stevens, 1996). The items comprising the three factors of the final version of the EIQ-AV are given in Table 3.

Cronbach's alphas calculated for the three factors for both samples ranged from .71 to .85, with one exception; the alpha value for Technique for sample 1 was .65. Finally, test-retest reliability of the EIQ—AV was satisfactory (r = .88).

General Discussion

The general purpose of the present research was to examine the nature of exercise imagery and develop a measure of it. Results revealed that most exercisers use imagery, they use imagery at a variety of times (e.g., before going to bed/sleep, during class/studying), and they do so for three main reasons. First, exercisers imagine themselves becoming healthier and improving their physical appearance. Second, they use imagery for psychological management (e.g., they get energized and/or psyched up). Third, they imagine doing the steps and patterns involved in the various exercises. An instrument, the EIQ—AV, was successfully developed to measure exercise imagery, and these three reasons for exercising are represented in the questionnaire by the three factors labeled Appearance, Energy, and Technique, respectively. It was also found that frequent exercisers use more imagery than less frequent exercisers. This finding suggests that imagery use may be related to exercise participation, as proposed by Hall (1995).

Despite the adequate psychometric properties of the EIQ—AV, there are a number of limitations with the present research that need to be taken into consideration when interpreting the findings and planning future research. One limitation is that the participants were participating in only one form of exercise—aerobic exercise. To increase the generalizability of the EIQ—AV, it would be valuable to assess other exercise activities (e.g., jogging, weightlifting) to determine if those exercisers use imagery for the same functions as aerobic participants. This would, of course, require the modification of the EIQ—AV to assess general exercise imagery.

A second limitation is that the present study was correlational in nature. Longitudinal and experimental studies are needed to examine the full utility of exercise imagery. Future studies might implement interventions based on an extended use of imagery over time. Knowing that exercisers use imagery extensively opens the possibility of changing their image content by having them participate in imagery training programs.

A third limitation is that the samples examined were largely female undergraduate students who were avid exercisers (i.e., exercising at least three times a week). Thus, to examine the generalizability of exercise imagery further research is needed with more diverse samples in regards to sex (i.e., males), age (e.g., children, adolescents, elderly), occupation (e.g., blue-collar and white-collar populations), and exercise activity level (e.g., sedentary, low exercise level, moderate exercise level). Further, the data collected were from a self-selected, motivated sample and relied exclusively on self-report for assessment. Future research is needed to verify the results of this study using more diverse methods such as random sampling and behavioral observation.

Given the intent and nature of the present study, it is not possible to determine the relationship between exercise imagery and exercise behavior. Moreover, this relationship may not be a direct one. Hall (1995) proposes that exercise imagery is related to other variables (e.g., self-efficacy and incentives for physical activity) that influence exercise behavior (Rodgers & Gauvin, 1998). Exercise imagery may be an important source of self-efficacy. Indeed, self-efficacy can be derived from numerous sources (i.e., actual and vicarious performance experiences, physiological arousal, verbal persuasion, and observing others) including imagery (Bandura, 1997). Given that self-efficacy is related to continuing and increased participation in exercise (Rodgers & Gauvin, 1998), the size or extent of the relationship between exercise imagery and self-efficacy, as well as the ultimate influence on behavior, warrants future investigation. Furthermore, exercise imagery and its relationships with variables such as self-efficacy may have implications for research and intervention programs concerned with exercise participation and adherence. For example, if individuals imagine themselves getting psyched up and energized when they exercise, this may actually motivate them to exercise either directly, or indirectly through increasing their self-efficacy; of course, research is needed to confirm this.

In conclusion, the present research provides some insight into the nature of exercise imagery. The study of exercise imagery has merit because it was found to distinguish between frequent and less frequent exercisers. It may also distinguish regular exercisers from less adherent exercisers and excessive exercisers as proposed by Hall (1995), but this awaits further research to be determined. The brevity and ease of administration of the EIQ—AV should readily permit researchers to investigate such issues and allow them to better understand the use of imagery associated with exercise. We feel that the EIQ—AV can serve as a foundation upon which future exercise imagery research and measurement can be based. Indeed, our goal in this initial phase of development was not to answer every possible question; rather, to examine the nature of exercise imagery and develop a questionnaire with adequate psychometric properties, one that would stimulate research in the area of imagery and exercise.

REFERENCES

Bandura, A. (1997). *Self-efficacy: The exercise of control.* New York: Freeman.

Barr, K., & Hall, C. (1992). The use of imagery by rowers. *International Journal of Sport Psychology, 23,* 243–261.

Byrne, B. M. (1989). *A primer of LISEREL. Basic applications and programming for confirmatory factor analytic models.* New York: Springer-Verlag.

Daw, J., & Burton, D. (1994). Evaluation of a comprehensive psychological skills training program for collegiate tennis players. *The Sport Psychologist, 8,* 37–57.

Gauvin, L., & Rejeski, W. J. (1993). The exercise-induced feeling inventory: Development and initial validation. *Journal of Sport & Exercise Psychology, 15,* 403–423.

Hall, C. (1995). The motivational function of mental imagery for participation in sport and exercise. In J. Annett, B. Cripps, & H. Steinberg (Eds.) *Exercise addiction: Motivation for participation in sport and exercise* (pp. 15–21). Leicester, UK: British Psychological Society.

Hall, C., Mack, D., Paivio, A., & Hausenblas, H. (1998). Imagery use by athletes: Development of the Sport Imagery Questionnaire. *International Journal of Sport Psychology, 29,* 73–89.

Hall, C. R., & Rodgers, W. M. (1989). Enhancing coaching effectiveness in figure skating through a mental skills training program. *The Sport Psychologist, 3,* 142–154.

Hall, C. R., Rodgers, W. M., & Barr, K. A. (1990). The use of imagery by athletes in selected sports. *The Sports Psychologist, 4,* 1–10.

Nunnally, J. C. (1978). *Psychometric theory* (2nd ed.) New York: McGraw-Hill.

Pipher, M. (1995). *Hunger pains. From fad diets to eating disorders—what every woman needs to know about food, dieting, and self-concept.* Massachusetts: Adams.

Rodgers, W. M., & Gauvin, L. (1998). Heterogeneity of incentives for physical activity and self-efficacy in high active and moderately active women exercisers. *Journal of Applied Social Psychology, 28,* 1016–1029.

Salmon, J., Hall, C., & Haslam, I. (1994). The use of imagery by soccer players. *Journal of Applied Sport Psychology, 6,* 116–133.

Stevens, J. (1996). *Applied multivariate statistics for the social sciences.* Mahwah, NJ: Lawrence Erlbaum Associates.

Manuscript received: May 15, 1998
Revision submitted: May 10, 1999

JOURNAL OF APPLIED SPORT PSYCHOLOGY **11,** 181–193 (1999)

A Personal Development Model of Sport Psychology for Athletes with Disabilities

JEFFREY J. MARTIN

Division of Health, Physical Education and Recreation, Wayne State University

Achieving superior sport performance is often the result of well developed psychological skills (Morris & Thomas, 1995). However, little is known about psychological skill development in athletes with disabilities (Hanrahan, 1998). The purpose of the present paper is to help sport psychologists in their work with athletes with physical disabilities. Although there are many similarities among athletes with and without disabilities, sport psychologists would benefit from an awareness of information unique to athletes with disabilities (Asken, 1991). I use a broad interpretation of psychological skills based on a holistic perspective and a personal development model (Vealey, 1988). Information is presented in the three areas of foundation, psychological, and facilitative skills, methods, and factors.

Achieving personal excellence in sport is dependent on athletes' cognitive and affective states (Morris & Thomas, 1995). However, psychological skill development for optimal performance states is typically presented in the context of able-bodied sport. Fortunately, sport psychologists have begun to note the importance of psychological skills training (PST) for athletes with physical disabilities (Asken, 1991; Hanrahan, 1998). However, few authors have discussed how sport psychologists may work with athletes with disabilities (e.g., Hanrahan, 1998) and most of that literature focuses on the development of specific psychological skills.

Jeffrey J. Martin, Division of Health, Physical Education and Recreation, College of Education, Wayne State University.

This manuscript was completed with the support of the Department of Human Movement and Exercise Science at the University of Western Australia while on sabbatical leave from Wayne State University. I would like to thank Ed Acevedo, Robert Eklund, Michael Sachs, Allan Smith, Robert Weinberg, two anonymous reviewers, and the section editor of the Journal of Applied Sport Psychology for their helpful comments during the preparation of this manuscript.

Correspondence concerning this article should be addressed to Jeffrey J. Martin, 266 Matthaei Building, Division of Health, Physical Education, and Recreation, College of Education, Wayne State University, Detroit, Michigan 48202.

1041-3200/99/0181–0193$1.00/0

Although there are many similarities among athletes with and without disabilities (Hanrahan, 1998), it is important to understand the unique psychological, social, and physiological factors associated with disability and disability sport. Most notable is the major physical and/or psychological trauma that is experienced (Asken, 1991). For instance, most athletes (i.e., 85%) with a disability have an acquired disability (e.g., car accident) as opposed to a congenital disability (i.e., born with a disability).

Athletes with disabilities are also socialized into sport differently from able bodied athletes (Sherrill, 1998; Williams & Taylor, 1994). Unlike able-bodied sport, more disability sport opportunities exist for adults compared to children (Steadward & Wheeler, 1996). Parents of children with disabilities may be particularly supportive of their childrens' athletic participation (Martin & Mushett, 1996) as well as worry that their children may get hurt in sport (Nixon, 1988).

Everyday activities can be quite challenging for many athletes. Transportation difficulties and architectural barriers can make getting to practice and competition difficult. Finally, individuals with disabilities are considered minorities (Shapiro, 1993) and are often stigmatized (Goffman, 1963), discriminated against (Yuker, 1987) and abused (Sobsey, 1994). Athletes with disabilities are subject to these practices and attitudes just as non-athletes are. In brief, it is important to be aware of athletes' psycho-social climate.

I refer to athletes with disabilities to denote athletes who have physical (e.g., paraplegic) and sensory (e.g., blindness) disabilities, as opposed to mental dysfunction (e.g., Special Olympians). I do not intend to diminish unique individual differences due to disability onset (i.e., congenital versus acquired), disability type (e.g., cerebral palsy), or severity (e.g., class A visual acuity). As with any athlete, sport psychologists should strive to understand what is unique about their clients.

Consistent with Hanrahan's (1998) suggestion, I urge the reader to think athlete first and disability second. Sport psychologists should also be aware that they may have ambivalent feelings toward working with athletes with disabilities (Sherrill, 1997). It is not uncommon for people to have feelings of aversion or discomfort while, at the same time, feel sympathy and compassion (Katz, Haas, & Bailey, 1988). Awareness and communication can aide in reducing discomfort and misunderstandings of expectations (Makas, 1988).

The remainder of the current paper is based on Vealey's (1988) human development model of PST. Vealey (1988) borrowed from Danish and Hale's (1981) human development perspective which suggests "interventions in sport psychology would not emphasize short-term cures, but lifelong enhancement of personal growth, development, and maximal athletic performance" (Danish & Hale, 1981, p. 94). This framework has also been used with elite athletes (Gordon, 1992), children (Weiss, 1991), intercollegiate athletes (Chartrand & Lent, 1987), and at-risk youth (Danish & Nellen, 1997). Vealey's (1988) framework revolves around foundation, performance, and facilitative skills and methods. Each of these areas is introduced and applied to disability sport in the following sections.

Foundation Skills

Vealey's (1988) model emphasizes the importance of developing self-awareness, self-esteem/self-concept, and self-determination, because these qualities influence athletes' PST and their sport experience. The value of developing such positive characteristics is vital for personal growth (Danish & Nellen, 1997; Weiss, 1987) and for performance (Vealey, 1988).

Personal growth and specific psychological skill development should not be considered mutually exclusive.

Self-awareness. Self-awareness in sport refers to self-knowledge of one's affective states, cognitions, and behaviors (Ravizza, 1998). In the PST literature self-awareness often pertains to knowledge of ideal performance states (Orlick, 1986). Awareness of one's athletic strengths and weaknesses forms a basis for setting performance goals and a lack of awareness is often the result of heightened concern with the outcome (Ravizza, 1998). Murphy and Tammen (1998) highlighted the importance of awareness as a pre-requisite to self-monitoring and self-regulation leading to performance management. Thus, enhanced self-awareness can contribute to both improved sport performance and the development of psychological skills.

Athletes with disabilities may have difficulty distinguishing between pain from their disability and pain from a sport injury (Davis & Ferrara, 1995). Pain or discomfort from fatigue and exertion may also contribute to uncertainty and confusion. Ravizza (1998) suggested that having athletes monitor their physiological systems can promote awareness. Helping healthy competitors learn to focus their attention on important muscle groups (e.g., shoulder muscles) when relaxed and stressed, and when energized and tired, should aid athletes in understanding the differences among muscle tension/relaxation and muscle freshness/fatigue.

This awareness should subsequently help athletes distinguish between muscle tension from anxiety, muscle fatigue, disability condition, and muscle pain indicative of an injury. Reducing injury rates and time off from injuries among athletes with disabilities may be especially critical given their often short careers (Wheeler, Malone, VanVlack, Nelson, & Steadward, 1996) and limited competitive opportunities (Steadward & Wheeler, 1996).

It is also important for sport psychologists to view self-awareness as it relates to motivation. Researchers have discovered that athletes with disabilities have goal orientations and goals similar to able bodied athletes. For example, cerebral palsy (CP) athletes hold both task/performance and ego/outcome goal orientations (Martin, Adams-Mushett, & Smith, 1995). Social goals (Brasile & Hedrick, 1991) and aesthetic goals (Cooper, Sherrill, & Marshall, 1986) are also prominent.

However, athletes with disabilities may have particularly complex motivations and helping athletes become aware of their motivations is important for personal growth (Asken, 1991). For instance, athletes may use sport as a vehicle to adjust to their disability (Kirkby, 1995), a means of self-advocacy (Martin, 1996), to overcome marginalization (Wheeler et al., 1996) and to further the disability sport movement (Asken, 1991). Athletes have reported using sport as a vehicle to be seen as normal as well as being "beyond normal" (Wheeler et al., 1996).

Sport psychologists can promote awareness of ideal performance states and sport motivation through a variety of techniques discussed by Ravizza (1998). Team and individual discussions led by the sport psychologist aimed at exploring athletes' goals should increase self-knowledge. Similarly, use of a sport journal and performance feedback sheets will also promote self-exploration.

In summary, sport psychologists should help athletes with disabilities become aware of any complex and unique motivations that are related to the experience of having a disability (Asken, 1991). Increased self-awareness should promote better sport performance and increased personal growth.

Self-esteem/Self-concept. Debate about the definitions of numerous self suffixes (e.g., self-esteem) has a long history (Baumeister, 1997). Similar to Baumeister (1997), I use self-concept to denote a persons' self-description and self-esteem as an overall evaluative assessment of one's self-concept.

Self-esteem is a critical component of mental health (Rosenberg, 1979), and life adjustment (Sonstroem, 1997), and sport has long been heralded as a vehicle for self-esteem development (Weiss & Ebbeck, 1996). Researchers examining multidimensional self-concept have suggested that sport is more likely to influence physical self-concept compared to global self-concept (Whitehead & Corbin, 1997).

Research in disability sport and adapted physical activity indicates that athletes possess adequate self-esteem (Hutzler & Bar-Eli, 1993; Martin, 1999). Researchers have also shown that participation in sports contributes to enhanced self-esteem (Greenwood, Dzewaltowski, & French, 1990; Patrick, 1986).

In summary, limited research suggests that sport can lead to physical self-concept development and enhanced self-esteem. Sport psychologists should not neglect the importance of self-esteem/self-concept development and sport psychologists should be familiar with the literature examining self-esteem/self-concept development in sport (e.g., Whitehead & Corbin, 1997).

Self-determination. Self-determination refers to people's ability to direct and manage their own lives. Self-determination is a laudable goal for adapted educators (Hoffman & Field, 1995), rehabilitation counselors (Condeluci, 1989), rehabilitative sport personnel (Hutzler, 1990), and recreation therapists (Martin, 1996). Sport psychologists can be added to the above list because sport as a vehicle for self-determination may be a particularly vital goal for individuals with disabilities because they often report feelings of powerlessness (Asch, 1986).

Lord and Hutchinson (1993) found individuals with disabilities experienced extended feelings of powerlessness as a result of social isolation, unresponsive social services, poverty, and abuse. Participants who developed a sense of self-determination were often spurred by an awareness of their strengths. Confidence development, social support, and the process of social participation were particularly important in promoting self-determination.

Clearly disability sport can be an effective avenue for developing confidence (Greenwood, Dzewaltowski, & French, 1990) and enhancing social integration. Blinde and McClung (1997) reported that participants in a recreation program developed increased confidence in their physical capabilities. Participants also expanded their social interactions and gained increased social confidence to initiate social contact. Moucha (1991), a gold medalist in the 1988 Seoul Paralympics, has noted that "if it were not for sport, I might, as a hemiplegic cerebral palsy athlete, still be 'within my shell'" (p. 37).

In a study examining empowerment, Hutzler (1990) found wheelchair athletes reported greater functional independence derived from increased wheelchair proficiency, enhanced confidence and self-esteem, and perceptions of social acceptance, as a result of sport participation. Hutzler (1990) concluded that increased physical ability and enhanced self-referent cognitions (e.g., confidence) led to empowerment. It appears that sport can promote self-determinism through increased confidence in interpersonal, functional, and sport skills, and sport psychologists should view the development of self-determination as a critical goal.

Summary. Self-awareness, self-esteem/self-concept, and self-determinism are not typically viewed as directly impacting on performance. In addition, they are related and possess similar antecedents. Increased self-efficacy can lead to both enhanced self-esteem and feelings of self-determination. When viewing performance enhancement from a personal development model they are important considerations. Sport psychologists may clearly benefit their clients by being sensitive to the development of such personal qualities.

The greatest value of sport for athletes with disabilities may well be its potential to facilitate social integration, increase fitness, and promote self-efficacy leading to enhanced self-esteem and self-determination. Armed with a strong and enduring sense of self-esteem and self-determination, athletes with disabilities may then enjoy an enhanced quality of life.

Psychological Skills and Methods

Limited research suggests that athletes with disabilities use psychological skills (Martin & Mushett, 1997), would like to learn about psychological skills (Kirkby, 1995), mentally prepare for competition (Watanabe,

Cooper, Vosse, Baldini, & Robertson, 1992) and are successful at developing their psychological skills (Henschen, Horvat, & Roswal, 1992). There is no empirical or logical reason to suggest that psychological skills are different for athletes with disabilities compared to athletes without disabilities. However, the methods (e.g., communication mode) used may vary depending on disability type or severity. For instance, Meyers (1997) successfully improvised a consultation with a deaf athlete by passing notes. In the following sections I first discuss unique challenges to optimal performance states and then how psychological methods (i.e., goal setting, imagery, self-talk, and competition planning) can be used to develop psychological skills (e.g., anxiety management) for performance enhancement.

Unique Challenges. Optimal levels of confidence and anxiety, and a clear task oriented focus promote superior performance (Morris & Thomas, 1995). However, for many athletes sport can be an anxious experience and athletes with disabilities face stressors that are unique to their sport and disability. For example, athletes with CP can have abnormal reflex activity during competition (Sherrill, 1998).

Reliance on equipment (e.g., wheelchairs), other people (e.g., transportation needs) and medication also present unique challenges. For example, wheelchair athletes have to contend with poor road surfaces that not only impair performance but pose safety threats (Dattilo & Guadagnolo, 1988). Awareness of these challenges by sport psychologists can aid in helping athletes develop coping responses in preparation for difficulties.

Goal Setting. Athletes with disabilities can benefit from setting appropriate goals as a method to enhance motivation and confidence. Similar to able-bodied athletes, adherence to effective goal setting principles is recommended. Watanabe et al. (1992) reported that although athletes with disabilities used mental preparation, they could benefit from setting goals for training, competition, and dietary behaviors. Hedrick and Morse (1991) discussed goal setting practices for wheelchair basketball and provided a feedback chart for offensive and defensive behavioral goals. As Gordon (1992) suggests, the key factor in all mental skill development may be goal setting for self-regulation.

Imagery. Little is known about imagery use for individuals with physical disabilities although Hanrahan (1998) offers many useful suggestions. For instance, athletes imaging missing limbs may get frustrated or angry (Hanrahan, 1998). Surburg (1989) suggested that visuomotor behavior rehearsal (VMBR) might be an ideal technique for athletes with CP because relaxation may reduce spasticity which could disrupt imagery. However, it should be noted that most research with able bodied athletes indicates relaxation is not considered critical to achieve imagery effects (Murphy & Jowdy, 1992).

Athletes with closed head injuries may also suffer cognitive damage due to brain trauma. Individuals who lose long term memory may have difficulty performing imagery (Farah, 1984). Imagery should focus on developing a plan for goal attainment and/or a plan for resolution of stressful events as opposed to simply imaging a successful outcome (Taylor, Pham, Rivkin, & Armor, 1998).

Self-talk. In this section I focus on self-talk for arousal moderation, technical proficiency, and the elimination/moderation of negative affect. First, self-talk may help athletes moderate their arousal as, unlike physiologically based techniques, they may have more control over cognition than body parts. For example, athletes with CP often experience uncontrollable muscle spasticity that worsens with fatigue, making muscular relaxation difficult. Deep breathing may prove difficult for athletes without use of their abdominal muscles although, surprisingly, Hanrahan (1998) found deep breathing for relaxation effective for athletes with no use of their abdominal muscles.

Second, self-talk can be used for correct technique and to promote visual images of correct movement (Webber, Fronske, & Wilson, 1997). Hutzler (1992) derived 12 cognitive strategies related to wheelchair tennis position and ball strike that could form the basis of self-talk for technique and strategy.

Finally, Sherrill (1997) suggested that athletes with disabilities may be overly self-critical. Wheeler et al. (1996) also reported that wheelchair users with multiple sclerosis were self critical. Henschen et al. (1992) indicated that over a four month PST program, nine Paralympic wheelchair basketball team members became less self-critical. Thus, self-talk may be helpful in negating self-critical cognitions.

Competition Plans. Athletes with disabilities often need to carefully plan and anticipate difficulties. Arranging for transportation to the competition site, dealing with equipment difficulties, facing unanticipated travel barriers that add additional travel time (e.g., lack of wheelchair ramps), all necessitate careful planning. At a recent world class road race wheelchair athletes missed the start of the race because they were unable to find an empty elevator from their upper story rooms. Sport psychologists need to incorporate these types of considerations into pre-competition plans that they develop with athletes. Hedrick and Morse (1993, 1995b) provided wheelchair specific precompetition and competition plans for focusing and refocusing and anticipating critical situations during wheelchair racing and basketball.

Summary. Athletes with disabilities, similar to all athletes, can use traditional psychological methods (e.g., goal setting) to develop psychological skills (e.g., confidence). Sport psychologists who understand the challenges of disability sport will enhance their ability to assist athletes in their PST and pursuit of personal excellence.

Facilitative Factors

Many factors outside of competition and training such as travel (Davis, 1988), nutritional practices (Williams & Devlin, 1992), sleep habits (Savis, 1994), and retirement issues (Martin, 1996), can affect performance.

The purpose of this section is to detail important considerations for disability sport participants in the areas of injury and illness, effective training, and leaving sport.

Injury and Illness. Although the fitness benefits of sport participation may be more valuable for athletes with disabilities, compared to able bodied athletes (Fallon, 1992), sport participation may also cause injuries (Davis & Ferrara, 1995). Obviously, to achieve sport success it is important to remain injury free (Laskowski, 1994).

Compared to able-bodied athletes, however, athletes with disabilities lose more training time due to injury (Davis & Ferrara, 1995). Many injuries involve damage to the shoulders and hands (e.g., carpal tunnel syndrome; Burnham, Newall, & Steadward, 1991). Training time is also lost to disability related illness (e.g., bladder infections) and injury (e.g., pressure sores).

It is also important to understand the increased risk of heat exhaustion and related outcomes (e.g., heat stroke) for athletes with spinal cord injuries (SCI). SCI athletes have difficulty regulating body temperature, particularly when competing in high temperatures (McCann, 1996). Finally, a major medical and ethical concern of competitive quadriplegic wheelchair athletics has been the practice of intentionally inducing autonomic dysreflexia (AD) in order to raise blood pressure (Burnham, et al. 1994). Inducing AD, called "boosting," is often achieved by overdistending the bladder and results in significant performance gains. However, this practice is extremely dangerous and can be life threatening.

Sport psychologists should attempt to prevent such practices. Although sport psychologists are ethically bound to maintain confidentiality, their ethical obligation to prevent their clients from harming themselves supersedes an obligation to confidentiality (Sachs, 1993).

In summary, sport psychologists should be aware of sport type and disability type that may predispose athletes to particular injuries. Should a client become injured it is important that sport psychologists are familiar with the growing body of literature examining the psychology of injury and disability sport injury (Davis & Ferrara, 1995) in order to provide competent service to their clients.

Effective Training. Athletes usually need intelligent coaching to achieve sport success. Research examining coaching practices in disability sport is not encouraging. Although coaches (N = 239) of athletes from the six national disability sport organizations in the USA indicated that they coached athletes on a regular basis (i.e., at least once a week), most other research is less supportive (DePauw & Gavron, 1995). For instance, only 58% of 319 elite adult athletes stated that they had coaches who directed their training sessions (Ferrara & Buckley, 1996).

One-third of an international group of wheelchair racers, throwers, and swimmers reported that they did not have a coach (Liow & Hopkins, 1996). Swimmers were coached regularly, whereas the throwers and wheelchair racers received little coaching (Liow & Hopkins, 1996). In the United Kingdom few wheelchair racers have coaches (Williams &

Taylor, 1994). In the United States most coaches are volunteers without a sport science background (Hedrick & Morse, 1995a), although they often have university educations (DePauw & Gavron, 1991). Many volunteers have training in rehabilitation, and physical and occupational therapy (Sherrill, 1998).

Athletes may train inappropriately regardless of whether they are coached or self-coached. Liow and Hopkins (1996) reported that many elite athletes with disabilities trained in ways that were not sport specific and they tapered poorly. Research by Watanabe et al. (1992), finding some athletes overtrained on recovery days, and by Hedrick, Morse, and Figoni (1988), indicating athletes trained inconsistently, also suggests that athletes would benefit from improved coaching. Athletes have also reported a lack of availability of training material specific to their sport (Williams & Taylor, 1994). Williams and Taylor (1994) found that non-elite wheelchair athletes often quit sport because of a lack of training information and feelings of isolation from training partners.

Sport psychologists need to understand the quality of their athletes' physical training. Helping athletes obtain quality coaching services and referring them to educational materials are appropriate actions. Textbooks discussing disability specific coaching principles and techniques exist (DePauw & Gavron, 1995) and Sports 'N Spokes, a monthly magazine publishes sport science information about wheelchair sports. Providing both coaching and sport psychology services is controversial and sport psychologists should be aware of the professional and ethical issues surrounding a decision to do both (Burke & Johnson, 1992; Sachs, 1993). Because of the dual relationship issues involved in being both a sport psychologist and coach, Sachs (1993) suggested avoiding such arrangements.

Leaving Sport. Elite athletes (i.e., Paralympians) often have very brief careers (e.g., 2 years) that start shortly after (e.g., 2 years) an acquired disability (Wheeler et al., 1996). Because of this unique timing, sport psychologists working with Paralympians, may also find themselves assisting athletes with the transition out of sport.

Acceptance and adjustment to a major trauma (e.g., SCI) often takes up to 2 years (Wheeler, et al., 1996), and self-concept stabilization for individuals with SCI may take up to 4 years (Trieschmann, 1988). Thus, athletes may be coping with their disability in addition to coping with transitioning out of sport (Wheeler, et al., 1996). Additionally, they may be dealing with a "secondary disability" in the form of a chronic injury (Wheeler et al. 1996). A small body of literature about transitions out of sport for athletes with disabilities exists (Martin, in press-a; Martin, in press-b; Martin, 1996).

Summary. Sport psychologists can increase their effectiveness by being aware that the athletes they work with may not train optimally due to a lack of effective coaching or because of injury difficulties. Issues associated with leaving sport may indirectly impact on current athletic performance as well as influence post sport quality of life. Sport psychologists familiar with these issues will be better equipped to offer quality service to their clients.

Conclusion

Athletes with disabilities have typically been underserved by professionals in sport psychology. This article was written to provide information to sport psychologists choosing to work with athletes who have physical disabilities. Sport psychologists can play an important role in helping athletes with disabilities achieve personal excellence in sport and in life. With these two goals in mind, it is my hope that sport psychologists will approach their work in disability sport from a personal development model that values clients first as people and second as athletes. Finally, similar to the challenge of being familiar with both psychological principles of athletic behavior and the sport sciences, sport psychologists desiring to work with athletes with disabilities have the additional challenge, and ethical responsibility, of understanding the world of disability and disability sport in order to be effective (Sachs, 1993).

REFERENCES

Asch, A. (1986). Will populism empower the disabled? *Social Policy, 16,* 12–18.

Asken, M. J.(1991). The challenge of the physically challenged: Delivering sport psychology services to physically disabled athletes. *The Sport Psychologist, 5,* 370–381.

Baumeister, R. F. (1997). Identity, self-concept, and self-esteem. In R. Hogan, J. Johnson, & S. Briggs. (Eds.). *Handbook of personality psychology.* (pp. 681–710). New York: Academic Press.

Blinde, E. M., & McClung, L. R. (1997). Enhancing the physical and social self through recreational activity: Accounts of individuals with physical disabilities. *Adapted Physical Activity Quarterly, 14,* 327–344.

Brasile, F., & Hedrick, B. N. (1991). A comparison of participation incentives between adult and youth wheelchair basketball players. *Palaestra, 7,* 40–46.

Burke, K, L., & Johnson, J. J. (1992). The sport psychologist-coach dual role position: A rebuttal to Ellickson and Brown (1990). *Journal of Applied Sport Psychology 4,* 51–55.

Burnham, R., Newell, E., & Steadward, R. (1991). Sports medicine for the physically disabled: The Canadian team experience at the 1988 Seoul Paralympic Games. *Clinical Journal of Sports Medicine, 3,* 193–196. Burnham, R., Wheeler, G., Bhambhani, Y., Belanger, M., Eriksson, P., & Steadward, R. (1994). Intentional induction of autonomic dysreflexia among quadriplegic athletes for performance enhancement: Efficacy, safety, and mechanisms of action. *Clinical Journal of Sports Medicine, 4,* 1–10.

Chartrand, J. M., & Lent, R. W. (1987). Sports counseling: Enhancing the development of the student athlete. *Journal of Counseling and Development, 66,* 164–167.

Condeluci, A. (1989). Empowering people with cerebral palsy. *Journal of Rehabilitation, April/May/June,* 15–16.

Cooper, M. A., Sherrill, C., & Marshall, D. (1986). Attitudes towards physical activity of elite cerebral palsy athletes. *Adapted Physical Activity Quarterly, 3,* 14–21.

Danish, S. J., & Hale, B. D. (1981). Toward an understanding of the practice of sport psychology. *Journal of Sport Psychology 3,* 90–99.

Danish, S. J., & Nellen, V. C. (1997). New roles for sport psychologists: Teaching life skills through sport to at-risk youth. *Quest 49,* 100–113.

Dattilo, J., & Guadagnolo, F. B. (1988). Perceptions of road races by participants in the challenged division. *Adapted Physical Activity Quarterly, 5,* 193–202.

Davis, J. O. (1988). Strategies for managing athletes' jet lag. *The Sport Psychologist 2,* 154–160.

Davis, R. W., & Ferrara, M. S. (1995). Sports medicine and athletes with disabilities. In K. P. DePauw and S. J. Gavron (Eds.). *Disability and Sport.* (Pp 133–149). Champaign, IL: Human Kinetics.

DePauw, K. P., & Gavron, S. J. (1995). *Disability and Sport.* Champaign, IL: Human Kinetics.

Fallon, K. E. (1992). The disabled athlete. In J. Bloomfield, P. A. Fricker, & K. D. Fitch (Eds.) *Textbook of science and medicine in sport.*(pp. 488–511). Melbourne: Blackwell Scientific Publications.

Farah, M. J. (1984). The neurological basis of mental imagery: A conceptual analysis. *Cognition, 18,* 245–272.

Ferrara, M. S., & Buckley, W. E. (1996). Athletes with disabilities injury registry. *Adapted Physical Activity Quarterly, 13,* 50–60.

Goffman, E. (1963). *Stigma: Notes on the management of spoiled identity.* New York: Simon & Schuster.

Gordon, A. M. D. (1992). Self-regulation and goal setting. In J. Bloomfield, P. A. Fricker, & K. D. Fitch (Eds.) *Textbook of science and medicine in sport.* (pp. 136–146). Melbourne: Blackwell Scientific Publications.

Greenwood, C. M., Dzewaltowski, D. A., & French, R. (1990). Self-efficacy and psychological well-being of wheelchair tennis participants and wheelchair non-tennis participants. *Adapted Physical Activity Quarterly, 7,* 12–21.

Hanrahan, S. J. (1998). Practical considerations for working with athletes with disabilities. *The Sport Psychologist, 12,* 346–357.

Hedrick, B., & Morse, M. (1995a). Coaching: Beyond good intentions. *Sports 'N Spokes, 21,* 16.

Hedrick, B., & Morse, M. (1995b). All psyched up. *Sports 'N Spokes, 21,* 70–71.

Hedrick, B., & Morse, M. (1993). Preparation: A key to successful racing. *Sports 'N Spokes, 19,* 77–79.

Hedrick, B., & Morse, M. (1991). Setting goals in wheelchair basketball. *Sports 'N Spokes, 17,* 64–67.

Hedrick, B, N., Morse, M. I., & Figoni, S. F. (1988). Training practices of elite wheelchair roadracers. *Adapted Physical Activity Quarterly, 5,* 140–153.

Henschen, K. P., Horvat, M., & Roswal, G. (1992). Psychological profiles of the United States wheelchair basketball team. *International Journal of Sport Psychology, 23,* 128–137.

Hoffman, A., & Field, S. (1995). Promoting self-determination through effective curriculum development. *Intervention in School and Clinic, 30,* 134–141.

Hutzler, Y. (1992). Cognitive strategies utilized for multiple action control in wheelchair tennis. *Therapeutic Recreation Journal, 26,* 36–45.

Hutzler, Y. (1990). The concept of empowerment in rehabilitative sports. In G. Doll-Tepper, C. Dahms, B. Doll, & H. von Selzam (Eds.). *Adapted Physical Activity: An interdisciplinary approach,* (pp 43–51).Berlin: Springer-Verlag.

Hutzler, Y., & Bar-Eli, M. (1993). Psychological benefits of sports for disabled people: A review. *Scandinavian Journal of Medical Science and Sports, 3,* 217–228.

Katz, I., Haas, R. G., & Bailey, J. (1988). Attitudinal ambivalence and behavior toward people with disabilities. In H. E. Yuker. (Ed.). *Attitudes towards persons with disabilities.* (pp. 47–57). New York: Springer.

Kirkby, R. J. (1995). Wheelchair netball: Motives and attitudes of competitors with and without disabilities. *Australian Psychologist, 30,* 109–112.

Laskowski, E. R. (1994). Rehabilitation of the physically challenged athlete. *Sports Medicine, 5,* 215–233.

Liow, D. K., & Hopkins, W. B. (1996). Training practices of athletes with disabilities. *Adopted Physical Activity Quarterly, 13,* 372–381.

Lord, J., & Hutchinson, P. (1993). The process of empowerment: Implications for theory and practice. *Canadian Journal of Community Mental Health, 12,* 5–22. Makas, E. (1988). Positive attitudes toward disabled people: Disabled and nondisabled persons' perspectives. *Journal of Social Issues, 44,* 49–61.

Martin, J. J. (1996). Transitions out of competitive sport for athletes with disabilities. *Therapeutic Recreation Journal, 30,* 128–136.

Martin, J. J. (1999). Predictors of social physique anxiety among adolescent swimmers with disabilities with disabilities. *Adapted Physical Activity Quarterly, 16,* 75–85.

Martin, J. J. (in press-a). Loss experiences in disability sport. *Journal of Loss and Interpersonal Loss.*

Martin, J. J. (in press-b). Transitions out of competitive sport for athletes with disabilities. Chapter in *Transitions out of Sport.* Morgantown, WV: Fitness Information Technology, Inc.

Martin, J. J., & Mushett, C. A. (1996). Social support mechanisms among athletes with disabilities. *Adapted Physical Activity Quarterly, 13,* 74–83.

Martin, J. J., & Mushett, C. (1997). *Mental skills of athletes with cerebral palsy.* Paper presented at the International Society of Sport Psychology Conference, Tel Aviv, Israel.

Martin, J. J., Adams-Mushett, C., & Smith, K. L. (1995). Athletic identity and sport orientation of adolescent swimmers with disabilities. *Adapted Physical Activity Quarterly, 12,* 113–123.

McCann, B. C. (1996). Thermoregulation in spinal cord injury: The challenge of the Atlanta Paralympics. *Spinal Cord, 34,* 433–436.

Meyers, A. W. (1997). Sport psychology service to the United States Olympic Festival: An experiential account. *The Sport Psychologist, 11,* 454–468.

Morris, T., & Thomas, P. (1995). Approaches to applied sport psychology. In T. Morris and J. Summers. (Eds.). *Sport psychology: Theory, applications and issues.* (pp. 215–258). New York: John Wiley & Sons.

Moucha, S. A. (1991). The disabled female athlete as a role model. *Journal of Physical Education, Recreation and Dance, 62,* 37–38.

Murphy, S. M., & Jowdy, D. P. (1992). Imagery and mental practice. In T. S. Horn. (Ed.). *Advances in sport psychology.* (pp. 221–250). Champaign IL: Human Kinetics.

Murphy, S., & Tammen, V. (1998). In search of psychological skills. In J. L. Duda. (Ed.). *Advances in sport and exercise psychology measurement.* (pp. 195–209). Morgantown, WV: Fitness Information Technology, Inc.

Nixon, H. L. (1988). Getting over the worry hurdle: Parental encouragement and the sports involvement of visually impaired children and youths. *Adapted Physical Activity Quarterly, 5,* 29–43.

Orlick, T. (1986). *Psyching for sport.* Champaign IL: Leisure Press.

Patrick, G. D. (1986). The effects of wheelchair competition on self-concept and acceptance of disability on novice athletes. *Therapeutic Recreation Journal, 20,* 61–71.

Ravizza, K. (1998). Increasing awareness for sport performance. In J. M. Williams (Ed.). *Applied sport psychology: Personal growth to peak performance.* (3rd. ed.) (pp. 171–181). Mountain View, CA: Mayfield Publishing Co.

Rosenberg, M. (1979). *Conceiving the self* (pp. 149–176). New York: Basic Books, Inc.

Sachs, M. (1993). Professional ethics in sport psychology. In R. N. Singer, M. Murphy, &

L. K. Tennant (Eds.). *Handbook of research in sport psychology.* (pp. 921–932). New York: MacMillan.

Savis, J. C. (1994). Sleep and athletic performance: Overview and implications for sport psychology. *The Sport Psychologist 8,* 111–125.

Shapiro, J. (1993). *No pity: People with disabilities forging a new civil rights movement.* New York, Random House, Inc.

Sherrill, C. (1998). *Adapted physical activity, recreation and sport: Crossdisciplinary and lifespan.* (5th. ed.). Madison, WI: WCB/McGraw Hill.

Sherrill, C. (1997). Disability, identity, and involvement in sport and exercise. In K. R. Fox (Ed.). *The physical self: From motivation to wellbeing.* (pp. 257–286). Champaign IL: Human Kinetics.

Sobsey, D. (1994). *Violence and abuse in the lives of people with disabilities.* Baltimore, ML: Brookes Publishing Co.

Sonstroem, R. J. (1997). The physical self-system: A mediator of exercise and self-esteem. In K. R. Fox (Ed.). *The physical self: From motivation to wellbeing.* (pp. 3–26). Champaign IL: Human Kinetics.

Steadward, R. D., & Wheeler, G. D. (1996). The young athlete with a motor disability. In O. D. Bar. (Ed.). *The child and adolescent athlete* (pp. 493–520). Champaign, IL: Human Kinetics.

Surburg, P. (1989). Application of imagery techniques to special populations. *Adapted Physical Activity Quarterly, 6,* 328–337.

Taylor, S. E., Pham, L. B., Rivkin, I. D., & Armor, D. A. (1998). Harnessing the imagination. *American Psychologist, 53,* 429–439.

Trieschmann, R. B., (1988). *Spinal cord injuries: Psychological, social and vocational rehabilitation.* (2nd ed.). New York: Demos.

Vealey, R. S. (1988). Future directions in psychological skills training. *The Sport Psychologist, 2,* 318–336.

Watanabe, K. T., Cooper, R. A. Vosse, A. J., Baldini, F. D., & Robertson, R. N. (1992). Training practices of athletes who participated in the national wheelchair athletic association training camps. *Adapted Physical Activity Quarterly, 9,* 249–260.

Webber, A. M., Fronske, H., & Wilson, R. (1997). Basketball? Get a cue. *Sports 'N Spokes, 23,* 63–66. Weiss, M. R. (1991). Psychological skill development in children and adolescents. *The Sport Psychologist, 5,* 335–354.

Weiss, M. R. & Ebbeck, V. (1996). Self-esteem and perceptions of competence in youth sport: Theory, research and enhancement strategies. In O. Bar-Or. (Ed.). *The child and adolescent athlete.* (pp. 364–382). London: Blackwell Science, Ltd.

Wheeler, G., Malone, L. A., VanVlack, S., Nelson, E. R., & Steadward, R. (1996). Retirement from disability sport: A pilot study. *Adapted Physical Activity Quarterly, 13,* 382–399.

Whitehead, J. R., & Corbin, C. B. (1997). Self-esteem in children and youth: The role of sport and physical education. In K. Fox. (Ed.). *The physical self: From motivation to well-being.* (pp. 175–203). Champaign IL: Human Kinetics.

Williams, C., & Devlin, J. T. (1992). *Foods, nutrition and sports performance.* London, GB: E & FN Spon.

Williams, T., & Taylor, D. (1994). Socialization, subculture, and wheelchair sport: The influence of peers in wheelchair racing. *Adapted Physical Activity Quarterly, 11,* 416–428.

Yuker, H. E. (1987). *Attitudes towards persons with disabilities.* New York: Springer Publishing.

Manuscript submitted: September 18, 1998
Revision received: February 12, 1999

JOURNAL OF APPLIED SPORT PSYCHOLOGY **11,** 194–209 (1999)

Primary Process in Competitive Archery Performance: Effects of Flotation REST

TORSTEN NORLANDER AND HENRIK BERGMAN

Karlstad University, Sweden

TREVOR ARCHER

Göteborg University, Sweden

The purpose of the present study was to investigate whether or nor the floating form of Restricted Environmental Stimulation Technique (REST) may be exploited within the field of competitive archery to reinforce primary process (inner-directed) orientation and thereby enhance the quality of coaching and training. Floatation REST consists of a procedure whereby an individual is immersed in a water-tank filled with saltwater of an extremely high salt concentration. The experiment was performed over the course of two weekends with a 6-week interval. Twenty participating archers, 13 male and 7 female, were recruited. The between-group factor was "adjudged skill." The within-group factor was provided by an Armchair condition in which the participants sat in an armchair for 45 min after which they were required to shoot four salvo series of three shots each, as a comparison to the Flotation-Rest condition whereby the participants were required to lie in a floating-tank for 45 min just prior to shooting. Results indicated that: (a) the participants experienced less perceived exertion during marksmanship in the floating condition, (b) the elite archers performed more consistently in the Flotation-REST condition, (c) the least and most proficient archers had lower muscle tension in the Extensor Digitorum in the Flotation REST condition.

A number of investigations strongly suggest that the ability to unreservedly concentrate mental effort is the key to successful performance in sport (e.g., Abernethy, 1993; Cox, 1994; Gordon 1990; Landers, Hans, Salazar, Petruzzello, Kubitz, & Gannon, 1994; Summers, Miller, & Ford, 1991). One generally-accepted way of defining concentration is to de-

---

Author note: This study was supported by grants from Karlstad University, Karlstad, from Olympic Support Center, Örebro, and from Swedish National Center for Research in Sports, Stockholm.

Correspondence should be addressed to Dr. Torsten Norlander, Department of Psychology, Karlstad University, SE-651 88 Karlstad, Sweden. Email: (at.norlander@mailbox.swipnet.se).

1041-3200/99/0194–0209$1.00/0

scribe it as the ability to focus one's attention on the task at hand and thereby not be disturbed or affected by irrelevant external and internal stimuli (Schmid & Peper, 1993).

Within sport psychology, a central role has been assigned to problems concerning concentration. Much effort has focussed upon the consequences of external/internal distractions, or putative improvements to "concentrative-effort" within sport (for a review, see Moran, 1996). A critical period for the athlete during ongoing performance occurs when negative preoccupations (pertaining to perceived failure) must be rejected for new opportunities. In this regard, these individual sports are most demanding whereas the fast and unpredictable team sports ensure the players' attention is drawn to events as they occur (Moran, 1996). Archery provides an example of an individual sport that may be studied within the context influenced by a "here-and-now" experience in concentration. Thus, Landers, Boutcher, and Wang (1986) found that archers who dwelt on earlier failures performed worse than those more focussed on the present. Other observations indicate that thinking about the future, rather than the present, also caused performance deterioration (Moran, 1996).

Electroencephalogram techniques may offer a neurophysiological correlate for the "here-and-now" experience wherein archers and shooters display cognitive shift from left to right hemisphere the instant after firing (e.g., Hatfield & Landers, 1987; Hatfield, Landers, & Ray, 1984; Salazar, Landers, Petruzzello, Crews, Kubitz, & Han, 1990). According to Summers and Ford (1995), this may be described as a shift from the verbally-based left hemisphere to the spatially-dominant right hemisphere. In traditional psychological terms the effect may be described as a cognitive shift from a more secondary process-oriented thinking to a more primary process orientation (Neisser, 1967). The secondary process-primary process continuum is here taken in a descriptive manner (Martindale & Dailey, 1996). As such, the primary process is a unconventional, instinctive thinking that tends to operate on concrete images rather than abstract concepts, while secondary process is associated with studied, logical, analytic, abstract, and reality-oriented thought. Hilgard (1968) postulates that primary and secondary thought may be considered two alternative states of awareness and concurrent processes and differentiates between (a) *fusion,* where both types of thought process are "fused" in differing proportions, and (b) *oscillation,* "quick shifts," where each part remains distinct and intact. Singer (1974) has implied that fantasy provides a continuous background to everything one endeavors, but that this is noticed first after attention upon the outer sources of stimulation begins to rescind.

It is reasonable to assume that different sports require a differential equilibrium between primary and secondary processes in order to ensure maximal performance. For instance, in a soccer match a player will most often "calculate" effects of a pass in the context of his/her and teammates' movements on the field (secondary process). In a different situation the same player may be required to concentrate upon a penalty whereby a well-rehearsed sequence of action is allowed to dominate (primary process). The former demonstrates a "broad-external," the latter a "narrow-internal" focus (Nideffer, 1986). A narrow focus of attention is a special necessity in closed skill and/or self-paced sports like archery, rifle shooting, diving, and ice-skating (Nideffer, 1993). Associated with the secondary-primary process continuum is that of arousal-control as a concentration technique. Performers in strength and power sports may favor "psych up" strategies while preparing for competition while precision sport performers, like archers, may prefer to engage in "psych down" or relaxation techniques (Moran, 1996). Relaxation techniques often lead to both less perceived exertion and less muscle tension (Borg, 1970).

Those athletes active in sports where a dominant and constant primary process-orientation is a requirement for optimal performance must develop techniques to ensure that the training facilities provide just these conditions. Noy (1969) suggests, with the support of Goldberger's (1961) experiments in sensory isolation, that sensory deprivation, or with the more modern terminology Restricted Environmental Stimulation Technique (REST), might be an effective technique for inducing a primary process condition. Much evidence indicates that following REST an "aftereffect," lasting about an hour, comprises a cognitive balance with a mainly primary process-orientation (Hutchison, 1984a; Norlander, Bergman, and Archer, 1998). The floatation-isolation technique is a special form of REST. The floating form of REST consists of a procedure whereby an individual is immersed in a water-tank filled with saltwater of an extremely high salt concentration. The complete technique centers upon reducing sensations to a minimum. In order to achieve this, the participant in question must lie down in the tank while a cover is closed down over the opening. This cover may be opened quite easily just through pushing it up. The floating tank is isolated from the inside in order to preserve the warmth and keep out both noise and light.

Experiments conducted earlier with REST often reported negative effects on participants (Zubeck, 1973), such as problems with logical thinking, concentration problems, higher levels of anxiety, and even hallucinations. Later research, however, has shown also the occurrence of positive effects, such as improved relaxation (Jacobs, Heilbronner, & Stanley, 1984), reduced anxiety (Fine & Turner, 1982), increased receptivity to information (Aquino, 1982), pain reduction (Turner & Fine, 1984), heart rate reduction (Jacobs, Heilbronner, & Stanley, 1984), and muscular tension reduction (Stanley & Francis, 1984). Corresponding positive effects have been reported for the floating form of REST (e.g., Best & Suedfeld, 1982; Hutchison, 1984a; Forgays & Belinson, 1986; Suedfeld, Metcalfe, & Bluck, 1987; Suedfeld & Bruno, 1990). Several studies (e.g., Lee & Hewitt, 1987; Suedfeld & Bruno, 1990; McAleney, Barabasz, & Barabasz, 1990; Wagaman, Barabasz, & Barabasz, 1991) provide strong support for the contention that the flotation-isolation procedure reinforces aspects of "imagery," a prerequisite to the creative process (Forgays and Forgays, 1992). At the same time, these effects may also be regarded as an expression of a primary process domination (Norlander, 1997, 1998). Flotation REST has been applied to a sport psychology context in order to attain a more effective control over the negative consequences of stress, to reinforce various visualization techniques, and to improve the restitution following training bouts and competition (Bond, 1988; Hutchison, 1984b; Lee & Hewitt, 1987; Suedfeld & Bruno, 1990). As yet we are not aware of any systematic attempt to study the direct and immediate influence of Flotation REST (i.e., without visualization and during aftereffects) upon precision sport performance.

The purpose of the present study was to investigate to what extent Flotation REST may be exploited within the field of competitive archery to reinforce primary process orientation in performers and thereby enhance the quality of coaching and training. During and directly after Flotation REST a condition consisting of a narrowed span of attention and relaxation was achieved. This condition provides the point of departure for the theoretical standpoints described above. Sensory isolation leads to a cognitive shift towards the primary process, which is associated with an increased psychological and muscular relaxation. These characteristics of relaxation are important for closed sports like archery (Moran, 1996). Thus, the following hypotheses were formulated: Flotation REST would lead to significantly less perceived exertion and less muscle tension. These changes would possibly lead to (c) improvements in performance.

Methods

Participants

The present experiment was performed over the course of two weekends (Saturday and Sunday) with a 6-week interval. The experiment was carried out at the Olympic Support Center in Örebro, Sweden, in collaboration with Karlstad University, Sweden. Twenty participants, 13 male and 7 female, were recruited through the auspices of the Swedish Archery Union (Svenska Bågskytteförbundet). The participating archers may be described as (a) those that maintained a good junior standard at district and club level, (b) those archers aspiring to belong to the category "Junior-elite" but had not quite reached that standard, and (c) those that had achieved Swedish Junior-elite standard. Mean age was 15.75 years (*SD* = 1.33, variation of age range = 13–18). Five of the participants used the so-called "compound-bow," 3 used the "classical bow," and 12 the "free-style bow." Each of these three types of archery bow define separate branches within the sport and would not normally compete with each other under standard competitive conditions. Only one of the participants had any previous experience of the flotation-REST technique but nine of them had experience of some type of mental training. Two of the participants were left-handed.

At the start of the experiment, four federal (national) coaches, universally recognized for their expertise and experience within the field of archery were assigned the task of separately assessing and grading the archers with regard to their skill. These assessments were later shown to indicate a high level of interjudge reliability (see "Interjudge Reliability" in Results section) and on this basis three groups could be identified and formulated as an independent variable: the least skillful archers, an intermediary group, and finally an elite, most skillful, group. The least skilled group consisted of seven participants, the intermediary group of seven, and the elite group of six participants. One-way ANOVA's did not show any group-differences with regard to either age, height, weight, degree of optimism (LOT), personal commitment (PCS), or maximum voluntary contraction (MVC), as measured by the EMG-apparatus ($ps > 0.089$). Kruskal-Wallis testing did not show any differences between groups with regard to type of bow used, gender, type of breakfast consumed, self-assessed performance level, marital status, health condition at the first weekend occasion, as well as at second weekend occasion, type of upbringing, type of school education, smoking/non-smoking habit, alcohol consumption, female participants' phase of the menstrual cycle, or amount of training ($ps > 0.065$). However, a significant effect of Type of lunch ($KW = 2.39$, $p = 0.044$) where a multiple comparisons procedure indicated that the least skilled group (*M* Rank = 7.71) showed evidence of lunch habits that were distinguished by an irregularity and lack of nourishment value in comparison with the intermediary group (Mean Rank = 12.00) and the elite group (*M* Rank = 12.00).

Design

This study presented a mixed effect design. The between-group factor was defined by the assignment of the participants into three experimental groups on the basis of "Adjudged Skill," the least skillful, the intermediate, and the elite. The within-group factor was provided by an Armchair condition in which the participants sat in an armchair for 45 min after which they were required to shoot four salvo series of three shots each, as a comparison to the Flotation-REST condition (Flotation condition), whereby the participants were required to lie in a floating-tank for 45 min just prior to shooting their four salvo series. The order in which the Armchair condition and the Flotation condition were presented was varied so that half of the participants began with the Armchair condition whereas the other half began with the Flotation condition and then reversed conditions for the next experimental session. Between conditions was a 6-week interval interspersed.

Instruments

Floating Tank. A floating tank (Pantarei Flytexperten, Stockholm) with measurements 2400 mm × 1,260 mm × 950 mm was used. Water depth varied between 200–300 mm, due to evaporation, volume of water 1 cubic meter. The floating tank was insulated on the inside so as to maintain a constant temperature and to isolate the participant from sound and sight. The water temperature was maintained at 34.2°C. Ambient (air) temperature was the same as the water temperature minimizing sense sensation. The water was saturated with magnesium sulphate in order to maintain a salt concentration of 1.3 g/cm3.

The Target. The target was a regular competitive archery target (1) i.e., it was ten-ringed with a total diagonal of 40 cm. The rings were graded from 1 point for the outermost ring to 10 points for hitting the bull's eye (the center point, diameter cm). The distance to the target was fixed at 18 meters which represents the international indoor competitive standard range. Each archer was required to shoot 4 series of 3 arrows to each series. Maximum time allowed was 120 sec per salvo series.

EMG (Electromyogram Analysis). These measurements were carried out using an EMG-apparatus Myo I (EMG-Konsult, Solna, Sweden). In order to measure contraction impulses from the chosen muscle (i.e., Extensor Digitorum), two electrodes were connected to the skin of the lower arm on the muscle (medial central) as well as a third, neutral electrode on the skin above the bone, os radius. For right-handed archers, the right arm was chosen, whereas the two left-handed archer received electrode placements on the left arm. The Extensor Digitorum muscle was chosen because this muscle has antagonist action to the Flexor Digitorum muscle which controls the flexion responses of the fingers and wrist, thereby exerting a critical influence on the arching of the bow when the bowstring is drawn. It was assumed (Jansson, 1995) that the antagonist of the Flexor Digitorum (i.e., Extensor Digitorum) is required to be as relaxed as possible in order to achieve maximal archery performance. For the EMG-measurements, Maximum Voluntary Contraction (MVC) was applied. In order to obtain calibration standards, each participant was instructed to tense Extensor Digitorum as much as possible. All the measured values of the participants were described as a percentage of each individual's MVC. For the present analysis two separate assessments for percent of MVC were employed: (a) Mean Tension (MT) as expressed by the total mean muscle tension during the four salvo series, and (b) Prerelease Tension (PT) as expressed by the mean value for muscle tension shortly before (0.1–0.5 sec) the bowstring was released on each of the 12 shots.

RPE—Ratings of Perceived Exertion. This scale (Borg, 1970; Borg, 1985; Borg, 1998) provides an assessment of perceived exertion (1 i.e., how heavy and strenuous particular exercises are experienced by the athlete). According to the RPE instructions, perceived exertion depends mainly on the strain and fatigue in the athletes' muscles. Each participant is instructed to use a scale from 6 to 20, where 6 symbolized "no exertion at all" and 20 "maximal exertion." A high reliability of ratings of perceived exertion has been found in many investigations applying different procedures (Borg, 1998). Parallel Test Reliability is reported to lie between 0.70 and 0.90, Intratest Reliability around 0.90, and Retest Reliability around 0.90. Similarly, RPE provides good values for different validity measures, including content validity (0.96) regarding self-versus observer-ratings, concurrent validity (0.77–0.94), as well as predictive validity (0.50–0.70) (Borg, 1998).

The Five-scale. The direct experiential effects of the presentation, from "bad" to "very good," were assessed on a five-graded scale (Janson, 1995). This scale is often used by coaches even though there are no analyses on reliability and validity data available. In an applied sport psychology study, however, it is important that the scale be tested.

LOT—Life Orientation Test. The test (Scheier & Carver, 1985) consists of eight items, plus four filler items. The task of each participant is to decide whether or not one is in agreement with each of the items described, ranging from 0 (*strongly disagree*) to 4 (*strongly agree*). The test measures dispositional optimism, defined in terms of generalized outcome expectancies. Parallel Test Reliability is reported to .76 and Internal Consistency to .76 (Scheier & Carver, 1985). LOT is also regarded to have an adequate level of convergent and discriminant validity (Scheier & Carver, 1985) demonstrated by correlation statistics and by using LISREL VI ($r = 0.64$).

PCS—Personal Commitment Scale. A 1–10 graded scale (Orlick, 1990) that indicates how highly individuals estimate and evaluate their interests in sports was used. A 10 on the scale indicates that it is the most important pastime in one's life whereas a mark of 1 indicates the minimal priority of the sport. Orlick (1990) has demonstrated from studies with marathon runners that those who rated marathon running highest showed better performances competitively compared with those who rated their own marathon running as being less important. Orlick (1990) does not present any reliability data but, regarding validity, it is indicated that when a large group of marathon runners responded to the PCS it was found that those individuals with the highest commitment were shown to the most proficient. "As the commitment score decreased, the performance level decreased proportionally. The same was true for athletes in a variety of other sports" (Orlick, 1990, p. 9).

Procedure

The experiment was performed during two weekends (Friday evening to Sunday evening), with a 6-week break, at the Olympic Support Center, Örebro, Sweden. On arrival at the first Friday evening, all the archers were received by the coaches and subsequently instructed by the experimenters on the experimental design and set-up. At the same time, the archers were informed which of them had been assigned, randomly, to either the Control (Armchair condition) or to the Floating conditions during each of the two occasions. It was indicated too that all task-associated data would be treated with strict confidentiality. The rest of that evening was assigned for shooting practices. On the following Saturday morning further information, pertaining to the period when they were not actively engaged in the experiment, was provided. Thus, they were told they were supposed to participate, pre- or post-performance, in theoretical or coaching exercises organized by national coaches.

At the start of the experiment, each participant was required to complete a questionnaire on background information as well as LOT. If he/she was in the Armchair condition the participant was shown to a separate room and instructed to sit in an armchair and read the newspapers available. Those included in the Flotation condition were shown to the house with the tank. Each participant was instructed to make a toilet visit, change to bathing clothes and shower. The participant was then instructed to dry carefully around the face in order to avoid drops of water disturbing relaxation. In order to introduce the participant to an immediate relaxed state in the tank following instruction (adapted from Benson, 1975) was given: "We require you to lie down in the water. Experience the comfort of the situation. Shut your eyes and let yor muscles simply relax. Allow the relaxation to start at you toes, then go slowly to your feet, legs, thighs, stomach, chest, arms, shoulders, and neck and finally try to also feel relaxation in your face muscles. Maintain this state of relaxation. Try to breath through your nose exclusively when you exhale and keep the word ONE in conscious awareness. For example breath IN . . . OUT, 'ONE'. IN . . . OUT, 'ONE'. If you maintain this procedure a few times then flotation will maintain your condition. You do not have to do anything yourself." The participant was then informed of how to remove the cover and how to climb in and out of the tank. So as not to be disturbed by the water and to further eliminate sounds, wax plugs were inserted into the participants' ears. Thereafter, the participant entered the tank and 45 minutes later the tank visit was interrupted and the participant was allowed to shower and put on training overalls.

Following the respective armchair-sitting and floating an experimenter instructed that full competition status was in force, requiring complete concentration. Then the participant proceeded to the Archery-hall. A different experimenter received the participant and mounted the EMG electrodes on the pulling-arm. An assistant explained that after each shot the participant was to rate the experience on a five-point scale. Then the participant was allowed to loose-off four series of three shots each. The time limit was 120 sec per series. When the participant had completed all four series he/she made an estimate of perceived exertion on the RPE scale. Finally, a short debriefing was organized whereby the participant communicated particular problems or viewpoints. The same procedure (except with reversed order of conditions) was maintained during the next weekend occasion, six weeks later, with the exception that the background questionnaire and LOT were replaced by the Personal Commitment scale.

Results

Data Reduction

In order to simplify the statistical analysis it was investigated as to whether or not one may obtain data reductions regarding marksmanship in the four shooting series, the five scale after the four series, the mean tension (EMG-MT) during the four series, the pre-release tension (EMG-PT) during the four series. Regression analysis (enter-method) were used for calculating Multiple R (*R*) which showed significant correlations between the four shooting series for *R* with regard to Marksmanship in the Armchair condition ($R = 0.75$, $p = 0.003$), Marksmanship in the Flotation condition ($R = 0.90$, $p < 0.001$), the Five-scale in the Flotation condition ($R = 0.66$, $p = 0.018$), EMG-MT in the Armchair condition ($R = 0.94$, $p < 0.001$), EMG-MT in the Flotation condition ($R = 0.96$, $p < 0.001$), EMG-PT in the Armchair condition ($R = 0.95$, $p < 0.001$), EMG-PT in the Flotation condition ($R = 0.96$, $p < 0.001$). There was however no significant correlation with regard to the Five-scales in the Armchair condition ($R = 0.43$, $p = 0.330$). Since the regression analysis indicated acceptable ($R > 0.70$) or high ($R > 0.90$) *R* values it was considered meaningful to summate the results for the Marksmanship from the four shooting series in both the Armchair and the Flotation conditions, summate the results for the EMG-MT measures from the four shooting series in both Armchair and Flotation conditions, and summate the results from the EMG-PT measures from the four shooting series in both Armchair and Flotation conditions. The scores from the Five-scales in the Armchair condition did not correlate significantly and it was also adjudged unnecessary to convert the scores in the Flotation condition to one variable as a comparison was no longer possible.

Reliabilities

Order Sequence of the Conditions. To examine whether or not the order sequence between conditions affected outcome participants who received floating on the first occasion were compared with those receiving floating on the second. Split-plot ANOVAs were used with the Armchair and Flotation conditions marksmanship, respectively, the RPE scale result, the EMG results expressed as Mean Tension (MT) and Pre-release Tension (PT), respectively, as the Within-Subject Factors and sequential order of conditions as the Between-Subject Factor. The analyses indicated that the order of conditions had no influence on either marksmanship ($p = 0.723$), the RPE scale ($p = 0.449$), EMG-MT ($p = 0.343$) or EMG-PT ($p = 0.319$). Nor were there any interactions between factors and within factors ($ps > 0.121$).

Interjudge Reliabilities. Regression analysis (enter-method) showed a significant multiple correlation between the four coaches ($R = 0.90$, $p < 0.001$). Thus it was deemed necessary to average the coaches' scoring for skill as well as apply the coaches' own group divisions.

Type of Bow. Three types of bow were used in the experiment. No significant group differences (Kruskal-Wallis) occurred with regard to type of bow ($p = 0.90$) and split-plot ANOVAs with Armchair and Flotation condition marksmanship, the RPE scale result, results of the EMG, MT and PT, respectively, as Within-Subject Factors and type of bow as Between-Subject Factor showed that type of bow had no influence for either marksmanship ($p = 0.224$), the RPE scale ($p = 0.208$), or EMG-MT ($p = 0.562$). However, type of bow did influence EMG-PT [$F(2,16)$

Table 1
Relationships between conditions (armchair and flotation) and skill level for different dependent variables

	Least skillful		Intermediate		Most skillful	
	A-condition	F-condition	A-condition	F-condition	A-condition	F-condition
Mark.ship						
Mean	91.29	77.86	105.57	99.71	105.50	108.67
SD	11.28	23.86	9.03	13.65	13.28	7.45
RPE						
Mean	12.86	10.57	12.86	12.14	9.50	9.50
SD	1.86	2.44	2.04	1.46	0.84	1.05
EMG-MT	17.00	13.12	15.45	17.48	15.48	13.70
Mean SD	3.53	3.15	6.22	6.08	1.30	1.83
EMG-PT						
Mean	25.15	18.07	20.21	25.31	18.41	17.44
SD	11.20	6.93	9.84	18.82	9.83	6.23

= 5.04, p = 0.020]. Further testing (one-way ANOVA's and the LSD-test) indicated in the Armchair condition a significant difference between the compound (M = 11.71, SD = 5.36) and the freestyle bow (M = 26.37, SD = 9.56), but not with regard to the classical bow (M = 19.71, SD = 7.13). No interaction effects occurred with respect to between-factors and within-factors ($ps > 0.680$).

Dependent Variables

In order to analyze the dependent variables split-plot ANCOVA's were used (controlling for the difference between groups in regard to lunch habits) and will be described below. For means and standard deviations se Table 1.

(a) Marksmanship. A split-plot ANCOVA was used with scores from marksmanship as the Within-Subject Factor and Group as the Between-Subject Factor. There was no interaction effect between Marksmanship and Group and no difference between conditions ($ps > 0.1$), but there were group differences [$F(2,17) = 9.92$, $p = 0.002$]. As post hoc analysis LSD-testing was applied to examine group differences (5% level), indicating that there was a significant difference in marksmanship between the least skilled group (Armchair condition: M = 91.29, SD = 11.28; Flotation condition: M = 77.86, SD = 23.86) and the intermediary group (Armchair condition: M = 105.57, SD = 9.03; Flotation condition: M = 99.71, SD = 13.65), and between the least skilled and the elite (Armchair condition: M = 105.50, SD = 13.28; Flotation condition: M = 108.67, SD = 7.45). Standard deviation may provide a measure of performance constancy, so a comparison (one-way ANOVA's) of these was derived: in the Armchair condition, no group-differences existed (p = 0.988), but in the Flotation condition there was a significant difference in deviance

for marksmanship [$F(2,17) = 3.00$, $p = 0.046$]. LSD-testing indicated group differences: The elite ($M = 1.28$, $SD = 0.41$) indicated significantly lower deviation than the least skilled ($M = 3.43$, $SD = 1.87$), but did not differ from the intermediary group ($M = 3.04$, $SD = 2.06$).

(b) RPE—Ratings of Perceived Exertion. A split-plot ANCOVA was used with scores from the RPE scale as Within-Subject Factor and with Groups as the Between-Subject Factor. Significant interaction effects were obtained between the RPE scale and Groups [$F(2,17) = 4.41$, $p = 0.029$) and between conditions on the RPE scale [$F(1,17) = 9.70$, $p = 0.006$], as well as group differences [$F(2,17) = 6.23$, $p = 0.010$]. In the Armchair condition, means ($M = 11.85$, $SD = 2.25$) were significantly higher than in the Flotation condition ($M = 10.80$, $SD = 2.02$) which may suggest that less effort was perceived necessary in the Flotation condition. Subsequent LSD-testing indicated, in the Armchair condition, a significant difference for the RPE scale between the elite ($M = 9.50$, $SD = 0.84$) and the least skilled ($M = 12.86$, $SD = 1.86$), and between the elite and the intermediary group ($M = 12.86$, $SD = 2.04$), whereas for the Flotation condition there was a difference between the elite ($M = 9.50$, $SD = 1.05$) and the intermediary group ($M = 12.14$, $SD = 1.46$), with the least skilled ($M = 10.57$, $SD = 2.44$) in between. To examine the interaction effects, the RPE scale results were analyzed under Armchair and Flotation conditions using the Wilcoxon Matched-Pairs Test. In the least skilled group there was a significant difference ($Z = -2.20$, $p = 0.028$) between conditions whereby the RPE scale in the Armchair condition gave a higher mean ($M = 12.86$, $SD = 1.86$) than in the Flotation condition ($M = 10.57$, $SD = 2.44$). There were no other significant differences within groups between Armchair and Flotation conditions regarding the RPE scale ($ps > 0.390$).

(c) Mean Tension (MT). A split-plot ANCOVA was used with scores from EMG-measures, in MT, as a Within-Subject Factor and Groups as Between-Subject Factor. There was a significant interaction between EMG-MT and group [$F(2,17) = 11.67$, $p = 0.001$] but there were no significant differences between conditions ($p = 0.127$) and no group difference ($p = 0.626$). Wilcoxon Matched-Pairs Test was used to examine the EMG-MT result under Armchair and Flotation conditions in each group. In the least skilled group there was a significant difference ($Z = -2.03$, $p = 0.043$) between conditions whereby EMG-MT, in the Armchair condition, gave a higher mean ($M = 17.00$, $SD = 3.53$) compared with that of the Flotation condition ($M = 13.12$, $SD = 3.15$). Further, in the elite group there was a significant difference ($Z = -2.20$, $p = 0.028$) between conditions such that EMG-MT, under the Armchair condition, showed a higher mean ($M = 15.48$, $SD = 1.30$) than in the Flotation condition ($M = 13.70$, $SD = 1.83$). For the intermediary group there were no significant differences ($p = 0.075$) between the Armchair condition ($M = 15.45$, $SD = 6.22$) and the Flotation condition ($M = 17.48$, $SD = 6.08$).

(d) Pre-release Tension (PT). A split-plot ANCOVA was used with

scores from the EMG-measures expressed with PT as Within-Subject Factor and group as Between-Subject Factor. No EMG-PT × Group interaction effect was indicated ($p = 0.197$) and no difference between conditions ($p = 0.772$), nor any Group difference ($p = 0.661$).

Correlation Statistics

Correlation coefficients (Pearson's r) were computed between variables (see Table 2). The results indicated that the connection between marksmanship (Mark) and the consistency of performance (Con) increased during Flotation condition (F) at the same time as the connection between ratings of perceived exertion (RPE) and adjudged skil (Skil) diminished.

Discussion

Statistical analyses indicated that the participants experienced a lesser *perceived exertion* effort during marksmanship in the Floating condition than in the Armchair condition, as measured by the RPE scale. The most proficient archers (the elite) distinguished themselves from the other two groups in the Armchair and Floating conditions through their significantly lower points on the RPE scale (i.e., the elite group experienced lower perceived exertion). The concept of perceived exertion (Borg, 1998) contains several components used to describe all exercises from exaggeratedly high overall physical exertion (e.g., distance running) to the exercising of small muscle groups or to exercises with short duration (e.g., archery). For archery, local strain sensations in the arm muscles involved disturb concentration so that a lower perceived exertion is an advantage (Janson, 1995), suggesting a practical value.

With regard to *average muscle tension* (EMG-MT) in the Extensor Digitorum during marksmanship, a between-conditions difference was obtained for the least and most proficient archers (the least skilled group and the elite group, respectively) whereby floating led to lower muscle tension. However, no significant difference between either group or condition regarding *pre-release tension* (EMG-PT) was obtained.

Marksmanship was not improved in the Flotation REST condition. One explanation may be that an improved marksmanship performance requires a period of training under conditions of relaxation induced by Flotation. On the other hand, it should be noted that the elite archers performed more *consistently* in the Flotation condition compared with the least skilled group.

Several studies appear to confirm the conclusion that Flotation REST induces a more conspicuous primary process condition (Norlander, 1997; Norlander, Bergman, & Archer, 1998). This condition (i.e., a deeper concentration) includes certain mechanisms (e.g., immediacy-focus, cognitive-shift from the verbal-based left hemisphere to the spatially-dominated right hemisphere, narrowed span of attention, and relaxation) that have been found to exert particular influence in "closed skills" and/or self-paced sports like archery, rifle marksmanship, diving, and ice-skating

Table 2

Correlations between different variables in armchair (A) and flotation (F) conditions. Significant correlations are indicated as follows: $p < 0.05$ (*), $p < 0.001$ (**)

	Mark A	Mark F	Con A	Con F	RPE A	RPE F	MT A	MT F	PT A	PT F	Skill
Mark A	1.00										
Mark F	.69**	1.00									
Con A	−.65*	−.21	1.00								
Con F	−.46*	−.77**	.09	1.00							
RPE A	−.24	−.33	.23	.22	1.00						
RPE F	.29	−.08	−.12	.05	.70*	1.00					
MT A	−.08	−.26	.02	.40	.18	.25	1.00				
MT F	.11	−.14	−.06	.39	.26	.42	.62*	1.00			
PT A	−.48*	−.35	.25	.09	.48*	.27	.42	.22	1.00		
PT F	−.01	−.27	−.01	.46*	.08	.29	.65*	.77**	.41	1.00	
Skill	.48*	.62*	−.03	−.48*	−.60*	−.20	−.17	.07	−.28	−.01	1.00

(Moran, 1996). Even though the present study did have some methodological limitations (the sample size was rather small and the Flotation condition included, for a couple of minutes, progressive relaxation which was not present in the Armchair condition), it indicates that clear dividends may be obtained through the exploitation of the "aftereffects" induced in the floating condition. In order to reinforce the quality of training in individual technically-based disciplines the technical advances offered by a floating procedure may possibly be applied to develop particular assemblies of responses (for example taking a penalty in soccer) in otherwise exclusively team sports. Well-rehearsed coaching with high technical and conceptual quality reinforces the probability of enhanced concentration and successful performance in the instant of competition (Railo, 1992).

Flotation REST may be applied as an instrument to improve coaching and to hone technique, as data discussed above suggest. Within competitive archery, there appears much importance placed upon the degree of relaxation encountered in the antagonist to the Flexor Digitorum (i.e., the Extensor Digitorum) during the performance of archery marksmanship such that further relaxation of this muscle optimizes performance. Flotation REST provided positive effects in this respect. The results indicated that even the most proficient archers were presented an opportunity to improve the consistency of their marksmanship. The technical opportunities for advancing quality of coaching and training ought to be reinforced through the combination of Flotation REST with visualization in the water-tank (Lee & Hewitt, 1987; Suedfeld & Bruno, 1990). Further, simulation training (Orlick, 1990), under the influence of the "aftereffect," assisted by external distractions (e.g., noise, applause) is expected to reinforce potential benefits.

In summary, the present data describes a treatment recipe for coaching and training that capitalizes on primary process reinforcement through concentration of effort in a highly individual sports discipline. Further experimentation is necessary to define the basic methodology in different sports. Longitudinal studies with athletes training after Flotation-REST compared with athletes training without REST might here be of great interest.

REFERENCES

Abernethy, B. (1993). Attention. In R. N. Singer, M. Murphey, & L. K. Tennant (Eds.), *Handbook of research in sport psychology* (pp. 127–170). New York: Macmillan.

Aquino, C. C. (1982). Relationships between stimulus depravation theory and creative communications. *Journal of Creative Behavior, 16,* 123–131.

Benson, H. (1975). *The relaxation response.* New York: Morrow.

Best, J. A., & Suedfeld, P. (1982). Restricted environmental stimulation therapy and behavioral self-management in smoking cessation. *Journal of Applied Social Psychology, 12,* 408–419.

Bond, J. W. (1988). Flotation therapy: Current concepts. *Excel, 4,* 2–4.

Borg, G. (1970). Perceived exertion as an indicator of somatic stress. *Scandinavian Journal of Rehabilitation Medicine, 2,* 92–98.

Borg, G. (1985). *An introduction to Borg's RPE-scale.* Ithaca, NY: Mouvement.

Borg, G. (1998). *Borg's perceived exertion and pain scales.* Champaign, IL: Human Kinetics.

Cox, R. H. (1994). *Sport psychology: Concepts and applications.* Madison, WI: Brown & Benchmark.

Fine, T. H., & Turner, J. W., Jr. (1982). The effect of brief restricted environmental stimulation therapy in the treatment of essential hypertension. *Behavioral Research Therapy, 20,* 567–570.

Forgays, D. G., & Belinson, M. J. (1986). Is flotation isolation a relaxing environment? *Journal of Environmental Psychology, 6,* 19–34.

Forgays, D. G., & Forgays, F. K. (1992). Creativity enhancement through flotation isolation. *Journal of Environmental Psychology, 12,* 329–335.

Goldberger, L. (1961). Reactions to perceptual isolation and Rorschach manifestations of the primary process. *Journal of Projective Techniques, 25,* 287–302.

Gordon, S. (1990). A mental skills training programme for the Western Australia State Cricket Team. *The Sport Psychologist, 4,* 386–399.

Hatfield, B. D., & Landers, D. M. (1987). Psychophysiology in exercise and sport research: An overview. *Exercise and Sport Science Reviews, 15,* 351–388.

Hatfield, B. D., Landers, D. M., & Ray, W. J. (1984). Cognitive processes during self-paced motor performance: An electroencephalographic study of elite rifle shooters. *Journal of Sport Psychology, 6,* 42–59.

Hilgard, E. R. (1968). *The experience of hypnosis.* New York: Hartcourt Brace Jovanovich.

Hutchison, M. (1984a). One man, one float: by using a flotation tank, athletes don't even have to move to improve. *Esquire, 11,* 29–30.

Hutchison, M. (1984b).*The book of floating: exploring the private sea.* New York: Morrow.

Jacobs, G. D., Heilbronner, R. L., & Stanley, J. M. (1984). The effects of short-term flotation REST on relaxation: a controlled study. *Healthy Psychology, 3,* 99–111.

Janson, L. (1995). Avspänd teknik [Relaxed technique]. Stockholm: SISU.

Landers, D. M., Boutcher, S. H., & Wang, M. Q. (1986). A psychobiological study of archery performance. *Research Quaterly for Exercise and Sport, 57,* 236–244.

Landers, D. M., Han, M., Salazar, W., Petruzzello, S. J., Kubitz, K. A., & Gannon, T. L. (1994). Effects on learning on electroencephalographic and electrocardiographic patterns in novice archers. *International Journal of Sport Psychology, 25,* 313–330.

Lee, J., & Hewitt, J. (1987). Using visual imagery in a flotation tank to improve gymnastic performance and reduce physical symptoms. *International Journal of Sport Psychology, 18,* 223–230.

Martindale, C., & Dailey, A. (1996). Creativity, primary process cognition and personality. *Personality and Individual Differences, 20,* 409–414.

McAleney, P. J., Barabasz, A., & Barabasz, M. (1990). Effects of flotation restricted environmental stimulation on inter-collegiate tennis performance. *Perceptual and Motor Skills, 71,* 1023–1028.

Moran, A. P. (1996). *The psychology of concentration in sport performers. A cognitive analysis.* Hove, UK: Psychology Press.

Neisser, U. (1967). *Cognitive Psychology.* New York: Appleton Century Crofts.

Nideffer, R. M. (1986). Concentration and attention in control training. In J. Williams (Ed.), *Applied sport psychology* (pp. 257–269). Palo Alto, CA: Mayfield.

Nideffer, R. M. (1993). Attention control training. In R. N. Singer, M. Murphey, & L. K. Tennant (Eds.), *Handbook of research in sport psychology* (pp. 542–556). New York: Macmillan.

Norlander, T. (1997). *Alcohol and the creative process. Frameworks of influence upon creative performance.* Örebro: Tryckverkstan, ISSN 1101–718X. (Doctorial dissertation at Göteborg University, Sweden).

Norlander, T. (1999). Inebriation and Inspiration? A Review of the research on alcohol and creativity. *Journal of Creative Behavior, 33,* 7–29.

Norlander, T., Bergman, H., & Archer, T. (1998). Effects of flotation REST on creative problem solving and originality. *Journal of Environmental Psychology, 18,* 000–000.

Noy, P. (1969). A revision of the psychoanalytic theory of the primary process. *International Journal of Psychoanalysis, 50,* 155–178.

Orlick, T. (1990). *In pursuit of excellence. How to win sport and life through mental training.* Champaign, IL: Leisure Press.

Railo, W. (1992). *Bäst när det gäller* [Best when needed]. Stockholm: SISU.

Salazar, T. A., Landers, D. M., Petruzzello, S. J., Crews, D. J., Kubitz, K. A., & Han, M. (1990). Hemispheric asymmetry, cardiac response and performance in elite archers. *Research Quarterly for Exercise and Sport, 61,* 351–359.

Scheier, M. F., & Carver, C. S. (1985). Optimism, coping, and health: Assessment, and implications of generalized outcome expectancies. *Health Psychology, 4,* 219–247.

Schmid, A., & Peper, E. (1993). Training strategies for concentration. In J. M. Williams (Ed.), *Applied sport psychology: Personal growth to peak performance* (pp. 262–273). Mountain View, CA: Mayfield.

Singer, J. (1974). *Imagery and daydream methods in psychoterapy and behaviour modification.* London: Academic Press.

Stanley, J. M., & Francis, W. D. (1984). The effects of REST and REST enhanced self-regulation on essential hypertension. Presented at the *XXIII International Congress of Psychology,* Alcapulco, Mexico, 3 September 1984.

Suedfeld, P., & Bruno, T. (1990). Flotation REST and imagery in the improvement of athletic performance. *Journal of Sport & Exercise Psychology, 12,* 82–85.

Suedfeld, P., Metcalfe, J., & Bluck, S. (1987). Enhancement of scientific creativity by flotation REST (Restricted Environmental Stimulation Technique). *Journal of Environmental Psychology, 7,* 219–231.

Summers, P., & Ford, S. K. (1995). The test of attentional and interpersonal style: An evaluation. *International Journal of Sport Psychology, 21,* 102–111.

Summers, J. J., Miller, K., & Ford, S. K. (1991). Attentional style and basketball performance. *Journal of Sport & Exercise Psychology, 8,* 239–253.

Turner, J. W., Jr., & Fine, T. H., (1984). REST-assisted relaxation and chronic pain. Presented at the *XXIII International Congress of Psychology,* Alcapulco, Mexico, 3 September 1984.

Wagaman, J., Barabasz, A., & Barabasz, M. (1991). Flotation rest and imagery in the improvement of collegiate basketball performance. *Perceptual and Motor Skills, 72,* 119–122.

Zubeck, J. P. (1973). Behavioral and physiological effects of prolonged sensory and perceptual deprivation: A review. In J. E. Rasmussen (ed.), *Man in isolation and confinement* (pp. 9–83). Chicago: Aldine.

Manuscript submitted: May 4, 1998
Final revision received: Jan 10, 1999

JOURNAL OF APPLIED SPORT PSYCHOLOGY **11,** 210–229 (1999)

The Changes in Psychological Characteristics and Reactions of Elite Athletes from Injury Onset until Full Recovery

ANN M. QUINN AND BARRY J. FALLON

University of Melbourne, Melbourne, Australia

The purpose of this investigation was to describe the psychological characteristics and reactions of injured athletes and to examine the changes in these reactions throughout their rehabilitation. This study examined 136 elite injured athletes from 25 sports at four phases: upon injury, partial recovery, semi-recovery, and full recovery. Injury appraisal, athlete's demographics, and emotional and psychological variables were measured. Duration of injuries ranged from 4 to 99 weeks (M = 19 weeks). Changes were examined through a series of repeated measure MANOVAs with polynomial contrasts. Findings were typically as expected: increased confidence and vigor and decreased negative emotional responses over the recovery period. The changes over the recovery period were not always at a constant rate. Confidence of adhering to rehabilitation, passive, and emotion-focused coping, remained stable over time. The initial injury appraisal, regarding anticipated loss of time and the psychological impact of this, needs to be examined further. The psychological state of the athlete at the various stages of recovery has important implications for those diagnosing injuries and implementing rehabilitation programs.

Regardless of experience or ability, no athlete is immune to injury (Steadman, 1993). For the elite athlete, a great deal of time and energy is invested in obtaining optimal performance in sport, hence any significant injury is likely to be perceived as a traumatic life event with physical and psychological ramifications. The psychological effects on a sport participant include the initial emotional responses of experiencing an injury, the psychological factors that influence the recovery process, and the psychological impact of an injury on the individual's future performance (Grove & Gordon, 1992; McDonald & Hardy, 1990).

Correspondence concerning this article should be addressed to Dr. A. Quinn and Dr B. Fallon, Department of Psychology, University of Melbourne, Parkville, Victoria, 3052, Australia, email: aquinn@tennisaustralia.com.au

This study formed part of the first author's doctoral dissertation research conducted in the Department of Psychology, University of Melbourne.

 1041-3200/99/0210–0229$1.00/0

Many factors can influence the recovery process of an injured athlete. Some authors (Gieck, 1990; Gordon, 1986; Rotella, 1988; Silva & Hardy, 1991) suggested that injured athletes progress through a grief cycle similar to that experienced by the terminally ill and have adapted the stage model proposed by Kubler-Ross (1969) to injured athletes. The one cross-sectional study in which emotional adjustment and injury duration data were gathered failed to support stage models (Brewer, Linder, & Phelps, 1995). On the other hand, Smith, Scott, O'Fallon, and Young (1990) and McDonald and Hardy (1990), reported in their research that global negative affective reactions diminished with time.

In summary, research has not supported the major claims of stage models. Behaviors consistent with the various stages hypothesised in stage models have been observed in injured athletes by sport medicine personnel (Gordon, Milios, & Grove, 1991), but a common sequence of discrete emotional reactions to athletic injury has not been documented. The evidence suggests that mood disturbances following injuries appear to be more global and varied across individuals than stage models would predict. The notion of a stereotypic pattern of distinct emotional responses to loss has not stood up to empirical scrutiny (Brewer, 1994).

Whereas stage models fail to account for individual differences in responses to athletic injuries, cognitive appraisal models have been developed to explain such differences (Brewer, 1994). Some examples of cognitive appraisal models which have relevance to psychological responses to injury include: Lazarus and Folkman's (1984) transactional model of stress; Weiss and Troxel's (1986) psychophysiological stress model; and Wiese-Bjornstal and Smith's (1993) cognitive-emotional-behavioral model. In each of these models, responses to injury are analyzed in the context of the stress process. It is proposed that the way the athlete appraises the injury determines the emotional responses, which in turn is thought to affect behavioral outcomes. However, there are little or no experimental or empirical data to support the applicability of these models to the recovery process. Additionally, due to the demands of competitive sport, it should be noted that athletes may face different issues compared to their non-athletic counterparts. The generalizability of non-athletic models to the athletic population is thus questionable (Rose & Jevne, 1993).

Regardless of how the response to injury is described, the basic implication in these theories is that athletes will manifest different reactions throughout their injury and may exhibit these reactions according to variable time lines. Thus, this study aimed to examine the changes in psychological characteristics and reactions of elite athletes from injury onset until full recovery. The variables examined in this study included: emotional responses, self-efficacy, coping skills, self-motivation, and confidence. The related literature pertaining to these variables will be discussed briefly.

Psychological Aspects

Emotional Responses. Emotional responses are mood states that athletes experience during injury and recovery. Significant mood disturbances, such as elevations in depression, tension, and anger, have been found in more seriously injured athletes (Grove, Stewart, & Gordon, 1990; Smith, Scott, O'Fallon, & Young, 1990). Smith, Scott, O'Fallon, and Young (1990) found that mood disturbance paralleled the rating of perceived recovery, that severity of injury was the major determinant of the emotional response, and that athletes with minor injuries actually had less mood disturbance than college norms. Connelly (1991) found that physical self-efficacy was affected by injury, but self-esteem and physical acceptance were not. McDonald and Hardy (1990) examined the affective response pattern of severely injured athletes and found there was a transition from an extremely negative state immediately following injury to an extremely positive state during the rehabilitation period, thus suggesting a two-stage process. Conversely, Yukelson (1986) believes that most seriously injured athletes seem to react by facillating through emotional highs and lows. These findings, illustrate the importance of avoiding the assumption that all injured athletes will experience the same cognitive and emotional responses.

Self-efficacy. Another variable that may affect one's responses to injury is self-efficacy (Kelley, 1990). Self-efficacy is defined as the strength of one's conviction that he or she can successfully execute a behavior required to produce a certain outcome (Bandura, 1977). Efficacy expectations determine how much effort people expend on a task and how long they will persist in the face of adversity or setbacks. Self-efficacy is not concerned with the skills an individual has, but rather with the judgements of what an individual can do with the skills he or she possesses (Bandura, 1986).

A number of studies have considered the relationship between self-efficacy and performance in competitive sport (Feltz, Bandura, & Lirrg, 1989; Weiss, Wiese, & Klint, 1989). In general, these studies indicated that higher levels of self-efficacy are associated with superior performance. It thus seems logical to hypothesize that higher self-efficacy may result in a quicker recovery time and/or more confident recovery.

Coping Skills. Coping skills comprise a wide range of behaviors and social networks that help the individual deal with the problems, joys, disappointments, and stresses of life (Andersen & Williams, 1988). Numerous authors have presumed the importance of coping during the injury rehabilitation process (Andersen & Williams, 1988; Gordon, Milios, & Grove, 1991), though little has been empirically studied to identify ways of coping with injury. Little is known about what types of coping strategies are used most frequently by injured athletes, and if these coping patterns change over the course of rehabilitation, or what types of strategies are most effective in facilitating adherence and recovery. This is certainly an important and potentially fruitful area of research (Madden, 1995).

Self-motivation. Self-motivation has been associated with better adherence to rehabilitation regimens (Duda, Smart, & Tappe, 1989; Fisher, Domm, & Wuest, 1988). The question of motivation during rehabilitation becomes particularly critical during inevitable setbacks and periods of little or no improvement, which will challenge the athlete's motivation and enthusiasm for treatment (Grove & Gordon, 1992).

Confidence. Physical recovery, however, is only a part of total recovery. Without successful psychological rehabilitation, recovery is incomplete. Some athletes, despite physical readiness, are not psychologically ready to return to competition (Wiese & Weiss, 1987). To them, even the suggestion of returning is a questioned challenge. Doubts, fears, and anxieties surface. Such anxiety and tension can lead to one or more of the following: reinjury; injury to another body part; lowered confidence resulting in a temporary or permanent performance decrement; general depression; and fear of further injury, which can sap motivation and the desire to return to competition. The literature clearly suggests that athletes should only be allowed to return to competition when they themselves consider that they are both physically and mentally ready to do so (Gordon & Lindgren, 1990; Rotella, 1985; Wiese & Weiss, 1987).

Need for this Study

"The future will demand that injury rehabilitation include both physical and psychological components" (Rotella & Heyman, 1986, p. 343). It is crucial to the ultimate goal of recovery and return to competition. However, at present, the psychological processes an injured athlete goes through during recovery is unclear. There is general agreement but little empirical evidence that injury results in emotional and behavioral reactions characteristic of the grief response. Smith, Scott, and Wiese (1990) have cautioned against too readily accepting grief response theories based on the experiences of the terminally ill and other health loss populations. Such groups differ in many ways from injured athletes.

It is interesting that despite all the theory published about coping, little is known about how injured athletes cope with injuries throughout rehabilitation, and if certain coping strategies are more advantageous with regard to injury rehabilitation and recovery. Research in this area is long overdue and much needed. This study will thus examine the psychological characteristics and reactions of elite injured athletes to long-term injury and the changes that occur from injury onset until full recovery.

Method

Participants

One-hundred-and-thirty-six elite injured athletes were surveyed throughout their rehabilitation. The sample comprised 118 (86.8%) male and 18 (13.2%) female elite injured athletes ranging in age from 18 years to 44 years, with a mean age of 24.6 years (SD = 4.5 years). The group included Olympic competitors and athletes competing at the international level, the national level, and at the highest level in their state. The participants represented 25 different sports, with 50% (n = 68) participating in contact sports and the remainder in non-contact sports. The majority

(73.5%) were involved in team sports, and the remaining 26.5% played individual sports. Participants had been involved in their sport at their current level for an average of 5.56 years (*SD* = 3.48; range = 1–16 years). Almost 90% of the sample trained 10 hours or more per week with the majority of athletes training somewhere between 10–25 hours each week.

One-third of the sample did not earn money from their sport, and only 17% earned their total income from their sport. The remaining 50% of the athletes in the sample, whose earnings were dependent on their successful sporting performance, derived an average of 67% of their income from their respective sports.

Types of Injuries. Each athlete and his or her medical personnel were required to give a brief description of the injury. Fifteen categories were formed. The predominant injuries were major ligamentous injuries of the knee (*n* = 32, 23.5% of injuries), injuries to the shoulder joint (*n* = 13, 9.6%), and stress fractures (*n* = 11, 8.1%). This was closely followed by the other fractures, and knee injury groups, lower back injuries and thigh muscle strains. Each of the remaining categories of injuries made up less than 5% of the total injuries.

Duration of Recovery. For the purpose of this study, the duration of recovery was defined as the actual number of weeks the athlete was injured and unable to participate at a full level of training (*M* = 19.25 weeks; *SD* = 17.91; range = 4–99 weeks).

Injury Variables. Injury was operationally defined as physical damage sustained as a result of sport participation. Time loss was the actual number of weeks the athlete was injured and unable to participate at a full level of training.

Procedure

Participants were required to be out of competition and/or training for a minimum of four weeks in order to be included in this research. Participants initially completed a demographic questionnaire assessing background information such as name, age, sex, type of sport, sport class, injury, level of play, years experience at current level, hours per week training, earnings, and injury history.

A sport injury survey was used to explore and identify psychological characteristics, conditions, or practices that relate to the recovery process. Data were collected at four different time points. The *Phase 1* portion of the survey was completed after evaluation of the injury by the medical personnel and within one week of the injury occurring. The doctor's estimated time to return (completed at initial appraisal) was used to determine when the athlete was required to fill out phases two (partial recovery), and three (semi-recovery) of the questionnaire. This was calculated by dividing the total expected weeks to recovery by three. *Phase 2* was thus completed at approximately one-third of the recovery time and *Phase 3* at two-thirds of the recovery time. *Phase 4* was completed when the athlete had reached full recovery. As the total length of time to recovery varied so greatly (Range = 4–99 weeks), this was seen as the only fair way of comparing athletes at various phases of their rehabilitation. If recovery was not proceeding as expected at Phase 2, then the estimated number of weeks to recovery was adjusted, so that Phases 3 and 4 would be completed at the appropriate times.

The medical personnel who was most familiar with each athlete was required to complete the corresponding medical questionnaire. This survey requested the doctor or physiotherapist to supply a description of the injury, the date it occurred, the rehabilitation requirements, and the estimated, and actual date of return to training and/or competition. Progress reports of the athlete's recovery were also collected at Phases 2 and 3.

Measures

Confidence. Two measures were used to assess self-confidence. At each data collection stage, Vealey's State Sport-Confidence Inventory (SSCI) was administered (Vealey, 1986). Participants were asked to compare their confidence to the most confident athlete they know when responding to each 9-point Likert scale item. The scores are additive. Also, the athletes were asked to indicate on a scale from 0 to 100 how confident they are right now in their ability to be successful at their sport.

Injury Appraisal. The injury appraisal was provided by the doctor and/or physiotherapist at each of the four time points during the injury rehabilitation. The medical personnel were asked to provide a brief description of the athlete's injury and estimate the length of time (in weeks) for the athletes return to full level of training or competition. The medical team were also required to estimate on a scale of 0–100 percent, the range of motion for the injured body part; the strength of the injured body part and surrounding tissues, as well as the athlete's functional use of the injured body part. The latter three components, combined, make up the variable "athletic function." At phases two and three, the medical team were required to assess the progress of the athlete's injury. Doctors were asked to circle one of three responses: slower than expected, as expected, or faster than expected. In the final three phases, they were also asked to indicate the percentage of recovery of the athlete (at that point in time), when compared to full recovery (100%). Finally, upon recovery, the doctor/or physiotherapist indicated by circling yes or no, if he or she was confident the athlete was then ready to return to full training and/or competition. The injured athlete was also asked to provide his or her estimate of how many weeks it would take to reach full recovery. This question was asked at each time point.

Emotional Responses. Schacham (1983) developed a short version of the well known mood state scale, Profile of Mood States (POMS; McNair, Lorr, & Droppleman, 1971) for use with hospital patients. Grove and Prapavessis (1992) made minor modifications to Schacham's scale to adapt it to a sport setting. This modified form of the POMS has acceptable psychometric properties for use in sport settings (Grove & Prapavessis, 1992). The revised scale consists of 40 adjectives that measure the six different mood states: tension, depression, fatigue, vigor, confusion, and anger. The POMS responses ranged from 0 (*not al all*) to 4 (*extremely*). It was administered at each of the four phases outlined earlier.

Self-efficacy. Participants were asked to indicate on a scale from 0 to 100 how confident they were of recovering in the estimated time and how confident they were of adhering to the rehabilitation program. These questions were administered at the first three phases of their recovery.

Coping Skills. The COPE inventory (Carver, Scheier, & Weintraub, 1989), incorporates 13 conceptually distinct scales. Five scales measure distinct aspects of problem focused coping (active coping, planning, suppression of competing activities, restraint coping, and seeking of instrumental social support); five scales measure aspects of emotion focused coping (seeking of emotional social support, positive reinterpretation, acceptance, denial, and turning to religion); and three scales measuring coping responses that are less useful (focus on and venting of emotions, behavioral disengagement, and mental disengagement).

Respondents were asked to read each statement carefully and circle the number that is most true of the coping strategies they have been using to deal with their injury. Response choices were: "I didn't do a lot," "I did a little bit," "I did a medium amount," and "I usually do this a lot" (scored from 1 to 4). Each scale total is computed as an unweighted sum of responses to the four items that make up each of the 13 scales. (R = 4–16, total score = 52–208). The COPE scale was administered at Phases 2 and 3 of the injury rehabilitation process.

Sound psychometric characteristics have been found for this instrument. Reliability coefficient values in general, were acceptably high, with one falling below .6 (the mental disengagement scale). This scale differs from the others in being more of a multiple-act-criterion, and thus this lower reliability is not entirely unexpected. Correlations of the test-retest reliability of the various scales suggest that the self-reports of coping tendencies that are measured by COPE are relatively stable (Carver, Scheier, & Weintraub, 1989). In this study, reliability coefficient values were between .73–.91, with a mean of .84. At both times of testing, the active coping scale had the highest reliability (.90, .91), followed by denial coping (.84, .85) and passive coping (.73, .79).

Rehabilitation Motivation Measures. Exercise intensity was defined as the degree of effort the athlete put forth while performing the rehabilitation exercises. In this study, participants were asked to indicate on a scale from 0 to 100, the intensity of effort they have applied to their rehabilitation program in the past few weeks.

Self-motivation. Participants were asked to indicate on a scale from 0 to 100 how much of the rehabilitation program which was prescribed to them by the medical support staff, and/or coaches during the last few weeks, had been completed. These rehabilitation motivation questions were administered at Phases 2, 3, and 4 of their recovery.

Results

Preliminary Analysis

Preliminary analyses were conducted to verify that the inventories used were psychometrically sound. Tests for skewness and kurtosis indicated that some of the variables were negatively skewed and as a consequence, transformations of the variables were undertaken. Square root transformations were performed on each of the mood states: tension, depression, anger, fatigue, confusion, and vigor, as well as the confidence measures. Inverse transformations were performed on each of the self-efficacy, rehabilitation motivation, and "confident of being successful" measures. This reduced the skewness in their distributions, reduced the number of outliers, and improved the normality, linearity, and homoscedasticity of residuals. The reliabilities for each of the emotion subscales (tension, depression, anger, fatigue, confusion, and vigor) were satisfactory (>.75). Cronbach alpha coefficients for the coping and confidence assessments all had adequate reliability and the variables were retained for subsequent analysis.

To reduce the number of variables in this study and to validate the scales, a principal components factor analysis was performed on the items of the COPE scale. Three factors were extracted. A factor structure was considered meaningful if a minimum of three items had a structure coefficient above .49 and an eigenvalue greater than 1.0. A minimum structure coefficient of .49 was used as a criterion cut-off point to ensure that the variable in question had a minimum of 25% shared variance with the derived factor. As no cross loading was found to exceed .40, variables were not dropped from the factor structure.

After varimax rotation, the first factor was labelled Active Coping because the scales within this factor signify action strategies to actively cope with injury (e.g., initiating direct action and increasing one's efforts). The second factor reflected Denial and Emotion Focused Coping methods. The items in this factor included: seeking of social support for emotional reasons, turning to religion, denial, behavioral disengagement, and focus on, and venting of emotions. The third factor was labelled Passive Coping because the three items within this factor reflect a passive approach to dealing with injury. The internal consistency of the extracted scales was found to be satisfactory, yielding alpha reliability coefficients ranging from .79 to .91, and a mean of .85.

Analyses

The data analysis focused on describing the psychological characteristics and reactions of injured athletes, and examining the changes in these reactions over the four phases of this investigation. Categories of variables examined included: demographics (type of injury, time loss, level of competition, history of injury, time in season, hours per week training, age, and sex), medical appraisal (weeks to recovery, overall athletic function, and progress), emotional responses (tension, depression, anger, fatigue, confusion, and vigor), and psychological variables, including: self-efficacy: confident of reaching full recovery in the estimated time, and confident of adhering to rehabilitation program; rehabilitation motivation (intensity of effort and completed rehabilitation), coping (active, passive, and denial); and confidence.

Two sources of data and analysis have been provided in an attempt to identify important characteristics and to ascertain whether significant changes over time in the variables of interest were apparent. First, means, standard deviations and ranges for each of the variables were calculated. Second, changes over time in the scales of interest were examined through a series of repeated measure MANOVAs with polynomial contrasts. Multivariate analyses were considered more appropriate than univariate analyses to control for type one errors. Trend analyses were used to investigate the functional relationship between the levels of the independent variable and the dependent variables. More specifically, the purpose of trend analysis was to determine whether the trend departs significantly from the linear and, if so, whether the trend is quadratic, or cubic, rather than determining the exact polynomial that describes the relationship.

Analyses of research with two time points can only indicate a linear relationship between the independent variable and the dependent variable. As this study has four time points, the non linear relationship over time can also be tested between injury and recovery. A linear increase or decrease may be an imprecise statement of the relationship between variables. Some variables for example, might undergo a more rapid rate of change between phases and then taper off. Analysis of cubic and quadratic trends will thus help the researcher determine how much the means deviate significantly from linearity. For example, a quadratic trend might look like an inverted "U" and a cubic trend is like an asymptote. In addition, the plot of coefficients for quadratic and cubic orthogonal polynomials assists in understanding the nature of the relationship, which in turn gives the medical team greater insight into, and comprehension of, some of the psychological aspects of injury recovery.

Medical Appraisal

As expected, athletic function (an estimate of the strength, range of motion, and functional use of the injured body part), which was lowest upon injury, increased at each subsequent phase (Phase 1: M = 96.80, SD = 73.39; Phase 2: M = 156.07, SD = 69.07; Phase 3: M = 227.19, SD = 48.47; Phase 4: M = 278.61, SD = 31.10). A repeated measures MANOVA of athletic function with a polynomial contrast resulted in a significant linear trend (t = 28.32, $p < .001$), indicating a constant increase in athletic function across the phases.

Progress of the injured athlete which was measured at Phases 2 and 3 also improved. A repeated measures MANOVA resulted in a significant time effect [F (1,135) = 6.78, $p < .01$]. Approximately 5% of the variance was accounted for by time effects (η^2 =.05).

Table 1
Means, standard deviations, and reliabilities for emotional responses at all phases

Emotional responses	Mean	*SD*	Cronbach alpha
Tension			
Phase 1	11.93	4.75	.75
Phase 2	10.40	4.72	.79
Phase 3	9.31	5.18	.84
Phase 4	7.91	5.16	.83
Depression			
Phase 1	11.24	5.93	.84
Phase 2	7.15	5.33	.85
Phase 3	5.27	5.25	.90
Phase 4	2.62	4.46	.92
Anger			
Phase 1	12.04	5.30	.84
Phase 2	8.29	5.50	.89
Phase 3	5.39	5.01	.90
Phase 4	2.96	4.40	.93
Fatigue			
Phase 1	5.66	5.06	.87
Phase 2	4.56	4.58	.90
Phase 3	4.46	4.61	.91
Phase 4	3.01	3.83	.89
Confusion			
Phase 1	8.21	5.17	.81
Phase 2	5.96	4.90	.86
Phase 3	5.16	4.97	.87
Phase 4	3.64	4.04	.83
Vigor			
Phase 1	6.93	6.04	.84
Phase 2	10.08	6.04	.88
Phase 3	11.57	5.98	.90
Phase 4	13.90	5.60	.86

Mood States

The means, standard deviations, and Cronbach alpha's for the Modified Profile Of Mood States scale by Grove and Prapavessis (1992) are shown in Table 1.

There was a decrease over time in each of the negative emotions: tension, depression, anger, fatigue, and confusion; and an increase in the positive emotion, vigor. Negative emotions were highest at Phase 1 and

Table 2
Polynomial contrasts for mood state variables

	Linear		Quadratic		Cubic	
Variable	t	*p*	t	*p*	t	*p*
Tension	−23.07	.001	−9.30	.001	−4.87	.001
Depression	−21.28	.001	17.98	.001	−15.46	.001
Anger	−24.63	.001	7.21	.001	7.37	.001
Fatigue	−5.57	.001	−1.41	.162	−1.69	.094
Confusion	−16.32	.001	14.33	.001	−11.82	.001
Vigor	24.94	.001	−8.30	.001	5.45	.001

decreased with each subsequent phase, and vigor was lowest upon becoming injured and increased throughout the recovery.

A series of repeated measure MANOVAs with polynomial contrasts was conducted to examine changes over time (see Table 2). For the positive emotion of vigor and the negative mood states, except fatigue, there were significant linear, quadratic, and cubic trends. The linear trend which normally indicates a constant rate of change across the phases, while significant, did not account for all the variance between the phases. The quadratic and cubic trends were also statistically significant indicating that the rate of change in the mood states between phases was not constant. That is, the notion of steady increases or decreases in the scores across the phases is too simplistic.

The means in Table 1 indicate that for tension, depression, anger, confusion, and vigor, the greatest amount of change occurred between Phase 1 and Phase 2, and the least amount of change occurred between Phases 2 and 3 for all the variables, except anger, which had the least amount of change between Phases 3 and 4. For tension, depression, confusion, and vigor, the rate of change increased again from Phase 3 to Phase 4. Fatigue exhibited only a linear trend which indicated a constant linear decrease between phases.

Self-Efficacy

There were no significant changes in the mean scores across all phases for athletes' confidence in adhering to their rehabilitation programs, Wilk's lambada, F (1,135) = .937, p = .72. At Phase 1, M = 88.81, SD = 16.60, Phase 2: M = 88.36, SD = 17.57, and Phase 3: M = 88.44, SD = 16.65.

Confidence of recovering in the estimated time was highest at Phase 1 (M = 81.58, SD = 20.40), and decreased at Phase 2 (M = 80.52, SD = 22.14), and Phase 3 (M = 79.06, SD = 23.82). A repeated measures MANOVA with polynomial contrast resulted in a significant linear trend (t = −9.55, $p < .001$) indicating a constant change between phases.

Table 3
Means, standard deviations, and reliabilities for coping scales at phases 2 and 3

Coping Scales	Mean	*SD*	Reliability
Active Coping 2	55.59	11.51	.90
Active Coping 3	56.98	11.82	.91
Denial Coping 2	23.39	5.96	.84
Denial Coping 3	23.65	6.73	.85
Passive Coping 2	28.26	5.83	.73
Passive Coping 3	27.93	6.30	.79

Rehabilitation Motivation

The rehabilitation motivation questions were administered at Phases 2, 3, and 4 of their recovery. Intensity of effort was lowest at Phase 2 ($M = 81.97$, $SD = 23.58$) early in the recovery process and progressively improved with each subsequent phase (Phase 3: $M = 86.60$, $SD = 15.79$; Phase 4: $M = 88.43$, SD 17.60). A repeated measures MANOVA with polynomial contrast showed that there was a significant linear trend from Phase 2 to Phase 4. Intensity of effort was lowest at Phase 2 and increased in a linear fashion to Phase 4 ($t = -3.61$, $p < .001$).

Completing rehabilitation also followed the same pattern as intensity of effort. It was lowest at Phase 2 ($M = 80.39$, $SD = 25.92$) and increased to highest at Phase 4 ($M = 88.45$, $SD = 19.10$). A repeated measures MANOVA with polynomial contrast resulted in a significant linear trend ($t = -3.04$, $p < .01$). Completing rehabilitation increased in a linear fashion from Phase 2 to Phase 4.

Coping Skills

The mean scores, standard deviations, and reliabilities for the COPE scale are displayed in Table 3. There was a slight increase in the use of active coping and denial/emotion based coping strategies from Phase 2 to Phase 3, and a very small decrease occurred in the use of passive coping methods over these two phases.

A paired t-test of the active coping scales resulted in a significant time effect, [F (1,135) = 4.13, $p < .05$]. Approximately 3% of the variance was accounted for by time effects ($\eta^2 = .03$), which was very small. A paired t-test of the denial/emotion focused coping scales resulted in a nonsignificant time effect, Wilk's lambda, F (1,135) = .66, n.s. Also a paired t-test of the passive coping scales resulted in a nonsignificant time effect, F (1,135)=.87, n.s.

Confidence

Results of Vealey's State Sport Confidence Inventory suggest that this sample was moderately confident in their ability to be successful in their sport, when compared to the most confident athlete they know. Minimal changes occurred in the mean confidence scores for Phase 1 (M = 92.24, SD = 14.73), Phase 2 (M = 90.15, SD = 17.60), and Phase 3 (M = 91.21, SD = 17.57), but there was a small increase upon recovery (M = 97.65, SD = 15.35). A repeated measures MANOVA with polynomial contrasts also explained these results. Although there was a significant linear trend (t = −5.35, $p < .001$) indicating a relatively constant rate of change between phases, the significant quadratic trend ($t = -4.75$, $p < .001$) indicated that the rate of change between phases varied. Part of this variation incorporates the initial reduction in confidence from Phase 1 to Phase 2, followed by a small increase, but the least amount of change between Phases 2 and 3, through to the greatest amount of change and increase in confidence between Phases 3 and 4.

Athletes were also asked at each phase to indicate on a scale from 0–100 how confident they were, at the time, in their ability to be successful at their sport. There was a significant correlation between this measure and Vealey's scale ($r = .46$, $p < .01$). The mean scores on this test suggest that these injured athletes were also very confident in their ability to be successful again in their respective sport.

Confident of being successful was high immediately after becoming injured (M = 88.79, SD = 15.32), and decreased at Phases 2 (M = 82.82, SD = 18.75), and 3 (M = 82.10, SD = 18.41). This was followed by a small increase at Phase 4 (M = 84.17, SD = 18.48). A repeated measures MANOVA with a polynomial contrast showed that there were significant linear ($t = 3.17$, $p < .05$) and quadratic trends ($t = -3.55$, $p < .001$) from Phase 1 to Phase 4. From an initial high mean at Phase 1, the greatest amount of change and decrease in confident of being successful occurred between Phases 1 and 2, and a further decrease again from Phase 2 to Phase 3, which was the least amount of change. A further increase occurred again between Phases 3 and 4.

In summary, both confidence measures indicated significant linear and quadratic trends, a decrease in confidence from time of injury to Phase 2 and an increase at Phase 4.

Summary

These results revealed many significant trends. As expected, there was a significant positive increase in athletic function. That is, athletes' strength, range of movement, and function improved as they recovered.

Each of the mood states depicted significant changes across the phases. Vigor increased and all the negative emotions: tension, depression, anger, fatigue, and confusion decreased across the phases. Anger, depression, and confusion all displayed higher scores at Phase 1, with a significant decrease to Phase 2, followed by a small decrease to Phase 3, and finally a larger decrease by final recovery. Tension showed a steady decrease to Phase 3, and further decreased at recovery. Conversely, vigor which was lowest upon becoming injured, showed a steady increase to Phase 3 and even more so to Phase 4.

There were no significant differences between the means, across all phases, for the self-efficacy measure, "confidence in adhering to their rehabilitation program." Conversely, as athletes recovered, they became less confident of reaching full recovery in the estimated time. The two rehabilitation motivation measures: (intensity of effort and completed rehabilitation), showed positive linear trends.

The two confidence variables showed significant linear and quadratic trends. There was a significant decrease in athletes being confident of being successful to Phase 3, but this increased in a positive direction to Phase 4. Similarly, Vealey's confidence scale showed a negative trend to Phase 2, but this trend changed to a positive direction from Phases 2–4.

Small, but significant time effects were shown on the progress scale and the active coping scale. Non-significant time effects occurred on the passive coping and the emotion focused/denial coping scales.

Discussion

The purpose of this investigation was to describe the psychological characteristics and reactions of injured athletes and examine the changes in these reactions over the four phases of this investigation. Findings relative to time changes and trends in medical appraisal, mood states, self-efficacy, rehabilitation motivation, coping skills, and confidence are discussed.

Medical Appraisal

As expected, significant time changes in the medical appraisal variables were observed over the course of rehabilitation. Athletic function, which was lowest upon injury, increased from Phase 1–4. Similarly, progress of the injury, as described by the doctor, significantly increased throughout injury recovery. No other injury studies have looked at changes in medical appraisal throughout the recovery. The findings, however, are not unexpected. As athletes are progressing with their recovery, the strength, range of motion, and athletic function of the injured body part should be increasing, as weeks to recover decrease.

Mood States

The data indicated that the participants in this study did not progress through a grief cycle similar to that proposed by Kubler-Ross, as some authors have suggested (Gieck, 1990; Gordon, 1986; Silva & Hardy, 1991). They also did not react by vacillating through emotional highs and lows as Yukelson (1986) suggested, nor did they demonstrate a transition from an extremely negative state immediately following injury to an extremely positive state during weeks 2 through 4 of the rehabilitation period, as found by McDonald and Hardy (1990).

The negative mood states were highest at Phase 1 and significantly decreased with each subsequent phase, and the positive emotion of vigor was lowest upon becoming injured and increased significantly throughout the weeks and months of their recovery. The trend for negative emotions to decrease over the course of rehabilitation is consistent with many findings in the athletic injury literature (Leddy, Lambert, & Ogles, 1994; Smith, Scott, O'Fallon, & Young, 1990; Udry, 1995), and has also been noted in the medical literature (Oldridge, Streiner, Hoffman, & Guyatt, 1995). These findings are important because knowing that the period immediately following injury occurrence is associated with the greatest negative moods and low vigor, may allow practitioners to streamline intervention efforts by targeting this period of the rehabilitation process. It was important to find that confusion was also high because it suggests that the athletes were not clear about the nature of their injury diagnosis and/or rehabilitation procedures. Medical practitioners can easily rectify this concern by explaining in more detail the nature of the injury and giving precise information regarding rehabilitation and what is required of the injured athlete.

Self-Efficacy

The injured athletes in this investigation maintained high confidence in adhering to the programs prescribed by their medical team and no significant changes occurred over time. This is not surprising considering the large number of elite athletes in this sample who play sport professionally and are dependent on their performances for their income. A large percentage of this sample do not have another job, which means they have plenty of time to adhere to their rehabilitation program.

Significant differences, however, were found across the phases in confidence of recovering in the estimated time. There was a significant decrease in confidence of reaching full recovery over time, which is surprising. As athletes recovered from their injury, the confidence that they would reach full recovery in the estimated time decreased. This may be able to be explained by the large difference that occurred between the doctor's first appraisal of the injury (length of expected recovery) and the actual length of recovery. In 9 of the 15 injury categories, the actual recovery time of the athletes took on average 10 weeks longer than the doctor's initial appraisal. In another category, head injuries, one athlete was out for more than a year longer! It is thus understandable that the athletes' confidence in recovering in the estimated time decreased from Phases 1 to 3. The mean expected length of recovery for this sample was 13.5 weeks, and the actual recovery time was 19.2 weeks. Perhaps, if the medical personnel were more conservative in their predictions of the expected length of recovery, athletes would have greater confidence in recovering in the estimated time.

Rehabilitation Motivation

The finding that the intensity of effort and amount of the rehabilitation program completed by the athletes, changed significantly over time is consistent with the work of Meichenbaum and Turk (1987) who have argued that adherence is best viewed as a process susceptible to fluctuations. From a practical perspective, an athlete's adherence and intensity of effort applied to completing the prescribed rehabilitation program, needs to be assessed and facilitated throughout the injury rehabilitation progress, particularly when the rehabilitation period is prolonged.

It is not surprising that intensity of effort, and the amount of rehabilitation program completed, increased over time. During the period from partial to semi-recovery, athletes may be limited in what they are able to do, and the skills they can perform. However, as athletes approach recovery and are able to be more active, they may be more motivated to want to get back and compete, and practice some specific sport skills. The time away from competition may also be a motivating factor to return, and hence their increase in intensity of effort and completing more of their rehabilitation program.

Coping Skills

There was little evidence that participants adopted a unidimensional approach to coping whereby they used only one strategy at any given time. This finding is consistent with the work of Folkman and Lazarus (1980) and Udry (1995). Although individuals responded to the stress of their injury using a varied arsenal of coping strategies, they consistently used active coping more than other forms of coping. This finding was expected. It has been the researchers' experience that elite athletes usually employ action strategies to actively cope with their injury. Their livelihood is dependent upon their successful return. Strategies such as planning, initiating direct action, and increasing one's efforts, are more likely to be employed than strategies such as denial, disengagement or venting of emotions.

The data also support the notion that the use of coping strategies remains relatively stable. Nonsignificant time effects were observed between denial/emotion focused coping and passive coping scales at Phases 2 and 3. Significant time effects were observed with the active coping scale, but only 3% of the variance was accounted for by time effects, thus the amount of variance explained by time changes was limited. It can also be noted that the active coping scale and the denial coping scale were consistent over time, which supports the argument that coping strategies remain stable over time.

Confidence

Both confidence measures indicated significant changes across time. In fact, confidence scores were high immediately after becoming injured, decreased to Phase 2, and increased from Phase 2 to Phase 4. It was expected that confidence would be lowest immediately after injury and increase as the athlete recovered. This was not the case. Confidence was higher immediately after injury compared to Phase 2. It thus decreased during the initial part of the recovery process. This may have been due to the fact that many of the injured athletes in this sample took longer to recover than they had originally estimated at Phase 1. The increase in confidence at Phase 4 when athletes had recovered was to be expected. Their strength, range of motion, and athletic function had all increased. They were now able to compete again and were ready to return. Their confidence in their ability to be successful again had also increased.

General Summary

To summarize, significant linear and quadratic trends were apparent in: the medical appraisal variable, weeks to return; the mood states: tension, depression, anger, confusion, and vigor; confident of recovering in the estimated time; completing rehabilitation; and the two confidence measures. Cubic trends were also evident in athletic function and all mood states except for fatigue. Small, but significant time effects were shown on the progress scale; and active coping. Alternatively, confident of adhering to rehabilitation; passive coping; and emotion focused/denial coping; remained more stable over time. Hence, changes over time in a number of important psychological variables were evident.

Strengths, Practical Implications, Limitations, and Recommendations for Future Research

There were many strengths in this investigation. Not only did this study have a large sample thus enabling good statistical power for analysis, but participants were all elite athletes from around the world. Moreover, the participants were from 25 different sports in all, making this an excellent representative sample of sports. Another strength of this study was the large number of long-term injuries that were obtained. Nineteen weeks was the mean number of weeks (loss of time) that participants were injured in this study. Valuable information was also obtained of the recovery process from a medical perspective, and the impact and effect of the medical appraisal on the athlete was assessed at each phase, which was a significant factor of recovery.

The collection of data at four different time points and the repeated measure MANOVAs with polynomial contrasts also enables a greater understanding of the rate of changes that occur throughout recovery. The increase in positive psychological factors and decrease in negative psychological factors were not constant throughout the rehabilitation process, which is critical to understand for all those involved in the rehabilitation process.

Finally, it can be said that this study appears to be the first of its kind to examine so many facets of the injury recovery process of elite athletes over a long period of time. As such, this study is a significant contribution to the literature and the information will assist coaches, athletes, and medical personnel to gain a clearer understanding of the injury recovery process.

A limitation of this study is that pre-injury profiles of all the variables tested were not obtained. This would have enabled a much clearer understanding of the full affective impact of injury on elite athletes. Some professional sporting teams today have pre-season physiological and psychological testing which may make it possible to obtain more pre-injury profiles in the future. A second limitation of the investigation resulted from the fact that no control group data were collected for this investigation and thus comparisons were unable to be made between the injured athletes and a control group, such as recreational athletes, with the same injury. Thirdly, there was extensive variation in injuries and recovery times that was unable to be controlled and thus contributed to error variance.

Follow up studies which use both quantitative and qualitative methods of assessment will provide further information and understanding of the injury recovery process. It is recommended that future researchers collect pre-injury profiles of subjects. Although sample sizes may not be as large, a greater knowledge and understanding of the full affective impact of injury would be gained. Utilizing the knowledge gained from such a study could then be further enriched by follow-up interviews.

It would also be exciting to evaluate the efficacy of psychological interventions in injury recovery. Skills such as relaxation, healing-imagery, goal setting techniques, and positive self talk, are just some examples of interventions that may assist athletes to full recovery. In the present study, it is not known how many, if any, were involved in such interventions. It would be reasonable to assume that some were, however a study of the efficacy of such interventions would be worthwhile. A control group and several intervention groups could be investigated to determine the effectiveness of strategies used. In a study of this type, it would be best to have participants with the same injury, so that injury status is held constant, and thus comparisons would be better able to be made.

Future research could also replicate this research on other injured populations, such as recreational athletes, more mature populations, high school athletes, wheelchair athletes, people with work related injuries, or even people suffering from other health conditions.

In conclusion, it is clear that further research is needed to provide more clarity and insight into the domain of athletic injury recovery. With the tremendous increase in sport participation, and consequently the increase in the numbers of injured athletes, it is crucial to the ultimate goal of recovery and return to competition that athletes are indeed rehabilitated both physically and psychologically.

REFERENCES

Andersen, M. B., & Williams, J. M. (1988). A model of stress and athletic injury: Prediction and prevention. *Journal of Sport & Exercise Psychology, 10,* 194–306.

Bandura, A. (1977). Self-efficacy: Toward a unifying theory of behavioral change. *Psychological Review, 84,* 191–215.

Bandura, A. (1986). *Social foundations of thought and action.* Englewood Cliffs, N.J: Prentice Hall.

Brewer, B. W. (1994). Review and critique of models of psychological adjustment to athletic injury. *Journal of Applied Sport Psychology, 6,* 87–100.

Brewer, B. W., Linder, D. E., & Phelps, C. M. (1995). Situational correlates of emotional adjustment to athletic injury. *Clinical Journal of Sports Medicine, 5,* 241–245.

Carver, C. S., Scheier, M. F., & Weintraub, J. K. (1989). Assessing coping strategies: A theoretically based approach. *Journal of Personality and Social Psychology, 56,* 267–283.

Connelly, S. L. (1991). *Injury and self-esteem: A test of Sonstroem and Morgan's model.* Unpublished masters thesis, South Dakota State University, Vermillion.

Duda, J. L., Smart, A. E., & Tappe, M. K. (1989). Predictors of adherence in the rehabilitation of athletic injuries: An application of personal investment theory. *Journal of Sport & Exercise Psychology, 11,* 367–381.

Feltz, D. L., Bandura, A., & Lirrg, C. D. (1989, August). Perceived collective efficacy in hockey. In D. Kendzierski (Chair), *Self-perceptions in sport and physical activity: Self-efficacy and self-image.* Symposium conducted at the meeting of the American Psychological Association, New Orleans.

Fisher, A., Domm, M., & Wuest, D. (1988). Adherence to sports-injury rehabilitation programs. *The Physician and Sports Medicine, 16,* 47–52.

Folkman, S., & Lazarus, R. S. (1980). An analysis of coping in a middle-aged community sample. *Journal of Health and Social Behavior, 21,* 219–239.

Gieck, J. (1990). Psychological considerations of rehabilitation. In W. E. Prentice (Ed.), *Rehabilitation techniques in sports medicine.* (pp. 107–122). St Louis, MO: Mosby.

Gordon, A. (1986, March). Sport psychology and the injured athlete: A cognitive-behavioral approach to injury response and injury rehabilitation. *Science Periodical on Research and Technology in Sport,* 1–10.

Gordon, A. M., & Lindgren, S. (1990). Psycho-physical rehabilitation from a serious sport injury: Case study of an elite fast bowler. *Australian Journal of Science and Medicine in Sport, 23,* 71–76.

Gordon, A., Milios, D., & Grove, R. (1991). Psychological aspects of the recovery process from sport injury: The perspective of sports physiotherapists. *The Australian Journal of Science and Medicine in Sport, 23,* 53–60.

Grove, J. R., & Gordon, A. M. D. (1992). The psychological aspects of injury in sport. In J. Bloomfield, P. A. Fricker, & K. D. Fitch (Eds.), *Textbook of Science and Medicine in Sport* (pp. 176–186). Carlton, Victoria, Australia: Blackwell.

Grove, J. R., & Prapavessis, H. (1992). Preliminary evidence for the reliability and validity of an abbreviated profile of mood states. *International Journal of Sport Psychology, 23,* 93–109.

Grove, J. R., Stewart, R. M. L., & Gordon, S. (1990, October). *Emotional reactions of athletes to knee rehabilitation.* Paper presented at the annual meeting of the Australian Sports Medicine Federation, Alice Springs, Australia.

Kelley, M. J. (1990). Psychological risk factors and sports injuries. *The Journal of Sports Medicine and Physical Fitness, 30,* 202–221.

Kubler-Ross, E. (1969). *On death and dying.* London: Tavistock.

Lazarus, R. S., & Folkman, S. (1984). *Stress, appraisal, and coping.* New York: Springer.

Leddy, M., Lambert, M., & Ogles, B. (1994). Psychological consequences of athletic injury among high school competitors. *Research Quarterly for Exercise and Sport, 65,* 347–354.

Madden, C. (1995). Ways of coping. In T. Morris & J. Summers (Eds.), *Sports psychology: Theory, applications and issues* (pp. 288–310). New York: John Wiley & Sons.

McDonald, S. A., & Hardy, C. J. (1990). Affective response patterns of the injured athlete: an exploratory analysis. *The Sport Psychologist, 4,* 261–274.

McNair, D. M., Lorr, M., & Droppleman, L. F. (1971). *Manual for Profile of Mood States.* San Diego: Educational and Industrial Testing Service.

Meichenbaum, D., & Turk, D. (1987). *Facilitating treatment adherence: A practitioner's guide.* New York: Plenum.

Oldridge, N., Streiner, D., Hoffman, R., & Guyatt, G. (1995). Profile of mood states and cardiac rehabilitation after acute myocardial infarction. *Medicine and Science in Sports and Exercise, 27,* 900–905.

Rose, J., & Jevne, R. F. J. (1993). Psychosocial processes associated with athletic injuries. *The Sport Psychologist, 7,* 309–328.

Rotella, R. J. (1985). The psychological care of the injured athlete. In L. K. Bunker, R. J. Rotella, & A. S. Reilly (Eds.), *Sport psychology: Psychological considerations in maximizing sport performance* (pp. 273–287). New York: Mouvement.

Rotella, R. J. (1988). Psychological care of the injured athlete. In D. N. Kulund (Ed.), *The injured athlete* (2nd ed., pp. 151–164). Philadelphia: J. B. Lippincott.

Rotella, R. J., & Heyman, S. R. (1986). Stress, injury, and the psychological rehabilitation of athletes. In J. M. Williams (Ed.), *Applied sport psychology: Personal growth to peak performance* (pp. 343–364). Palo Alto, CA: Mayfield.

Schacham, S. (1983). A shortened version of the Profile of Mood States. *Journal of Personality Assessment, 47,* 305–306.

Silva, J. M., & Hardy, C. J. (1991). The sport psychologist: Psychological aspects of injury in sport. In F. O. Mueller & A. J. Ryan (Eds.), *The sports medicine team and athletic injury prevention* (pp. 114–132). Philadelphia: F.A. Davis.

Smith, A. M., Scott, S. G., O'Fallon, W. M., & Young, M. L. (1990). The emotional responses of athletes to injury. *Mayo Clinic Proceedings, 65,* 38–50.

Smith, A. M., Scott, S. G., & Wiese, D. M. (1990). The psychological effects of sports injuries. Coping. *Sports Medicine, 9,* 352–369.

Steadman, R. (1993). A physician's approach to the psychology of injury. In J. Heil (Ed.), *Psychology of sport injury* (pp. 25–31). Champaign, IL: Human Kinetics.

Udry, E. M. (1995). *Examining mood, coping and social support in the context of athletic injuries.* Unpublished doctoral dissertation, University of North Carolina, Greensboro.

Vealey, R. S. (1986). Conceptualization of sport-confidence and competitive orientation: preliminary investigation and instrument development. *Journal of Sport Psychology, 8,* 221–246.

Weiss, M. R., & Troxel, R. K. (1986). Psychology of the injured athlete. *Athletic Training, 21,* 104.

Weiss, M. R., Wiese, D. M., & Klint, K. A. (1989). Head over heels with success: The relationship between self-efficacy and performance in competitive youth gymnastics. *Journal of Sport & Exercise Psychology, 11,* 441–451.

Wiese, D. M., & Weiss, M. R. (1987). Psychological rehabilitation and physical injury: Implications for the sports medicine team. *The Sport Psychologist, 1,* 318–330.

Wiese-Bjornstal, D., & Smith, A. (1993). Counselling strategies for enhanced recovery of injured athletes within a team approach. In D. Pargman (Ed.), *Psychological bases of sport injuries* (pp. 149–182). Morgantown, WV: Fitness Information Technology.

Yukelson, D. (1986). Psychology of sports and the injured athlete. In D. B. Bernhardt, (Ed.), *Clinics in physical therapy: Vol 10. Sport physical therapy.* (pp. 173–195). New York: Churchill Livingstone.

Manuscript submitted: April 30, 1998
Revision received: January 11, 1999

JOURNAL OF APPLIED SPORT PSYCHOLOGY **11,** 230–246 (1999)

The Effect of Multiple-Goal Strategies on Performance Outcomes in Training and Competition

WILLIAM C. D. FILBY, IAN W. MAYNARD AND JAN K. GRAYDON

University College Chichester

Many sport psychologists have been fighting against the pervasive "winning is everything" mentality and have encouraged athletes to set only self-referenced performance and process goals. However, studies that have explored the practices of successful performers have found that they do in fact make effective use of outcome goals (Weinberg, Burton, Yukelson, & Weigand, 1993; Jones & Hanton, 1996). The aim of this study was to examine empirically Hardy, Jones, and Gould's (1996) suggestion, that consultants should now be promoting the use of a multiple-goal strategy. Forty participants were split into five groups of equal number and matched for ability on a soccer task. Four of the groups used different combinations of outcome, performance, and process goals while the other acted as a control group. Performance on the soccer task was measured over a 5-week training period, and then in a competition. Two-factor (Group X Test) ANOVA's indicated significant differences ($p < .05$) between the groups for both training and competition performance. The superior performance of the groups using multiple-goal strategies provided evidence to support the efficacy of maintaining a balance between the use of outcome, performance, and process goals.

Goal-setting has long been accepted as a practical technique to increase and direct motivation in achievement-oriented fields, such as business, education and sport (Burton, 1992). Enthusiasm for the use of goal-setting has grown as a result of overwhelming evidence for the motivational and performance enhancing effects of goals, particularly from the management and organizational research literature (Locke & Latham, 1990). Locke and Latham (1985) first asserted that the findings from goal-setting research could be applied effectively in the sports environment, and goal-setting has subsequently emerged as a popular intervention strategy of-

---

William C. D. Filby, School of Sports Studies; Ian W. Maynard, School of Sports Studies, Jan K. Graydon, School of Sports Studies.

Correspondence concerning this article should be addressed to William C.D. Filby, at the School of Sports Studies, University Collese Chichester, College Lane, Chichester, West Sussex, PO19 4PE, United Kingdom. Electronic mail may be sent via Internet to b.filby@chihe.ac.uk

1041-3200/99/0230–0246$1.00/0

fered by sport psychology consultants. Indeed, Gould, Hodge, Peterson, and Giannini (1989) found that goal-setting is the most often used psychological intervention during athlete and coach consultations.

However, the introduction of goal-setting to sport has also resulted in the emergence of equivocal findings in the research literature. Although many studies have shown that participants in goal-setting conditions perform better than participants given "do your best" instructions, several investigations have also failed to find the expected performance differences (Hall, Weinberg, & Jackson, 1987; Weinberg, Bruya, & Jackson, 1985; Weinberg, Bruya, Jackson, & Garland, 1987). It has been proposed that the lack of goal-setting effects in such studies might be the result of differences between the sport and industrial settings. High levels of achievement orientation, competitiveness, and self-management skills are commonly found in sports performers, but are not typical in the industrial setting (Beggs, 1990). The absence of goal-setting effects on performance in some studies has also partly been attributed to the tendency of researchers to isolate single aspects of performance goals, such as specificity, difficulty, and proximity. The suggestion being that the absence of complete and longitudinal training programs is responsible for eroding potential goal-setting effects in these studies (Kingston & Hardy, 1997).

More recent research, however, has begun to stress the importance of distinguishing between three types of goals (outcome, performance, and process) and to investigate the possible benefits of emphasizing the relative salience of each goal type in different situations (Jones & Hanton, 1996; Kingston & Hardy, 1994, 1997). Outcome goals usually measure success by making a comparison with other competitors; for example, finishing first in a race or league table. Performance goals are set by identifying an end product of performance that can be achieved relatively independently of others; for example, running a certain time over the race distance. Process goals are less easily defined, but are usually specific about the behaviors necessary for successful performance. Examples of process goals might include "staying relaxed" during a race, or "watching the ball" in a striking game (Hardy, Jones, & Gould, 1996).

Before the advent of studies comparing different types of goals, most research into goal-setting in sport had been based on the use of performance goals. This limitation applied equally to investigations conducted in experimenter-controlled settings, and to the more ecologically valid field-based studies (e.g., Burton, 1989; Swain & Jones, 1995). The predominance of performance goals in research studies was also reflected in the practice of sport psychology consultants encouraging the use of such goals instead of outcome goals (Burton, 1992). This promotion of the use of performance goals being underpinned by a belief that beneficially increased levels of perceived control would result. Support for this view was provided by Jones and Hanton (1996), in a study which assessed swimmers using three types of goals. They found that the predictions of Jones' (1995) control model of debilitative and facilitative anxiety were best supported in the case of performance goals. However, the enthusiasm for the use of exclusively performance goals has proved relatively short-lived after Beggs (1990), and then Burton (1992), pointed out how even self-referenced performance standards may actually be dysfunctional in certain circumstances.

Zimmerman and Kitsantas (1996) examined the use of process goals during self-regulated learning of dart throwing and found that process goals improved skill acquisition more than did product goals. The process goals in this study required the participants to concentrate on successfully achieving the final three steps in each throw which, having been described in detail, were labeled as "sighting," "throwing," and "follow through." The finding that such goals were beneficial to performance would appear to support the recommendation that process goals should be "holistic" in order to encourage chunking and automaticity (Kingston & Hardy, 1994).

The findings of Zimmerman and Kitsantas (1996) were supported and extended by Kingston and Hardy's (1997) study, which compared the relative efficacy of two types of goal-setting training programs on the performance of club golfers over a whole season. A group using process goals showed an improvement in skill level, as measured by handicap, at an earlier stage in the season than did a group using performance goals. This study also measured processes that support performance and found that, relative to the group using performance goals, the process goals group demonstrated significant improvements in self-efficacy, cognitive anxiety control, and concentration. The authors concluded that there is no rationale for assuming that the effects of process goals on performance are mediated only by anxiety changes. The content of process goals may lead to improved performance through enhanced attentional focus, regardless of whether performers are consciously aware of using the information. Kingston and Hardy (1994) stressed the importance of recognizing that the work of Masters (1992) would actually predict performance decrements as a result of focusing consciously on specific aspects of a complex movement.

Hardy, Jones, and Gould (1996) reviewed the state of goal-setting research and drew several conclusions that have yet to be fully investigated. Their suggestions included the following hypotheses: Outcome goals, made explicit several weeks before a competition, will motivate effort and strategy development; performance goals aid self-confidence; process goals should be used during both practice and performance, to aid the allocation of attentional resources and to increase self-efficacy; outcome and performance goals should not be emphasized immediately before performance; and process goals should focus on holistic aspects of technique during skill execution.

Goal commitment has also been proposed as an important moderating factor in the relationship between goals and performance (Erez & Zidon, 1984; Locke, Shaw, Saari, & Latham, 1981). Goals will only have an impact on performance if the performer is committed to the particular goal. Indeed, Theodorakis (1996) used path analysis to reveal a direct effect from goal commitment to performance, and recommended that all goal-setting research studies should include a goal commitment measure. Hollenbeck and Klein (1987) suggested that goal commitment is determined by the attractiveness of attaining the goal and the belief that one can successfully achieve the goal.

Locke and Latham (1990) argued that assigned, as opposed to participative, goal-setting would not result in reduced goal commitment as long as the person using the goals perceives them to be reasonable and they are presented in a supportive manner. Fairall and Rodgers (1997) conducted a field experiment using track and field athletes which examined the effect of three methods of goal setting (participative, assigned, and self-set) on various goal attributes. They found no difference between the three conditions in terms of goal commitment as measured immediately after a single goal-setting session. However, they did suggest that variations in goal attributes, due to goal-setting method, might emerge over time.

Giannini, Weinberg, and Jackson (1988) highlighted, as a limiting factor in the goal-setting research literature, the predominance of studies employing goals that only encourage mastery and improvement. Specifically, they pointed to the importance in sport of competitive goals in which the goal becomes the performance of another person (i.e., competitor), and the level of the goal can be flexible in response to changes in the competitor's performance. Giannini et al. (1988) failed to find a difference in basketball shooting performance between groups using competitive goals and mastery goals. The competitive goal in this study was to score higher than a training partner, and the mastery goal was to achieve a personal best score on the task. It would, therefore, seem reasonable to regard these goals as equivalent to an outcome goal and a performance goal, using Hardy, Jones, and Gould's (1996) definitions. As the participants in this study were recreational basketball players, who were required only to complete two 3-minute shooting tasks, the lack of a goal-setting effect is perhaps understandable. The types of goal used by Giannini et al. (1988) could be hypothesized as having potentially differential effects on motivation in the longer term, depending on goal achievement and perceived ability. However, the relative power of outcome and performance goals to motivate effort would be unlikely to have resulted in the immediate accrual of a significant advantage for either group, in terms of current shooting performance.

A recent study by Kingston and Hardy (1997) compared the goal orientations of professional, county amateur, low handicap amateur, and high handicap amateur golfers across pre-season, pre-practice, and pre-competition situations. They found that, as competition approached, the professionals and high handicap golfers significantly increased their ego orientation. Ego orientations of the low handicap and county amateur golfers remained stable across the three situations. Interestingly, only the high handicap golfers exhibited a significant reduction in task orientation before competition. It appears that the professional golfers in this study tried to use the competition as an extra source of motivation, but not at the expense of focusing on the controllable aspects of their performance. The absence of an increase in ego orientation for the intermediate golfers may be the result of just trying to replicate the feel of a practice performance in a competitive setting; whereas perhaps the high handicap golfer tends to prioritize an outcome goal to the detriment of their performance (Hardy, 1997).

Sport psychology consultants are increasingly valuing the perceived advantage of process-oriented goal setting, when compared to the more traditionally used performance or outcome goals. Recently published sport psychology handbooks have reflected this favoring of a process-orientation and some have gone so far as to recommend that outcome goals, such as "Finish in the top three" (Butler, 1996, p. 23), should be rejected as inappropriate. Empirical studies testing the effects of different types of goals have also begun to provide evidence for the positive impact of process goals in competitive situations (e.g., Kingston & Hardy, 1997). However, in spite of these developments, Hardy, Jones, and Gould (1996) pointed to the relative lack of information available about setting goals for performance on complex tasks such as sports skills, and they could only provide "educated guesses" (p. 109) regarding best practice. The aim of the current study was to examine the suggestion made by Kingston and Hardy (1997) that sportsmen and women should in fact be encouraged to use multiple-goal strategies to maximize their level of performance in training and competition. This study compared the effect of four different goal-setting strategies, and a no goals control condition, on performance of a soccer task during training sessions and in competition. It was hypothesized that performance in both situations would be affected most beneficially by a multiple-goal strategy that made use of an outcome goal, a performance goal, and a process goal. It was also expected that using a process goal in conjunction with an outcome goal would be of more benefit than singly using either type of goal.

METHOD

Participants

The sample consisted of 40 (23 male and 17 female) students of Chichester Institute (mean age = 21.68 years, SD = 2.36 years). All the students were reading for sport related degrees and all participants volunteered to be involved in the study.

Experimental Task

The sport-related task used in this study was a variation of McDonald's (1951) Wall Volley Test, first used by McMorris, Gibbs, Palmer, Payne, and Torpey (1994), in which participants had continuously to kick a soccer ball at a target 7.6 meters away. The target was 30 cms wide and a hit scored 10 points. Either side of the 10-point zone were two 8-point zones, also 30 cms wide. Outside of these zones there were 6-, 4-, and 2-point zones, also 30 cms wide. Any kick hitting outside of the 2-point zone scored zero points. For a score to be recorded the ball had, not only, to hit the target but also to rebound back over the 7.6 meter line. The participant had 1 min 30 secs to score as many points as possible. McMorris et al. (1994) measured reliability using a test re-test method and demonstrated an intra-class correlation coefficient of 0.79 for total points scored. McMorris et al. also suggested that the test should be accepted as a valid and objective measure of passing accuracy in soccer. It should be noted that, in contrast with the present study, McMorris et al. used experienced male soccer players as participants. In the present study it was expected that there would be a learning effect on the task, and that this would be observable through the extent of the improvement in the control group.

Quantitative Data Collection

Wall Volley Test Performance Measures. Performance on the Wall Volley Test was measured by recording the total score achieved by the participant in each trial.

Goal Commitment Questionnaire. Goal commitment was assessed using a 4-item scale derived from a scale used by Weingart and Weldon (1991). The participants were required to respond, using a 6-point scale ranging from 1 (*strongly disagree*) to 6 (*strongly agree*), to the following statements: "I was strongly committed to pursuing this goal," "I didn't care if I achieved this goal or not" (reverse scored), "I was highly motivated to meet my goal," and "It was very important to me that I achieved my goal." The scale produced a total goal commitment score ranging from 4 (very low commitment to that goal) to 24 (very high commitment). Cronbach's alpha coefficients for the scale ranged from $\alpha = 0.83$ to $\alpha = 0.93$.

Qualitative Data Collection

Semi-structured Interviews. Two members of each of the intervention groups, 10 participants in total, were randomly selected to participate in a semi-structured interview after the final competition. The purpose of the interviews was to provide an alternative form of evaluation of the effectiveness of the intervention strategies, and also to gain insights into the participant's experiences during a "goal-setting study." An issue of particular importance was the examination of the extent to which participants had ignored externally assigned goals and set their own covert goals, as this has been identified as a significant methodological flaw within the sport psychology literature (Locke & Latham, 1990).

Interviews lasted for about 20 minutes each, and were all based on the same series of open-ended questions. The schedule of questions ensured a similar structure to all interviews and that all participants were treated in a standard way. The potential for interviewer bias was further addressed by asking each participant, at the conclusion of the interview, "How did you think the interview went?", "Did you feel you could fully outline your experiences?", and "Did I lead you or influence your responses in any way?" (Orlick & Partington, 1988, p. 108). All participants reported that they were not unduly influenced in their responses by the interviewer.

Goal Conditions

Outcome Goal Only. Participants were told that they had been entered into a competition, based on a simple soccer skill and involving nine other participants of similar ability to them. They were informed of the date of the competition, the schedule of training sessions, and that there was a cash prize for the winner of the competition. Participants in this group were also informed that the experiment was concerned with the effectiveness of different approaches to goal setting. Approximately one week before the first of the 10 training sessions, the experimenter worked with participants to develop an individually tailored, four-step pre-performance routine: Step One, Goal Statement; Step Two, Centering; Step Three, Positive Thought; and Step Four, Goal Statement. The development of the routine consisted of firstly, instruction on how to use the centering technique as described by Hardy and Fazey (1990). This technique is a relaxation strategy that requires participants to change their center of consciousness from their head to their center of gravity (a point just below the navel). Centering provides a mechanism for quickly relaxing and then focusing attention on what needs to be done and how it is going to be achieved (Hardy & Fazey, 1990). Secondly, participants were required to generate a task relevant positive thought for inclusion at step three of their routine. Participants were guided towards the use of a positive statement that was materially similar to "I'm feeling good" or "I'm ready." Finally, the participants were told that their goal statement, at both Step One and Step Four, should be to affirm "my aim is to win first prize in the competition."

The learning stage began with a one hour group session on centering, positive thinking, goal-setting, and pre-performance routines. This group session was followed by an individual meeting with each participant of about half an hour, during which their routines were developed and recorded. Participants were then told to practice using their routine, initially being encouraged to verbalize their thoughts at each step. Before the start of the training phase, all participants reported that they were able to use their pre-performance routine accurately without assistance. The purpose of the centering and positive thought steps was to add substance to the pre-performance routine without confounding goal effects. Because the second and third steps in the routine were standard across experimental groups, the internal validity of the study was maintained.

Outcome Goal and Process Goal. This protocol was identical to that for the outcome goal only group except for the goal statements in the pre-performance routine. Participants were given information regarding the use of process goals, and then they were helped to generate a process goal statement that could be used in their routine. Examples of the process goals arising included "low and straight," "pace," "concentrate for the whole 90 seconds," "focus on the ten," and "first time every time." Following this, participants were instructed that the goal statement at Step One should be "my long-term aim is to win first prize in the competition, and my short-term aim is to achieve my process goal," and that the goal statement at Step Four should be their individual process goal statement.

Process Goal Only. Participants in this group were informed only that the experiment was concerned with the effectiveness of different approaches to goal setting (i.e., they were not told about the competition). The protocol was then the same as that for the outcome goal and process goal group, except for the goal statement at Step One being "my aim is to achieve my process goal."

Outcome Goal, Performance Goal, and Process Goal. The protocol for this group was similar to that for the outcome goal and process goal group except for the goal statements in the pre-performance routine. In addition to information about process goals, participants were told that part of their routine should include setting a performance goal of achieving a personal best score. Finally, participants were instructed that the goal statement at Step One should be "my long-term aim is to win first prize in the competition, and my short-term aims are to achieve my process goal and a personal best score," and that the goal statement at Step Four should be their individual process goal statement.

No Goals Condition. Participants in this group were informed only that the experiment was concerned with the efficacy of pre-performance routines (i.e., they were not told about the competition, and they completed the experimental tasks without the use of explicit goal statements). They used a two-step pre-performance routine: Step One, Centering; and Step Two, Positive Thought.

Procedure

Initially all participants performed the Wall Volley Test and were ranked by their score. All testing was conducted at the same outdoor location and participants attended individually to eliminate any audience effects. The Wall Volley Test performance ranking was then used as the basis for the selection of five matched ability groups (n = 8).

All participants completed the learning stage of the study and then attended two training sessions in each of the next five weeks. Each training session consisted of participants rehearsing their pre-performance routine and then using the routine before performing the Wall Volley Test. Goal Commitment Questionnaires were used to investigate changes in commitment to the different types of goal during the training phase. Participants in the four goal setting groups also completed the Goal Commitment Questionnaire before training sessions 1, 5, and 10. Separate Goal Commitment Questionnaires were completed for each type of goal being used by the participant.

Table 1
Means and standard deviations of wall volley test performance scores

Goal-setting group	Pre-test		Training		Competition	
	M	*SD*	*M*	*SD*	*M*	*SD*
Outcome goal only	128.6	53.0	147.5	52.6	150.6	49.6
Process goal only	128.3	50.3	152.6	61.8	167.2	60.1
Outcome and process goals	129.0	48.0	179.6	48.6	194.5	57.9
Outcome, performance, and process goals	130.0	49.2	182.1	54.6	194.3	54.0
No goals control	130.4	55.1	154.4	49.8	171.8	47.8

The post-training phase competition comprised one trial of the Wall Volley Test for which participants were instructed to use the pre-performance routine that they had been using in the training phase of the study. All participants were in attendance throughout the competition and trophies, including cash prizes, were awarded to the winners of each group in the competition. After the competition, two participants were randomly selected from each experimental group to take part in a semi-structured interview. Qualitative data reported in this study was generated by the participants' responses to a series of open-ended questions.

RESULTS

Quantitative Data

Wall Volley Test Performance Scores. The means and standard deviations for Wall Volley Test performance scores are presented in Table 1. The score for the training stage of the study represents the participant's average Wall Volley Test performance score for the 10 trials performed.

Suitable homogeneity of variance was established prior to statistical manipulation (p values ranged from 0.128 to 0.997). Scores for Wall Volley Test performance scores were compared between the five intervention groups at the three stages of the experiment using a two-way analysis of variance (ANOVA) (group and test), with repeated measures on the second factor. Mauchly sphericity tests were conducted on the data used in all of the ANOVAs to ensure that the assumption of sphericity was not violated in any of the analyses. In accord with Schutz and Gessaroli (1993) a critical e value of 0.70 was set, and where applicable the Huynh-Feldt epsilon correction factor was used. Following Huck, Cormier, and Bounds (1974), where significant interactions were evident, interpretations of main effects were considered inappropriate. Post-hoc Fisher LSD tests were employed to determine between which means the significant differences were evident.

The intervention group by test interaction for Wall Volley Test performance score was significant, $F_{(8,70)} = 3.14$, $p < 0.05$ (see Figure 1). The results from the follow-up tests indicated that, for all groups, both average

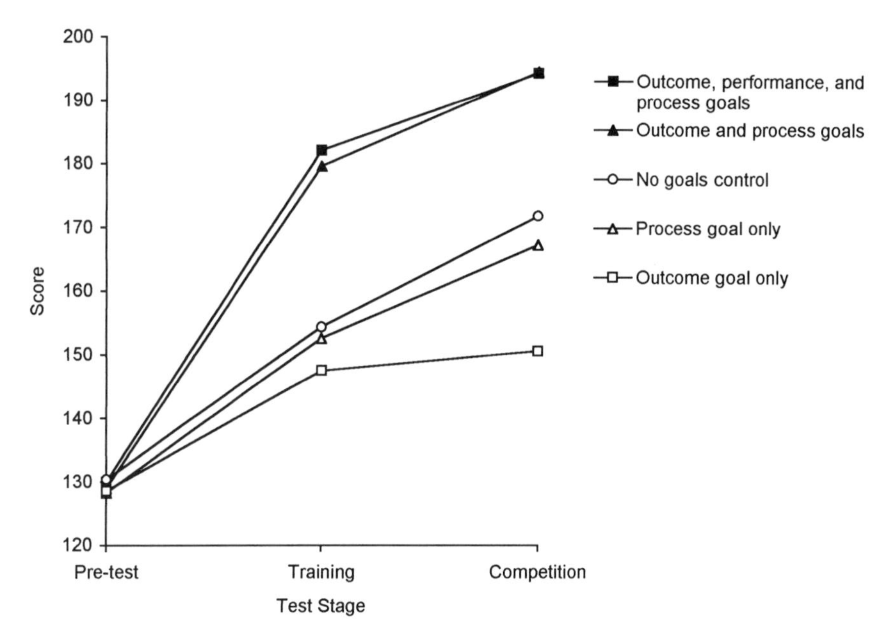

Figure 1. The intervention group by test interaction for Wall Volley test performance.

training performance and competition performance were significantly higher than was pre-test performance. As expected, due to the matching procedure employed, there were no significant differences between any of the groups for pre-test performance. The two groups using multiple-goal strategies performed significantly better during the training phase of the study when compared to each of the other three groups. The only group to improve significantly from average training performance to competition performance was the no goals control group.

Comparison between the groups for performance in competition also revealed that the two groups using multiple-goal strategies performed significantly better than each of the other three groups. Additionally at this stage, both the process goal only group, and the no goals control group, scored significantly better than did the outcome goal only group.

Goal Commitment. The means and standard deviations for the Goal Commitment Questionnaires are presented in Table 2. Scores for commitment to outcome and process goals were compared between the three relevant intervention groups at the three stages of the training phase of the experiment using separate two-way analyses of variance (ANOVA) (group and stage), with repeated measures on the second factor. Scores for commitment to a performance goal were compared between three stages of the training phase of the experiment using a one-way ANOVA with one repeated measure and no main effect was found for trials. Significant main effects were found, however, for trials for both commitment

Table 2
Means and standard deviations of goal commitment questionnaire scores for each type of goal, measured after training sessions one, five, and ten

	Session One		Session Five		Session Ten	
Type of goal	*M*	*SD*	*M*	*SD*	*M*	*SD*
Process goal	16.2	3.2	18.8	3.5	19.9	3.5
Outcome goal	16.8	3.6	19.0	2.5	19.3	2.8
Performance goal	19.0	3.9	21.6	2.4	21.0	3.2

to an outcome goal, $F_{(2,42)} = 13.24$, $p < .05$, and commitment to a process goal, $F_{(2,42)} = 11.50$, $p < .05$. Post-hoc Fisher LSD tests indicated that commitment to an outcome goal was significantly higher at training sessions 5 and 10 than it had been at training session 1. Similarly, commitment to a process goal was found to be significantly higher at training sessions 5 and 10 than it had been at training session 1. No significant interaction effects were found for either outcome or process goals.

Qualitative Data

Questions addressed to participants in the interview situation specifically referred to issues related to the content, format, adherence, and effect on performance in both training and competition of the various goal-setting interventions. Due to the length of each interview, it was impossible to report all of the information obtained. Consequently, only representative interview quotes are presented to illustrate the basis upon which statements are formulated.

All the participants interviewed reported that they had accepted and adhered to the pre-performance routine developed for them to use in this study. They said that they had understood the steps in the routine and felt they had generally been successful in carrying out the correct sequence. Additionally, they all thought that the "positive thought" and "centering" steps were probably beneficial in terms of preparing to perform. In line with the guidance given to them, the positive thought statements used were mainly of a general nature (e.g., "I'm feeling good," "I can do well at this"). Several of those interviewed reported that they had occasionally used slightly different forms of wording, but that the statements had remained conceptually very similar. Centering was regarded by all of the participants as a useful step in the routine. Typical observations were, "the centering bit was good because it settled you down" and "it made it easier to focus on what you're meant to be doing."

With respect to the goal statements, the general view of those interviewed was that the use of a routine was a successful strategy for controlling which goals were being prioritized. Possibly due to this, the reported incidence of covert goal setting was relatively low. There were, however, still times when participants thought that they had not conformed exactly to the expected procedure. The most frequent breach reported was the occasional spontaneous use of a personal best performance goal. This is perhaps not surprising given the nature of the task and the fact that all participants received knowledge of results feedback. Importantly, all of the four participants, who had not been assigned an outcome goal, reported that they had been unaware that there was going to be competition at the end of the training phase of the study. Furthermore, none of the selected participants reported using explicit process goal statements which were not part of their routine.

A valuable aspect of each interview was the part when participants were invited to comment on how they felt their goal setting might have influenced performance. Interestingly, both participants who had used only an outcome goal clearly expressed the feeling that the prioritization of such a goal had been an ineffective strategy. One of them reported that during the training phase he had been "worried about whether I was scoring high enough against the opposition" and that "if a ball went wide . . . it was like a downward spiral . . . what I needed to do was refocus." The other participant echoed this feeling and also felt that she had performed worse in the competition due to "extra pressure" that meant "I didn't take my time . . . when it went wrong I just started whacking it."

The two participants from the process goal only group reported that they felt their routine had had a positive effect on performance in training. When asked about their experience of the competition, however, there was a difference of opinion. One of them said that his/her process goal had "helped with confidence" and "helped with focus . . . every time the ball came back, I aimed at the 10." By contrast, the other participant felt that in the competition "other peoples' scores created pressure" and that "I think that the process goal got forgotten really."

All four participants who had used a multiple-goal strategy reported that they felt the pre-performance routine had been effective in creating a strong tendency to prioritize their process goal immediately before training performance. Their comments on process goals reflected those made by members of the other groups and included observations such as, "it helped you focus on what you were trying to do," and "I liked the challenge of trying to stick to my process goal for the whole minute and a half." In addition, they all considered their outcome goal to have been beneficial, in terms of providing an incentive to improve. A typical comment was, "I think that knowing that there was going to be a competition made me try harder." Finally, the two participants who had set performance goals both seemed to feel that this had also influenced their performance in training. One of this pair suggested that "trying to beat my best score was a good idea. . . . I really wanted to do it each time," while the other reported that "any mistakes meant I started to think negatively . . . that I'm not going to make my P.B. [personal best]."

CONCLUSIONS AND DISCUSSION

The results of this study clearly support the hypothesis that multiple-goal strategies are significantly advantageous when compared to methods that do not combine different types of goal. Statistically significant group by test interactions were found which indicated that groups using multiple-goal strategies performed better, both in training and in competition, than did groups using only one type of goal or no goals. Evidence was also provided to reinforce the opinion that using outcome goals immediately prior to competition may be detrimental to performance. Commitment to both process and outcome goals was found to increase with time spent using the goals as part of a pre-performance routine in practice sessions.

As expected, due to a learning effect on the performance task, the no goals control group did improve across the three periods tested. It is important, therefore, to consider comparisons with the control group when assessing the performance of the other groups. This line of analysis reveals that the process goal only, and outcome goal only groups both failed to outperform the control group, during any period of testing. Indeed, at the competition stage, the performance of the outcome goal only group was significantly supressed compared with the control group. The poor performance of the process goal only group and the outcome goal only group, when compared with the control group, suggest the potential for a negative effect on performance if such goals are used in the absence of complementary strategies. The use of a process goal only strategy might result in under-performance if the strategy causes the diminution of other components of performance such as a competitive sense of urgency, or commitment to expending high levels of effort during training periods. In contrast, the negative effect of an outcome goal only strategy might be derived from increased levels of competitive state anxiety and degraded attentional focus during performance.

The qualitative data produced within this study also revealed some considerations that may be important for practitioners when advising performers on how best to implement an effective goal-setting training program. Support has been demonstrated for Hardy's (1997) suggestion that outcome goals may have a significant role to play through motivating effort during periods of training. However, it appears that the benefits of adopting an outcome goal are realized only when the outcome goal is combined with the prioritization of a "process orientation" immediately before, and during performance. The potential for a performance goal to be a "double-edged sword" (Beggs, 1990) was confirmed, and the difficulty of maintaining a focus on process goals when under pressure (Hardy, 1997) was also highlighted.

The superior performance of both multiple-goal strategy groups, when compared to the process goal only group, supports the view of Hardy (1997) that a balance should be maintained between setting outcome, performance, and process goals. The qualitative data generated in this study also provided evidence for the beneficial role of different types of goals in facilitating competitive preparation and performance. Furthermore, these findings appear to support the suggestion of Kingston and Hardy (1997) that the most important factor in goal-setting training is the extent to which performers learn to prioritize their different goals. An outcome goal of winning a competition may provide the motivation necessary to approach difficult training periods in a positive frame of mind. Performance goals might be used in a number of ways as intermediate product measures. For example, to monitor progress, build confidence, or simulate a competitive situation. Finally, the value of process goals, used during both practice and competition, may lie in the provision of a mechanism for directing attention and limiting anxiety.

The use of a pre-performance routine, as a means for controlling the prioritization of goals before training and competition, was a strength of the present study. Additionally, the fact that the soccer task chosen was of comparatively short duration may have contributed to participants reporting that they felt the goal prioritized immediately before performance had, in most cases, exerted an influence throughout. Over a longer period of time, and under more stressful conditions, participants may have experienced more problems in maintaining the required focus of attention. Facilitating the development of strategies that enable the performer to maintain an appropriate process orientation, particularly when under extreme pressure, should be a priority for sport psychologists and coaches.

The result that commitment to the goals being used increased over the course of the training stage of the experiment is interesting. This could be due to the effect of continued use resulting in the participant becoming more accepting of a goal that had initially been partially rejected. Initially, participants were perhaps less accepting of goals which conflicted with their usual goal-setting style. Performance goal commitment was initially relatively high and the lack of an increase in this instance may therefore have been due to a ceiling effect. The higher commitment may have been present because the performance goal of a personal best score was readily acceptable to more of the participants in the first instance, as it already formed part of their goal-setting style.

The mechanism by which process goals might exert an influence on performance is an issue currently open to debate. One of the difficulties in this area is a lack of definition in terms of what a process goal comprises exactly. For instance, Hardy, Mullen, and Jones (1996, p. 623), reported the current goal-setting literature as suggesting that "athletes should be encouraged to use process goals which involve consciously attending to specific aspects of a movement in order to remain focused during performance." But if proposals such as Masters' (1992) explicit knowledge hypothesis, Baumeister's (1984) conscious monitoring explanation of the effect of stress on performance, and Singer, Lidor, and Cauraugh's (1993) conclusions about the problems associated with awareness during performance are accepted, it is hard to explain how such a process goal could actually be beneficial. Nevertheless, several studies have provided support for the use of process goals (e.g., Orlick & Partington, 1988; Kingston, Hardy, & Markland, 1992; Kingston & Hardy, 1994, 1997; Zimmerman & Kitsantas, 1996). Examination of the "process goals" used in such studies suggests that, rather than attending consciously to any specific aspect of a movement, performers should be encouraged to focus attention using cues of a more holistic nature. Zimmerman and Kitsantas (1996) proposed that this type of process goal should involve a single context relevant cue, such as the center of a target, and that this would not result in the predicted reduction in automaticity. Similarly, Kingston and Hardy (1997) suggested that the use during performance of holistic conceptual cues, such as "tempo," may actually encourage "chunking" and allow the implicit generation of subactions.

Dissatisfaction with the use of outcome goals to motivate performers has largely arisen as a result of research examining achievement goal orientations. In the goal orientations literature there are two different types of goal orientation which describe the mechanism by which performers measure their achievements (Duda, 1992). Task-oriented performers base their perceptions of competence on personal improvement or absolute measures of performance, whereas the perceptions of competence of ego-oriented performers are formulated by comparing their own ability with that of others. The bulk of research into the effect of achievement goal orientation on motivation and performance has contrasted the advantages that result from performers developing a strong task orientation with the possible negative effects associated with high ego orientations (Duda, 1992). The tendency of achievement goal orientation researchers to equate the setting of outcome goals with "ego-orientation" and to label both negatively has resulted in considerable debate. Hardy, Jones, and Gould (1996) strongly criticized the trend towards the denigration of an ego orientation and the implied rejection of outcome goals as a method for enhancing motivation. Hardy, Jones, and Gould (1996) referred to the practices of elite athletes and concluded that "it is difficult to see how one could become a genuinely elite performer without having a strong ego orientation" (p. 78). A further viewpoint, which perhaps offers a compromise position between the extremes, has been offered by Hall and Kerr (1997, p. 37), who suggested that "outcomes are important when adopting a task orientation, they just do not reflect on one's self-worth."

In conclusion, the growing body of research attesting to the effectiveness of process goals and the benefits of developing a process orientation has been strengthened by this study. The current findings also confirm the potential for outcome and performance goals to be dysfunctional if used inappropriately. Most importantly, however, empirical evidence is provided to support the proposal of Kingston and Hardy (1994) that process goals are most beneficially used within a hierarchy of goals that should also include both performance and outcome goals. It is the need to combine effectively, and subsequently prioritize, goals that should be stressed to performers. Such a strategy is likely to have significant advantages, when compared to pursuing the current trend of presenting a "process good"/"outcome bad" dichotomy in the area of goal-setting.

REFERENCES

Baumeister, R. F. (1984). Choking under pressure: Self-consciousness and paradoxical effects of incentives on skilful performance. *Journal of Personality and Social Psychology, 46,* 610–620.

Beggs, A. (1990). Goal setting in sport. In G. Jones and L. Hardy (Eds.), *Stress and performance in sport.* John Wiley, Chichester.

Boutcher, S. (1990). The role of performance routines in sport. In G. Jones and L. Hardy (Eds.), *Stress and performance in sport.* John Wiley, Chichester.

Burton, D. (1989). Winning isn't everything: Examining the impact of performance goals on collegiate swimmers' cognitions and performance. *The Sports Psychologist, 3,* 105–132.

Burton, D. (1992). The Jeckyll/Hyde nature of goals: Reconceptualizing goal setting in sport. In T. Horn (Ed.), *Advances in Sport Psychology* (pp. 267–297). Human Kinetics, Champaign, IL.

Butler, R. J. (1996). *Sport Psychology in Action.* Butterworth-Heinmann, Oxford.

Duda, J. L. (1992). Motivation in sports settings: A goal perspective approach. In G. Roberts (Ed.), *Motivation in sport and exercise.* Human Kinetics, Champaign, IL.

Erez, M., & Zidon, I. (1984). Effects of goal acceptance on the relationship of goal difficulty to performance. *Journal of Applied Psychology, 69,* 69–78.

Fairall, D. G., & Rodgers, W. M. (1997). The effects of goal-setting method on goal attributes in athletes: A field experiment. *Journal of Sport & Exercise Psychology, 19,* 1–16.

Giannini, J. M., Weinberg, R. S., & Jackson, A. J. (1988). The effects of mastery, competitive, and co-operative goals on the performance of simple and complex basketball skills. *Journal of Sport & Exercise Psychology, 10,* 408–417.

Gould, D. (1993). Goal setting for peak performance. In J. M. Williams (Ed.), *Applied sport psychology: Personal growth to peak performance.* (2nd ed., pp. 158–169). Mayfield, Mountain View, CA.

Gould, D., Hodge, K., Peterson, K., & Giannini, J. (1989). An exploratory examination of strategies used by elite coaches to enhance self efficacy in athletes. *Journal of Sport & Exercise Psychology, 11,* 128–140.

Hall, H. K., & Kerr, A. W. (1997). Motivational antecedents of precompetitive anxiety in youth sport. *The Sport Psychologist, 11,* 24–42.

Hall, H. K., Weinberg, R. S., & Jackson, A. (1987). Effects of goal specificity, goal difficulty, and information feedback on endurance performance. *Journal of Sport Psychology, 9,* 43–54.

Hardy, L. (1997). The Coleman Roberts Griffith address: Three myths about applied consultancy work. *Journal of Applied Sport Psychology, 9,* 277–294.

Hardy, L., & Fazey, J. (1990). *Mental Training.* National Coaching Foundation, Leeds.

Hardy, L., Jones, J. G., & Gould, D. (1996). *Understanding psychological preparation for sport: Theory and practice of elite performers.* John Wiley, Chichester.

Hardy, L., Mullen, R., & Jones, J. G. (1996). Knowledge and conscious control of motor actions under stress. *British Journal of Psychology, 87,* 621–636.

Hollenbeck, J. R., & Klein, H. J. (1987). Goal commitment and the goal-setting process: Problems, prospects and proposals for future research. *Journal of Applied Psychology, 72,* 212–220.

Huck, S. W., Cormier, W. H., & Bounds, W. G. (1974). *Reading statistics and research.* Harper Row, New York.

Jones, G. (1995). More than just a game: Research developments and issues in competitive anxiety in sport. *British Journal of Psychology, 86,* 449–478.

Jones, G., & Hanton, S. (1996). Interpretation of competitive anxiety symptoms and goal attainment expectancies. *Journal of Sport & Exercise Psychology, 18,* 144–157.

Kingston, K. M., & Hardy, L. (1994). Factors affecting the salience of outcome, performance, and process goals in golf. In A. Cochran & M. Farrally (Eds.), *Science and golf 2* (pp. 144–149).

Kingston, K. M., & Hardy, L. (1997). Effects of different types of goals on the processes that support performance. *The Sport Psychologist, 11,* 277–293.

Kingston, K. M., Hardy, L., & Markland, D. (1992). Study to compare the effect of two different goal orientations and stress levels on a number of situationally relevant performance subcomponents. *Journal of Sports Sciences, 10,* 610–611.

Locke, E. A., & Latham, G. P. (1985). The application of goal setting to sports. *Journal of Sport Psychology, 7,* 205–222.

Locke, E. A., & Latham, G. P. (1990). *A theory of goal setting and task performance.* Prentice-Hall, Englewood Cliffs, NJ.

Locke, E. A., Shaw, K. N., Saari, L. M., & Latham, G. P. (1981). Goal setting and task performance: 1969–1980. *Psychological Bulletin, 90,* 125–152.

McDonald, L. G. (1951). The construction of a kicking skill test as an index of general soccer ability. Unpublished Master's Thesis, Springfield College.

McMorris, T., Gibbs, C., Palmer, J., Payne, A., and Torpey, N. (1994). Exercise and performance of a motor skill. *British Journal of Physical Education Research Supplement, 15,* 23–27.

Masters, R. S. W. (1992). Knowledge, knerves, and know-how. *British Journal of Psychology, 83,* 343–358.

Orlick, T., & Partington, J. (1988). Mental links to excellence. *The Sport Psychologist, 2,* 105–131.

Schutz, R. W., & Gessaroli, M. E. (1993). Use, misuse and abuse of psychometrics in sport psychology research. In R. N. Singer, N. Murphey, and L. K. Tennant (Eds.), *Handbook of Research on Sport Psychology* (pp. 901–917). Macmillan, New York.

Singer, R. N., Lidor, R., & Cauragh, J. H. (1993). To be aware or not aware? What to think about while learning and performing a motor skill. *The Sport Psychologist, 7,* 19–30.

Swain, A., & Jones, J. G. (1995). Effects of goal-setting interventions on selected basketball skills: A single subject design. *Research Quarterly for Exercise and Sport, 1,* 51–63.

Theodorakis, Y. (1996). The influence of goals, commitment, self-efficacy and self-satisfaction on motor performance. *Journal of Applied Sport Psychology, 8,* 171–182.

Weinberg, R. S., Burton, D., Yukelson, D., & Weigand, D. (1993). Goal setting in competitive sport: An exploratory investigation of practices of collegiate athletes. *The Sport Psychologist, 7,* 275–289.

Weinberg, R. S., Bruya, L., & Jackson, A. (1985). The effects of goal proximity and goal specificity on endurance performance. *Journal of Sport Psychology, 7,* 296–305.

Weinberg, R. S., Bruya, L., Jackson, A., & Garland, H. (1987). Goal difficulty and endurance performance: A challenge to the goal atttainability assumption. *Journal of Sport Behavior, 10,* 82–92.

Weingart, L. R., & Weldon, E. (1991). Processes that mediate the relationship between a group goal and group member performance. *Human Performance, 4,* 34–54.

Zimmerman, B. J., & Kitsantas, A. (1996). Self-regulated learning of a motoric skill: The role of goal setting and self-monitoring. *Journal of Applied Sport Psychology, 8,* 60–75.

Manuscript received: February 20, 1998
Revision submitted: October 12, 1998

JOURNAL OF APPLIED SPORT PSYCHOLOGY **11,** 247–262 (1999)

Coaching Preferences of Adolescent Youths and Their Parents

SCOTT B. MARTIN, ALLEN W. JACKSON, PEGGY A. RICHARDSON, AND KAREN H. WEILLER

Department of Kinesiology, Health Promotion, and Recreation, University of North Texas, Denton, TX 76203-1337

This study compared preferred coaching styles of children and their parents using the Leadership Scale for Sport (LSS; Chelladurai & Saleh, 1980). The LSS preferred form was revised and then administered to children ranging from 10 to 18 years of age who competed in summer youth sport leagues and to one parent within each family unit (n = 239). A doubly multivariate repeated measure MANOVA revealed a significant multivariate difference for adolescent athletes and their parents on the five subscales of the LSS. Discriminant function and univariate analyses indicated that male and female children and their parents differed on autocratic and democratic behavior and children had a significantly higher score on democratic behavior and social support than did their parents. Parents, coaches, and researchers in youth sports could use the revised LSS to determine children-athletes' preferences for coaching styles and for developing more effective programs.

Organized sport programs for youths have been in existence in the United States since the 1920s (Brown, 1985). During the early years, these youth sport programs were established and directed by public school personnel. As the popularity and acceptance of youth sport participation increased, agencies outside the school initiated sport-related opportunities

---

Scott B. Martin, Allen W. Jackson, Peggy A. Richardson, and Karen H. Weiller are with the Department of Kinesiology, Health Promotion, and Recreation at the University of North Texas, Denton.

The authors thank Packianathan Chelladurai for allowing us to use the Leadership for Sport Scale. Appreciation is also extended to the adolescent-athletes and parents for their participation in the study. In addition, special thanks go to Jim Jackson for assistance with the data entry and to Bob Weinberg and the anonymous reviewers for their valuable feedback on a previous version of the manuscript.

Correspondence concerning this paper should be addressed to Scott B. Martin, Department of Kinesiology, Health Promotion, and Recreation at the University of North Texas, Denton, TX 76203-1337. Electronic mail may be sent via Internet to smartin@coefs.coe.unt.edu.

1041-3200/99/0247–0262$1.00/0

for children (Berryman, 1988). Recent figures suggest that each year over 30 million youngsters between 10 and 18 years of age spend 10 hours or more weekly participating in organized youth sport programs (American Academy of Pediatrics, Committees on Sports Medicine and School Health, 1989; Ewing & Seefeldt, 1996). The individuals involved in these agency-sponsored and community-based youth sport programs are program designers, administrators, officials, media representatives, coaches, parents or guardians, and the young athletes themselves. The primary individuals directly involved in the youth sport experience are parents/guardians, coaches, and athletes. This triad has been referred to as the "primary family of sport" (Scanlan & Lewthwaite, 1988) and/or the "athletic triangle" (Smith, Smoll, & Smith, 1989). Although this particular triad has been of interest to scholars, limited research attention has been given to the family unit's perspective of preferred coaching behavior. Thus unanswered questions linger. For example, how congruent are the perceptions of young athletes and their parents about appropriate and/or preferred coaching styles? Does parental toning or parents' roles in socializing young children into sport influence children's preference for particular coaching behaviors? Should parents and young athletes have some direct avenue for input related to preferred leadership with those individuals who direct youth sport programs, because generally neither the athletes nor the parents select their coaches?

Early Influence and Sport Involvement

Arguably the most important people in children's lives are their parents or parental figures, and although parental influence varies over the life cycle, it is paramount during early childhood and adolescence (Greendorfer & Lewko, 1978; Stewart, 1994; "11th Annual Special Teen Report: Teens and Self-Image: Survey Results," 1998). Additionally, empirical research suggests that parents influence their children's motivation to engage in sport and exercise (Brustad, 1993, 1996b; Eccles & Harold, 1991; Weiss & Hayashi, 1995). Typically, parents make the initial decision to enroll their children in youth sport programs (Howard & Madrigal, 1990) and may even play an important role in making sure the program is properly organized. Some research also indicates that parents who are physically active are more likely to socialize their children into sport and exercise than those who are not (Moore, Lombardi, White, Campbell, Oliveria, & Ellison, 1991). Furthermore, research suggests that parents' interests in sports can lead to an indirect teaching of the value of sport to children (Brustad, 1993, 1996b; Green & Chalip, 1997). Thus, parents or parental figures may pass on their attitudes about the importance and appropriateness of sports and physical activity intentionally or unintentionally to their children (Eccles & Harold, 1991).

In addition to parents, coaches in youth sport programs are influential figures for children (Harris, 1994; Hopper & Jeffries, 1990; Smith & Smoll, 1996). Coaches may spend a considerable amount of time with young athletes. The time spent with the athletes may include more than just the regularly scheduled practices and competitive events. Additional time may be required before or after practice sessions and/or competition, for eating, traveling, and attending fund raising events. In as much as coaches' relationships with athletes are considered multidimensional in nature, the coach may take on roles such as teacher, friend, counselor, and parent (Ryckman & Hamel, 1995). Indeed, many of these coaches are parents that give their time freely without financial reward (Green & Chalip, 1997). A good coach-athlete relationship tends to enhance motivation, induce pleasant emotions, and create a satisfactory and positive climate (Bortoli, Robazza, & Giabardo, 1995) while decreasing stress and burnout (Smoll & Smith, 1996). However, Kenow and Williams (1992) found that athletes perceived several specific coaching behaviors more negatively than did the coach. These results indicated that coaches of youth leagues need to be more aware of their behavior or coaching style to be effective in maintaining each individual child's interest and motivation to learn and participate in sports.

Most parents and coaches have good intentions and want to be supportive of young athletes; however, many place greater importance on winning than do the young participants. For example, many coaches and parents assume that acquiring high levels of skill and winning are the major reasons that young athletes participate in organized sport programs (Smoll & Smith, 1996). In contrast, Ewing and Seefeldt (1996) provided the top five reasons reported by adolescents for participating or continuing in organized sport programs: (a) to have fun, (b) to improve skills, (c) to stay in shape, (d) to do something they are good at, and (e) for the excitement of competition. These different orientations and expectations may cause stress between the groups. Thus, some coaches and parents may be unaware or unprepared to meet the needs and challenges of guiding children through the sport experience (Kenow & Williams, 1992; Ryckman & Hamel, 1995).

It appears that parental involvement and the coach's behavior are important at critical developmental stages of children and adolescents. Brustad (1996a) found that parents and coaches have different expectations for boys than for girls. Other research suggests that males between early and late adolescence are more competitive and oriented toward winning than females (e.g., Gill, 1988; Ryckman & Hamel, 1995). Furthermore, boys were found to receive more encouragement and motivation from peers in sport settings due to their larger social network than do girls (Kirshnit, Ham, & Richards, 1989). These findings suggest that boys may receive more support and encouragement from parents and coaches than do girls (see President's Council on Physical Fitness and Sports, 1997; Wilson Sporting Goods Company & Women's Sports Foundation, 1988). It has also been reported that many developmental changes occur for boys and girls during adolescence which may influence self-perceptions of their sport competence (Horn, Glenn, & Wentzell, 1993). Generally, girls have been found to have lower self-perceptions of their abilities than do boys (see Black & Weiss, 1992; Eccles & Harold, 1991). These findings suggest that early adolescent and late adolescent boys and girls may need different types of support from their parents and different coaching styles when participating in sports.

The Athletic Triangle

Understanding the relationship between the individuals involved in the "athletic triangle" (i.e., coaches and athletes, parents and athletes, and parents and coaches) has been of interest to sport sociologists and psychologists for several decades. A plethora of research articles concerning reasons for youth sport participation (e.g., Black & Weiss, 1992; Brustad, 1993, 1996a; Ewing & Seefeldt, 1996) and athletes' preference for coaching behaviors (see Chelladurai 1990, 1993) exists. Generally, research in this area indicates that young athletes "like" coaches who are supportive and encouraging, knowledgeable and instructive, honest and sincere, empathic and understanding, enthusiastic, motivated, reliable, fair, and consistent (Kenow & Williams, 1992; Martens, 1990). Also, research has found that female athletes tend to prefer a democratic and participatory coaching style allowing them to help make decisions more than do male athletes (see Chelladurai, 1993). Since leader effectiveness is a function of the congruence between actual leader behavior and preferred leader behavior (Chelladurai, 1990), it may be important to determine whether young athletes' and their parents' coaching preferences vary.

The concept of the athletic triangle parallels the "educational triangle" (i.e., teacher, child, and parent) in schools. Limited research related to the educational triangle indicates that teachers, parents, and children may perceive leader behavior differently and may also prefer different leadership styles (Sistrunk, Johnson, & Kennebrew, 1989). Epstein and Connors (1997) suggests that well-designed programs that involve teachers, parents, and children can lead to a better understanding of each individual's role and needs. Reduced ambiguity between these individuals may in turn have a positive influence on the child's academic achievement (Epstein & Connors, 1997). However, no studies have investigated leadership (i.e., coaching) preferences from the family unit perspective (i.e., child and parent) in youth sports. Therefore, the specific influence that a parent has on his/her child's preferences for coaching behavior still remains relatively unknown. Clearly, more investigation of the interdependencies among family influence, sport participation, and coaching styles is needed.

Concurrently, examining coaching and/or leadership preferences of children and their parents may provide additional information on the role parents have in forming their children's attitudes toward youth sport participation and physical activity as well as the interactions and insights between parents and children. Thus, the primary purpose of the current study was to examine the coaching preferences of early adolescent and late adolescent athletes and their parents (i.e., family unit). In accordance with previous research on the antecedents of leadership (see Chelladurai,

1990, 1993), it was hypothesized that there would be (a) a significant difference between coaching preferences of early adolescent and late adolescent athletes, and (b) a significant difference for boys and girls participating in youth sport programs. Based on parental socialization research (e.g., Brustad, 1996b), it was expected that there would be a significant difference for coaching preferences between children and their parents.

METHOD

Participants

The participants in this study were Dallas-Fort Worth Metroplex summer youth sport athletes ranging from 10 to 18 years of age and one parent from each family unit. All the athletes and their parents volunteered to participate in the study. Of the 270 family unit questionnaires (i.e., child and one of his/her parents) distributed at youth sport summer programs, 239 complete and usable family unit questionnaires were returned, representing an 88.5% response rate. Therefore, a total of 478 preferred versions of the LSS (children = 239, parents = 239) were returned and analyzed. Of the 239 youth sport participants that responded, 113 (74 males and 39 females) ranged from 10 to 13 years of age which represented the early adolescent group and 126 (72 males and 54 females) ranged from 14 to 18 years of age which represented the late adolescent group. Overall, the youth sport participants had a mean age of 14.0 years (SD = 2.2) and had 6.4 years (SD = 2.8) of sport participation. Represented in the sample were adolescents who participated primarily in the sports of baseball, basketball, cross country, American football, golf, gymnastics, karate, soccer, softball, swimming, tennis, track and field, and volleyball. The parents (118 females and 121 males) of the youth sport participants ranged from 30 to 56 years of age with a mean age of 41.3 years (SD = 5.1) and had 7.2 years (SD = 3.5) of sport participation. None of the parents were currently coaching their child in the organized youth sport program. Of the 239 child-parent pairs, 78 father-son, 43 father-daughter, 68 mother-son, and 50 mother-daughter combinations existed. In addition, 215 (90%) of the child-parent pairs were Caucasian, 13 (5%) were African-American, 9 (4%) were Latino, and 2 (1%) were Asian.

Instrument

The preferred version of the Leadership Scale for Sport (LSS) designed by Chelladurai and Saleh (1980) was used to determine adolescents' and their parents' preferences for coaching behavior. The LSS preferred version is a 40-item instrument representing five dimensions of leadership behavior. The five subscales are Training and Instruction (TI), Democratic Behavior (DB), Autocratic Behavior (AB), Social Support (SS), and Positive Feedback (PF). Participants respond to each item by selecting one of the response categories of "always," "often," "occasionally," "seldom," or "never." These response categories were anchored at 100%, 75%, 50%, 25%, and 0% of the time, respectively. Chelladurai and Saleh (1980) reported test-retest reliability for the preferred version of the LSS over a 4-week period that ranged from .71 for SS to .82 for DB. Also, they reported internal consistency estimates of .83, .75, .45, .70, and .82 for TI, DB, AB, SS, and PF, respectively. Chelladurai and Saleh (1980) found that the identical five factors emerged for physical education majors and varsity athletes. This supported the construct validity of the LSS. Furthermore, scores on the subscales of the LSS have been shown to discriminate between male and female respondents and between novice and athletically skilled respondents, thus providing evidence of construct validity (Chelladurai, 1990).

Prior to administration, a panel of nine youth coaches and two elementary classroom teachers read each item and made slight wording changes to 18 of the 40 items to reduce ambiguity for early adolescent and late adolescent athletes (e.g., "Keep aloof from the athletes" to "Keep distant from the athletes"). These changes were minor and did not alter the psychometric properties of the instrument (Martin, Jackson, Weiller, & Richardson, 1997). The LSS was revised to not only request young athletes to provide their preference for coaching behaviors (i.e., "I prefer my coach to . . .") but also to request their parents' preference for coaching behaviors (i.e., "I prefer my child's coach to . . .") on all five subscales. This revised LSS was reviewed for readability and clarity by 13 early adolescent athletes (i.e., ranging from 10 to 13 years of age) and their parents. The final revised preferred versions of the LSS (i.e., child and parent) included demographic questions (i.e., age, gender, race, education level, favorite sport, number of years participating in favorite sport, and sport organization type) and questions related to gender and age preference of the coach.

Procedures

The human subjects institutional review board approval was received prior to collecting data. Administration of the revised LSS to youth sport athletes and their parents was conducted during summer youth sport programs. The directors and coaches agreed to participate in the study and to recruit children and parents involved in their summer programs. The investigators read instructions for completion of the inventory and informed athletes and their parents that participation was voluntary. Informed consent was received prior to completion of the questionnaire. Anonymity was guaranteed and assurance that all data would be kept strictly confidential was given. Thus, aggregate group data were reported. Each participant was given an answer sheet and a question sheet. The instructions directed respondents to individually report (i.e., parent and child were instructed to complete the questionnaires separately) their preferred coaching behaviors (e.g., "I prefer my child's coach to see to it that athletes work as hard as they can."). The test administrator answered

Table 1
Test-retest reliabilities and internal consistency estimates for the LSS subscales

	Test-rest reliabilities		Internal consistency estimates	
Subscales	Children (n = 15)	Parents (n = 15)	Children (n = 239)	Parents (n = 239)
Training & Instruction	.78	.82	.77	.76
Democratic Behavior	.85	.87	.75	.78
Autocratic Behavior	.77	.83	.55	.50
Social Support	.91	.80	.63	.62
Positive Feedback	.89	.86	.68	.72

any questions and instructed the participants to answer each item as honestly as possible. The questionnaire took approximately 15 minutes to complete.

Data Analysis

Children (early adolescent and late adolescent) and parents' responses on the revised LSS was evaluated using a 2 × 2 × 2 × 2 (Adolescent Age Group × Child's Gender × Parent's Gender × Child/Parent Pair) doubly multivariate repeated measures analysis of variance (DM MANOVA; Schultz & Gessaroli, 1987). DM MANOVA was used to analyze child/parent responses on the LSS jointly (i.e., parent-child combination is the repeated measure) because this "family unit" relationship is not independent of one another and is considered to be a correlated factor. Thus, the child/parent pair was the within-subject factor and the child's age group (i.e., early adolescent and late adolescent), child's gender and parent's gender were the between-subject factors. Follow-up discriminant function analysis and univariate ANOVAs were then conducted to identify which factors maximized differences among the groups.

RESULTS

Reliability of the LSS

Internal consistency reliabilities based on the responses from 239 youth athletes and their parents were evaluated. The coefficient alpha, internal-consistency reliabilities of the scales, associated with the responses from the 239 youth athletes and their parents compared favorably with the internal consistency estimates for athletes reported by Chelladurai and Saleh (1980) in their original study. Table 1 shows the internal-consistency reliabilities for the five subscales. As reported in many other studies using the LSS (see Chelladurai, 1993), the internal consistency estimates are slightly low for the AB subscale. Applying more than one reliability-estimation procedure enriches the understanding of the instrument's measurement qualities. Therefore, an additional sample involving 15 child-

Table 2
Descriptive statistics for early adolescent and late adolescent athletes on the LSS

	Early adolescent athletes				Late adolescent athletes			
	Males (n = 74)		Females (n = 39)		Males (n = 72)		Females (n = 54)	
Subscales	*M*	*SD*	*M*	*SD*	*M*	*SD*	*M*	*SD*
Training & Instruction	4.25	.51	4.17	.50	4.25	.46	4.09	.64
Democratic Behavior	3.57	.63	3.83	.47	3.46	.57	3.78	.51
Autocratic Behavior	2.72	.63	2.55	.89	2.86	.95	2.72	1.14
Social Support	3.56	.59	3.41	.47	3.40	.57	3.51	.60
Positive Feedback	4.39	.63	4.44	.57	4.23	.62	4.34	.52

parent pairs was administered the LSS to determine stability over time. The test-retest reliabilities for a 1-month interval range from .60 to .93 with a median of .79 for 15 youth sport participants and their 15 parents (see Table 1). It appears that the LSS preferred form had acceptable stability over time for young athletes and their parents. Based on the two reliability-estimate procedures the AB subscale was retained. However, the AB subscale may need further modification and the results associated with this subscale may need to be viewed with caution.

Descriptive Statistics

The means and standard deviations for early adolescent and late adolescent athletes and their parents for each subscale on the LSS are shown in Tables 2 and 3, respectively. In addition, descriptive statistics for male and female athletes and their parents for each subscale on the LSS are shown in Table 4. An examination of these means reveals that positive feedback and training and instruction were very important to the children

Table 3
Descriptive statistics for parents by adolescent group on the LSS

	Early adolescent athletes				Late adolescent athletes			
	Males (n = 74)		Females (n = 39)		Males (n = 72)		Females (n = 54)	
Subscales	*M*	*SD*	*M*	*SD*	*M*	*SD*	*M*	*SD*
Training & Instruction	4.32	.43	4.28	.50	4.25	.50	4.10	.57
Democratic Behavior	3.23	.65	3.28	.41	3.25	.55	3.33	.52
Autocratic Behavior	2.49	.56	2.75	.79	2.76	.77	2.78	1.01
Social Support	3.26	.48	3.26	.53	3.38	.48	3.31	.59
Positive Feedback	4.47	.50	4.45	.42	4.34	.57	4.39	.51

Table 4
Descriptive statistics for children and their parents on the LSS

Subscales	Children						Parents					
	Males (n = 146)		Females (n = 93)		Both (n = 239)		Males (n = 121)		Females (n = 118)		Both (n = 239)	
	M	*SD*	*M*	*SD*	*M*	*SD*	*M*	*SD*	*M*	*SD*	*M*	*SD*
Training & Instruction	4.25	.48	4.12	.58	4.20	.53	4.28	.46	4.17	.55	4.24	.50
Democratic Behavior	3.51	.60	3.80	.49	3.62	.58	3.24	.60	3.31	.47	3.27	.55
Autocratic Behavior	2.79	.80	2.65	1.04	2.74	.90	2.62	.68	2.77	.92	2.68	.78
Social Support	3.48	.59	3.47	.55	3.47	.57	3.32	.48	3.29	.57	3.31	.52
Positive Feedback	4.31	.63	4.38	.54	4.34	.60	4.40	.56	4.42	.47	4.41	.53

and their parents. Children reported that they wanted to receive positive feedback and improve their skills. Similarly, parents desired that the coaches compliment their child and provide effective methods for improving their child's performance. In addition, the findings indicate that parents and their children want a coach that provides athletes with some opportunity to help in the decision making process. Likewise, children and parents want a coach who provides athletes with some nurturing and support. Conversely, the means revealed that children and their parents were less likely to prefer an autocratic coaching style. Parents and children want the coach to be directive only when providing instructional feedback and at times when making decisions that concern the overall group of youth participants.

Although many similarities existed, there were a few differences. The descriptive statistics indicate that boys (M = 2.79, SD = .80) preferred an autocratic coaching style slightly more than did fathers (M = 2.62, SD = .68). Conversely, girls (M = 2.65, SD = 1.04) preferred an autocratic coaching style slightly less than did mothers (M = 2.77, SD = .92). Also, the girls (M = 3.80, SD = .49) had higher means on DB than did boys (M = 3.51, SD = .60) In addition, the girls and boys preferred a democratic style of coaching more than did fathers (M = 3.24, SD = .60) and mothers (M = 3.31, SD = .47). Likewise, the boys (M = 3.48, SD = .59) and girls (M = 3.47, SD = .55) preferred a coach to provide social support more than did fathers (M = 3.32, SD = .48) and mothers (M = 3.29, SD = .57).

Adolescent Age Group × Child's Gender × Parent's Gender × Child/Parent Pair DM MANOVA

In order to examine coaching behavior preference differences among children participating in youth sport programs and their parents on the LSS, mean scores on all five subscales for each child and parent were calculated and used as dependent variables. A doubly multivariate repeated measure analysis of variance (DM MANOVA) using the child/parent pair as the within-subject factor and child's age group (i.e., early adolescent and late adolescent), parent's gender, and child's gender as the between-subject factors was conducted. The DM MANOVA revealed a significant child/parent by child's gender interaction, Wilks's lambda = .937, $F(5,227) = 3.03$, $p = .011$, $\eta^2 = .06$. Follow-up discriminant function analysis and univariate ANOVAs were then conducted to identify subscales that maximized differences among the groups. Based on the discriminant analysis, correlations between dependent variables and the effect were calculated. The discriminant function correlations among the dependent variables and effects and the univariate Fs are reported in Table 5. The univariate analyses indicated a significant effect for AB, $F(1,231) = 6.79$, $p < .010$, and DB, $F(1,231) = 5.29$, $p < .022$. The magnitude of the difference was low for AB and DB, $\eta^2 = .03$ and .02, respectively. Boys preferred an autocratic coaching style that involves dependent de-

Table 5
Discriminant function correlations and univariate Fs

Dependent variables	Child's gender	*F*	Child-Parent pair	*F*	Interaction	*F*
Training & Instruction	−.37	2.94	.16	1.82	−.12	.24
Democratic Behavior	.59	7.63**	−.89	59.61***	.59	5.29*
Autocratic Behavior	−.06	.08	−.07	.34	−.66	6.79**
Social Support	−.11	.27	−.50	18.94***	.04	.02
Positive Feedback	.16	.58	.17	2.24	.13	.26

* $p < .05$
** $p < .01$
*** $p < .001$

cision making and stresses personal authority slightly more than did fathers. On the contrary, girls preferred an autocratic coaching style slightly less than did mothers.

In addition, the DM MANOVA revealed a significant multivariate difference, Wilks's lambda = .749, $F(5,227) = 4.27$, $p = .001$, $\eta^2 = .09$; for child's gender on the five subscales. The discriminant function and univariate analyses (see Table 5) indicated a significant effect for DB, $F(1,231) = 7.63$, $p < .006$, $\eta^2 = .03$. Girls scored significantly higher on DB than did boys. Specifically, the scores of the girls revealed that they were more likely to want a coach that allowed athletes to assist in making decisions pertaining to practices and games than were boys.

Finally, results revealed a significant multivariate difference, Wilks's lambda = .754, $F(5,227) = 14.84$, $p = .001$, $\eta^2 = .25$; for the child/parent pair on the five subscales. The discriminant function and univariate analyses (see Table 5) indicated a significant effect for DB, $F(1,231) = 59.61$, $p < .001$, and SS, $F(1,231) = 18.94$, $p < .001$. The magnitude of the difference was low to moderate for DB, $\eta^2 = .21$, and low for SS, $\eta^2 = .08$. Specifically, this indicates that boys and girls preferred coaching behavior that allows greater decision making participation by the athletes more than did fathers and mothers. Also, the boys and girls preferred coaching behavior characterized by a concern for the welfare of individual athletes, positive group atmosphere, and warm interpersonal relations with athletes more than did fathers and mothers.

DISCUSSION AND CONCLUSION

The purpose of this study was to examine coaching preferences of early adolescent and late adolescent athletes and determine whether parents' coaching preferences influenced their children's preferences. Individuals that have been underrepresented in the coaching preference research, early adolescent and late adolescent athletes and their parents participated in this study. By exploring coaching preferences of children and parents, it was anticipated that greater insight would be gained on how parental socialization influences children participating in youth sport programs.

Coaching Preferences by Age of Early and Late Adolescent Athletes

In the present study, the findings indicate that early adolescent athletes 10 to 13 years of age and late adolescent athletes 14 to 18 years of age participating in youth sport programs tend to prefer similar coaching behaviors and characteristics. This suggests that early adolescent and late adolescent children in this study, regardless of age, want a coach that allows athletes greater participation in making decisions pertaining to group goals, practice methods, and game tactics. Furthermore, these athletes preferred a coach who develops warm interpersonal relations with team members and creates a positive group atmosphere. Thus, the coach should be someone who provides effective instruction in addition to positive individual and group experiences. At first glance, these findings may seem to contradict previous research that suggests less experienced athletes have different coaching preferences than more experienced athletes (Neil & Kirby, 1985) and that development of motor and psychosocial skills parallel each other in a sport setting to maximize improvement in these areas (Weiss & Duncan, 1992). However, the early adolescent and late adolescent athletes in the current study had various sport experiences and athletic maturity levels. Therefore, athletic maturity and past sport experience, as related to coaching preference, may need to be explored in more depth in the future.

Coaching Preferences Related to Gender

As anticipated, gender differences emerged for the child/parent pair. The LSS subscales that best discriminated between boys and girls based on the child/parent pair involved democratic coaching behaviors. Both boys and girls preferred a democratic style of coaching more than did their parents. The girls, as compared to boys, had a greater preference for having input into team activities, team goals, and team strategies. Mothers had a slightly greater preference for democratic behavior than did fathers. These findings are consistent with past research (see Chelladurai, 1993; Eccles & Harold, 1991) indicating that, in general, females prefer a democratic and participatory coaching style allowing them to help make decisions more than do males. Parents and coaches should try to determine what the child needs. A greater understanding of the possible gender differences related to preferred coaching behaviors could enhance the enjoyment that male and female young sport participant's experience.

Coaching Preferences of Adolescent Athletes and Their Parents

The results of this study indicated that there are some similarities between children and their parents for coaching preferences. The findings suggest that positive feedback and training, and instruction were very important to the children and their parents. Children want to receive positive feedback and improve their skills. Likewise, parents desire that a coach congratulate and praise their child and provide effective methods for improving their child's performance. Thus, it seems that children want to learn skills that help them be just as good, if not better than their peers (Ewing & Seefeldt, 1996) and most parents want their children to be skilled or at least as good as other young athletes who match their child's age (Brustad, 1996b).

Moreover, the current study does support previous literature (e.g., Ewing & Seefeldt, 1996) indicating that there are some differences between children and their parents on youth sports. Specifically, the results based on the child/parent pair indicated that adolescent athletes, more so than did their parents, prefer to have a coach who provides social support and allows athletes to help make decisions. Even though age, past experience, and maturity are not equivalent concepts, the measurements of these concepts in coaching studies have corresponded to one another (Chelladurai, 1993). Serpa (1990) found that basketball players ranging from 12 to 15 years of age preferred more social support and democratic behavior than did older players ranging from 17 to 29 years of age (as cited in Chelladurai, 1993). These findings suggest that younger athletes, relative to older athletes, want an opportunity to help set team goals and determine how these goals will be attained. Also, children want to have a coach who is empathetic and sympathetic to the needs of the athletes. This supports Kenow and Williams' (1992) findings which indicated coaches of youth leagues may need to be more empathic and supportive and less negative, especially with high anxious and low self-confident athletes. Parents and coaches should recognize that children want and need to make some decisions on their own and need to receive support to be truly satisfied and fully enjoy their sport (Orlick & Zitzelsberger, 1996).

In the social psychology of sport literature many cases have been presented that highlight how organized youth sport participation brings families together, however numerous other examples have been cited that show how participation in these programs can cause family problems (see Smoll & Smith, 1996). Coakley (1994) maintains that organized youth sport programs may simply provide another avenue for children and parents to establish their relationships. If coaches and administrators of youth sport programs had a greater understanding of the coaching preferences of children and their parents, then changes could be made to impact all the individuals involved, especially the children and their parents (Green & Chalip, 1990; Ryckman & Hamel, 1995).

Future Research Directions

The present study focused on the family unit and attempted to determine whether coaching preferences existed for parents and their children participating in youth sport programs. The results revealed that the revised preference version of the LSS demonstrated acceptable to marginal reliability for young athletes. Findings indicated that similar coaching behavior preferences exist between parents and children. Young male and female athletes and their parents prefer coaches who provide support, encouragement, information and strategies for improvement, and opportunities to make decisions. However, the results also revealed that differences exist for the groups on some aspects of preferred coaching styles. Therefore, parents, coaches, and researchers could use the LSS to determine athletes' preferences for coaching behaviors and for developing more effective youth sport programs.

At the time the present study was conducted, none of the parents were coaching their own child in a youth sport program. The authors also did not attempt to determine whether parents had coached their child in the past. Responses made by a parent and child might be different if the parent is also and/or has ever been their child's coach. The parent's dual role (i.e., parent-coach) may convolute the child-parent relationship and influence how the athlete and parent respond on the LSS. Therefore, additional research is necessary to determine how a parent coaching his/her own child influences the coaching preferences of the child and parent. In addition, research is needed on how involvement in a particular sport (e.g., American football, basketball, tennis, and golf) and the level of competition influences the coaching preferences of children and their parents. The current research investigated boys and girls during adolescence that had different sport interests and skill abilities. It is likely that the relative coaching preferences of children and parents are related to the type of sport that the child prefers to participate in most and the child's level of ability. A final recommendation for future work is to conduct longitudinal research to examine when and how significant others (e.g., parents) influence a child's coaching preferences. In the present study, parents and children provided information on coaching preferences during a single season. It is also probable, based on research related to age and coaching style preferences (see Chelladurai, 1993), that the coaching preferences of children and parents would change over time.

REFERENCES

American Academy of Pediatrics, Committees on Sports Medicine and School Health (1989). Organized athletics for preadolescent children. *Pediatrics, 84*(3), 1–3.

Berryman, J. W. (1988). The rise of highly organized sports for preadolescent boys. In F. L. Smoll, R. A. Magill, & H. J. Ash (Eds.), *Children in sport* (pp. 3–16). Champaign, IL: Human Kinetics.

Black, S. J., & Weiss, M. R. (1992). The relationship among perceived coaching behaviors, perceptions of ability, and motivation in competitive age-group swimmers. *Journal of Sport & Exercise Psychology, 14,* 309–325.

Bortoli, L., Robazza, C., & Giabardo, S. (1995). Young athletes' perception of coaches' behavior. *Perceptual and Motor Skills, 81,* 1217–1218.

Brown, E. W. (1985). Recruiting youth sports personnel. *Parks and Recreation, 20*(3), 65.

Brustad, R. J. (1993). Who will go out and play? Parental and psychological influences on children's attraction to physical activity. *Pediatric Exercise Science, 5,* 210–223.

Brustad, R. J. (1996a). Attraction to physical activity in urban schoolchildren: Parental socialization and gender influences. *Research Quarterly for Exercise and Sport, 67,* 316–323.

Brustad, R. J. (1996b). Parental and peer influence on children's psychological development through sport. In F. L. Smoll & R. E. Smith (Eds.), *Children and youth in sport: A biopsychosocial perspective.* (pp. 112–124). Dubuque, IA: Brown & Benchmark.

Chelladurai, P. (1990). Leadership in sports: A review. *International Journal of Sport Psychology, 21,* 328–354.

Chelladurai, P. (1993). Leadership. In R. N. Singer, M. Murphey, & L. K. Tennant (Eds.). *Handbook of research on sport psychology.* (pp. 647–671). New York: Macmillan.

Chelladurai, P., & Saleh, S. (1980). Dimensions of leader behavior in sports: Development of a leadership scale. *Journal of Sport Psychology, 2,* 34–45.

Coakley, J. (1994). *Sport in society: Issues and controversies.* (5th ed.). Colorado Springs, CO: Mosby.

Eccles, J. S., & Harold, R. D. (1991). Gender differences in sport involvement: Applying the Eccles' Expectancy-Value Model. *Journal of Applied Sport Psychology, 3,* 7–35.

11th annual special teen report: Teens and self-image: Survey results. (1998, May 3). *USA Weekend,* p. 18.

Epstein, J., & Connors, L. J. (1997). School and family partnerships in middle grades and high schools. In J. L. Epstein, L. Coates, K. C. Salinas, M. G. Sanders, & B. S. Simon (Eds.), *School, family, and community partnerships: Your handbook for action* (pp. 177–190). Thousand Oaks, CA: Corwin Press.

Ewing, M. E., & Seefeldt, V. (1996). Patterns and attrition in American agency-sponsored youth sports. In F. L. Smoll & R. E. Smith (Eds.), *Children and youth in sport: A biopsychosocial perspective* (pp. 31–44). Dubuque, IA: Brown & Benchmark.

Gill, D. (1988). Gender differences in competitive orientation and sport participation. *International Journal of Sport Psychology, 19,* 145–159.

Green, B. C., & Chalip, L. (1997). Enduring involvement in youth soccer: The socialization of parent and child. *Journal of Leisure Research, 29,* 61–77.

Greendorfer, S. L., & Lewko, J. (1978). Role of family members in sport socialization of children. *Research Quarterly, 49,* 146–152.

Harris, O. (1994). Race, sport, and social support. *Sociology of Sport Journal, 11,* 40–50.

Hopper, C., & Jeffries, S. (1990). Coach-parent relations in sport. *The Journal of Physical Education, Recreation and Dance, 61*(4), 28–32.

Horn, T. S., Glenn, S. D., & Wentzell, A. B. (1993). Sources of information underlying personal ability judgments in high school athletes. *Pediatrics Exercise Science, 5,* 263–274.

Howard, D., & Madrigal, R. (1990). Who makes the decision: The parent or child? *Journal of Leisure Research, 22,* 244–258.

Kenow, L. J., & Williams, J. M. (1992). Relationship between anxiety, self-confidence, and evaluation of coaching behaviors. *The Sport Psychologist, 6,* 344–357.

Kirshnit, C. E., Ham, M., & Richards, M. H. (1989). The sporting life: Athletic activities during early adolescence. *Journal of Youth and Adolescence, 18,* 601–615.

Martens, R. (1990). *Successful coaching* (2nd ed.). Champaign, IL: Leisure Press.

Martin, S.B., Jackson, A.W., Weiller, K.H., Richardson, P.A. (1997). Preferred coaching styles of adolescent athletes [Abstract]. *Journal of Sport & Exercise Psychology, 19,* S-86.

Moore, L. L., Lombardi, D. A., White, M. J., Campbell, J. L., Oliveria, S. A., & Ellison, R. C. (1991). Influence of parents' physical activity levels on activity levels of young children. *Journal of Pediatrics, 118,* 215–219.

Neil, G. I., & Kirby, S. L. (1985). Coaching styles and preferred leadership among rowers and paddlers. *Journal of Sport Behavior, 8,* 3–17.

Orlick, T. D., & Zitzelsberger, L. (1996). Enhancing children's sport experiences. In F. L. Smoll & R. E. Smith (Eds.), *Children and youth in sport: A biopsychosocial perspective* (pp. 330–337). Dubuque, IA: Brown & Benchmark.

President's Council on Physical Fitness and Sports (1997). *Physical activity and sport in the lives of girls: Executive summary.* Washington, DC: U.S. Department of Health and Human Services.

Ryckman, R. M., & Hamel, J., (1995). Male and female adolescents' motives related to involvement in organized team sports. *International Journal of Sport Psychology, 26,* 383–397.

Scanlan, T. K., & Lewthwaite, R. (1988). From stress to enjoyment: Parental and coach influences on young participants. In E. W. Brown & C. F. Branta (Eds.), *Competitive sports for children and youth: An overview of the research and issues* (pp. 41–48). Champaign, IL: Human Kinetics.

Schutz, R. W., & Gessaroli, M. E. (1987). The analysis of repeated measures designs involving multiple dependent measures. *Research Quarterly for Exercise and Sport, 58,* 132–149.

Sistrunk, W. E., Johnson, L., & Kennebrew, J. L. (1989). *The leadership style of a junior high school principal, the school climate, and group interaction.* Paper presented at the Annual Meeting of the Mid-South Educational Research Association, Little Rock, AR. (ERIC Document Reproduction Service No. ED 312 761)

Smith, R. E., & Smoll, F. L., (1996). The coach as a focus of research and intervention in youth sports. In F. L. Smoll & R. E. Smith (Eds.), *Children and youth in sport: A biopsychosocial perspective* (pp. 125–141). Dubuque, IA: Brown & Benchmark.

Smith, R. E., & Smoll, F. L., & Smith, N. J. (1989). *Parents' complete guide to youth sports* (pp. 3–5). Costa Mesa, CA: HDL Publishing.

Smoll, F. L., & Smith, R. E. (Eds.). (1996). *Children and youth in sport: A biopsychosocial perspective.* Dubuque, IA: Brown & Benchmark.

Stewart, C. C. (1994). Parents and coaches: Expectations, attitudes and communication. *Physical Educator, 51*(3), 130–137.

Weiss, M. R., & Duncan, S. C. (1992). The relationship between physical competence and peer acceptance in the context of children's sports participation. *Journal of Sport & Exercise Psychology, 14,* 177–191.

Weiss, M. R., & Hayashi, C. T. (1995). All in the family: Parent-child influences in competitive gymnastics. *Pediatric Exercise Science, 7,* 36–48.

Wilson Sporting Goods Company & Women's Sports Foundation (1988). *The Wilson report: Moms, dads, daughters and sports.* Los Angeles: Diagnostic Research, Inc.

Manuscript received: May 28, 1998
Revision submitted: January 26, 1999

JOURNAL OF APPLIED SPORT PSYCHOLOGY **11,** 263–282 (1999)

The Influence of Self-Talk on the Performance of Skilled Female Tennis Players

DENNIS LANDIN

Louisiana State University

EDWARD P. HEBERT

Southeastern Louisiana University

This paper reports on the development and implementation of a self-talk (ST) strategy designed to improve the volleying skill of collegiate tennis players (N = 5). A two-word ST strategy was developed, implemented, and evaluated using a single-case, multiple-baseline design. Dependent measures were movement patterns and outcome scores. After intervention, four players displayed immediate, positive changes with no overlapping datapoints on movement patterns. Notable improvements in outcome scores were also observed in all players, however, overlapping datapoints occurred for three players. Visual inspection of plotted values was supplemented by quantitative analysis using one-way ANOVAs to analyze four datapoints: the two baseline days just prior to intervention, and the two days immediately post intervention. Significant differences were found between phases, with both movement pattern and outcome scores higher following intervention. Qualitative data were collected via surveys and interviews. Players reported increased confidence following intervention, and offered explanations for its success conforming to theoretical positions that ST directs attentional focus and can prompt movement patterns.

Observers of athletic events often witness athletes talking to themselves at various times in the contest. Telecasts often show athletes berating or exhorting themselves at the conclusion of a play or point, and descriptions

---

Dennis Landin is with the Department of Kinesiology at Louisiana State University, Baton Rouge, LA 70803, USA. Edward P. Hebert is with the Department of Kinesiology and Health Studies, Southeastern Louisiana University, Hammond, LA 70402, USA.

Data from this project were presented at the 1995 AAASP Annual Conference in New Orleans, LA, USA.

Address correspondence to: Dennis Landin, Department of Kinesiology, 101 Long Fieldhouse, Louisiana State University, Baton Rouge, LA 70803, USA, Phone: (225) 388-2916, FAX: (225) 388-3680, E-mail: dlandin@lsu.edu

1041-3200/99/0263–0282$1.00/0

of this self-talk (ST) frequently appear in the print media. In addition to anecdotal reports, descriptive research dating back to the 1970s has consistently shown that athletes use ST in practice and competition in three ways: (a) to prompt critical elements of the movement pattern, (b) to increase motivation, and (c) to build self-confidence (e.g., Mahoney & Avener, 1977; Meyers, Cooke, Cullen, & Liles, 1979; Van Raalte, Brewer, Rivera, & Petitpas, 1994; Zinsser et al., 1998). Furthermore, it is fairly well established that ST can be a positive or negative influence on performance, so how athletes talk to themselves in practice and competition is important (Zinsser et al.).

Recent articles have focused on ST from theoretical, descriptive, and experimental perspectives (e.g., Landin, 1994; Van Raalte et al., 1994; Ziegler, 1987; Zinsser et al., 1998). Theoretically, mechanisms for the effects of ST are grounded in the concepts of attention and information processing and, while discussed in detail elsewhere (Landin, 1994), a brief review is pertinent here. Nideffer (1993) and Nideffer and Sagal (1998) describe eight principles of attention control training (ACT), two of which have been linked with ST in previous sport related research (Landin, 1994; Madigan, Frey, & Matlock, 1992; Mahoney & Avener, 1977; Ziegler, 1987). The first of these is that attentional focus varies across width and directional continua. The *width* continuum involves broad or narrow foci and relates to the amount of information the athlete attends to at a particular moment. The *direction* component refers to an internal (i.e., rehearsal, or analysis of options) or external (i.e., assessing the environment or "watching the ball") orientation. Based on these two continua, four categories of attention are possible: (a) broad—external, (b) broad—internal, (c) narrow—external, and (d) narrow—internal. These categories are characterized by assessment, analysis, performance, and rehearsal, respectively (Nideffer, 1993).

During competition athletes need proficiency in each category at varying times, and success hinges on the prompt, precise shifting of the attentional focus (Nideffer, 1981, 1993; Nideffer & Sagal, 1998). The nature of sport, open sports in particular, reveals the importance of these two elements of ACT. Athletes are often required to assess a changing situation whether it is ball flight, opponents' position, the direction of the wind, etc. Then, there has to be a rapid shift to the analysis mode, which prompts response selection. This in turn will be followed by one more shift to the performance mode, to ensure the best possible execution of the response. For example, a soccer player while dribbling the ball upfield and surveying the array of teammates and opponents should be in a broad-external mode of attention. Then, as the opportunity to pass or shoot on goal materializes, the athlete should shift to a narrow-external attentional mode. The demand for attentional shifting arises countless times in most sports and athletes may well benefit from interventions which prompt shifting to, or maintaining of, the preferred attentional mode (e.g., Ziegler, 1987).

In addition to the attention work of Nideffer and Sagal (1998), a second theoretical base of ST comes from the information processing literature. Related to the width/direction characteristic described above is the degree to which attention is voluntarily directed toward elements of the movement. Wrisberg (1993) points out that as skill develops, learners progressively decrease the amount of attention devoted to specific movements. This is explained by an increased ability to "chunk" information that reduces the number of elements in a skill, or series of skills, requiring attention. In effect, the athlete apparently can attend to triggering mechanisms which govern successful performance of a task (Magill, 1993; Zinsser et al., 1998). Descriptive evidence tends to support this perspective, as athletes report that their ST typically consists of short, verbal reminders, or cues, which prompt attention to one or two critical aspects of the task (Madigan et al., 1992).

Anecdotal evidence for the effects of ST, and how it can direct the performer's attentional focus, first appeared in the early 1970s in Gallwey's (1974) The *Inner Game of Tennis*. In this work, the author described instructing beginning tennis players to use verbal reminders during practice (e.g., "watch the seams"), which in effect, prompted a narrow-external attentional focus. His observations and experience led him to conclude that this form of task directed ST enhanced learning. Shortly thereafter, researchers began to empirically examine the impact of ST on the performance of sport skills.

Rushall (1984) described three primary categories of ST that athletes might use in practice and competition: (a) task specific, which related to the technique of the task; (b) positive self-talk for encouragement, effort, etc.; and (c) mood words that described the nature of the performance, such as "hard" and "blast." Furthermore, Rushall suggested that a combination of task-specific and positive ST would be most useful and proposed a distribution of thought content of 70% task-specific and 30% of positive ST and mood words. The task-specific statements are closely linked to Nideffer's (1981, 1993) ACT work. This is evidenced in Rushall's conclusion that findings from research on task-specific ST "have shown the beneficial effects on performance of using thoughts that focus on nature, conduct, and efficiency of the task" (p. 285). This work served as an impetus for subsequent descriptive and experimental research.

Research with ST has often focused on describing the nature, or content, of an athlete's thoughts (e.g., Mahoney & Avener, 1977; Rotella, Gansneder, Ojala, & Billing, 1980), while experimental assessments of its effects have been infrequent. Furthermore, in the existing research, a commonly used paradigm compares positive ST with various cognitive strategies on task performance (e.g., Weinberg, Smith, Jackson, & Gould, 1984), with the findings being somewhat mixed. The results from this research generally point to the superiority of positive ST (Van Raalte et al., 1995), however negative ST may act as a motivator and influence future performance (Van Raalte et al., 1994). Direct experimental assessments of the effects of task-specific ST remain few in number as most recent ST research has focused on the relative effects of positive versus negative ST (e.g., Van Raalte et al., 1995).

In the present study, we were interested in the effects of task-specific ST as a remediator to movement pattern problems. This form of ST research was initiated by Ziegler (1987) who explored the effects of ST on learning tennis groundstrokes. Ziegler devised a set of four cues, which prompted a narrow-external mode of attention throughout the task in effort to speed learning, and implemented the cues in beginning tennis classes. The first cue was "ball" which focused attention on the most important stimulus in the environment. This cue was vocalized the moment the ball was propelled from the ball machine. The second cue encouraged the students to attend to the flight of the ball by verbalizing "bounce" at the moment the ball hit the court. The narrow-external focus was then reinforced by the third cue "hit" which the students said as close as possible to the moment of ball/racket contact. The fourth and final cue "ready" returned attention to the ball machine, the source of the task's primary stimulus. The results showed that the ST led to dramatic and long-lasting improvements in the performance of the forehand and backhand groundstrokes. Furthermore, these results point to the importance of beginning tennis players maintaining the proper attentional focus, which is a central feature of Nideffer's ACT (1993). Each cue devised by Ziegler was designed to keep the students' attention on the most critical element in the environment, that is, the ball. By avoiding distraction by less important stimuli, the students displayed significant, lasting improvements.

Another example of using ST to maintain attentional focus and facilitate movement pattern performance can be found in Rushall, Hall, Roux, Sasseville, and Rushall (1988). These investigators devised three distinct ST interventions and compared the relative effectiveness when used by elite cross-country skiers. The three categories were: (a) task-relevant, which focused on technical aspects of skiing, (b) mood words that had a direct motor or emotional meaning, and (c) positive self-statements which were evaluative in nature. All three forms of ST led to significant improvements in elapsed skiing time over "normal" no ST conditions; however, the task-relevant category produced the largest gains. The authors concluded that for cross-country skiers "thought control content is very important for enhancing success" (p. 293). By maintaining the appropriate attentional focus, and prompting the preferred movement patterns, the skiers were able to traverse the course significantly faster than under conditions when thought content control was not used.

To maximize the utility of ST it is important to carefully select the cues. Landin (1994) provided guidelines for designing ST stressing that cues should be: (a) brief and phonetically simple, (b) logically associated with the referent element of the skill, and (c) compatible with the sequential timing pattern of the task. Brevity is essential for disruption of performance is a possibility whenever a skilled athlete begins to think excessively during the activity. However, Landin argues that ST which consists of one or two simple words will not disrupt performance and there is self-report evidence (e.g., Mahoney & Avener, 1977; Madigan et al., 1992) which supports this position. Second, ST cues need to be directly and logically related to the movement elements. Verbalizing the cue should create a powerful mental image, provide clear directions regarding the movement performance, or focus attention on the most important stimuli. A prime example of this is found in Ziegler's (1987) study in which the word "hit" was used to keep the beginning tennis players from averting their head and eyes prior to ball/racket contact. This is consistent with Nideffer's (1993) narrow-external mode of concentration. Third, movement patterns frequently have unique rhythms that influence performance. If the ST matches the rhythm of the movement, it has the potential to facilitate performance, if not, the motor activity will suffer (Thornton & Peters, 1982).

In summary, research to date indicates that athletes use ST during practice and competition, and suggests that ST can be motivational (Rushall, 1984) and enhance learning in novices (Ziegler, 1987). However, aside from Rushall et al. (1988), little experimental research has examined the impact of teaching skilled athletes to use ST when performing (Mallet & Hanrahan, 1997). Consequently, it is not yet possible to offer firm conclusions regarding how ST may enhance skilled performance. In the present study, we sought to extend research in this area by designing instructional ST for a particular skill, teach skilled tennis players how to use it, and have them implement it their natural practice environment. We sought to determine its impact on their performance, confidence, and style of play during competition, as well as explore their perceptions of using ST and explanations for any potential benefits. It was predicted that the onset of ST would improve the athletes' performances and lead to higher levels of self-reported confidence in their volleying ability.

METHOD

Participants and Setting

Participants for this study were five members of a women's NCAA Division I tennis team (age range = 18–21 years), each of whom read and signed an informed consent document prior to the start of data collection. Although the team was composed of 7 players, 2 had class and competition schedules, which prevented them from regularly attending practice. Therefore, the sample consisted of 5 players who were able to attend the majority of the practice sessions during the study. All participants were accomplished players with an average of 8.5 years of experience. Based on the National Tennis Rating Program (Johnson and Xanthos, 1997), these players held ratings of 6.0 out of a possible 7.0. A "6.0 player" has had "intensive training for national tournaments at the junior and collegiate levels, and has obtained sectional and/or national rankings." By definition a ranking of 7.0 indicates a "world class player" whose income is based on international tournaments. Still, the coaches

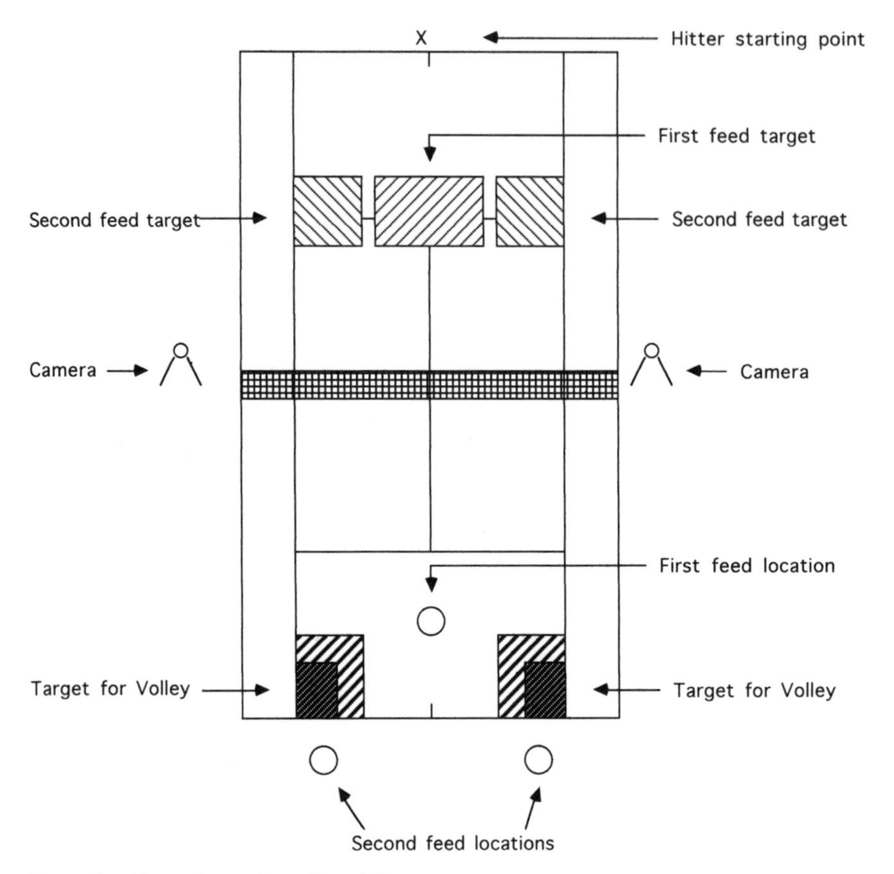

Figure 1. Court layout for volley drill.

had identified the volley as a team weakness and decided to devote considerable Fall (off-season) practice time to this skill. The coaching staff approached the investigators for assistance and collaborated on the design of the ST strategy and the study itself. Experimental procedures were incorporated into the team's normal practice routine, and data were collected during 10 of the 21 practice sessions allowed by the NCAA.

Task and Equipment

In conjunction with the coaches, a drill was designed which addressed the players' inconsistent volleys. The drill required players to hit a "down-the-line" approach shot, move to the net, and volley the returning ball to the same corner. The purpose of this sequence was to teach the players to exploit the lateral movement of their opponents by "hitting behind" them. Players began behind the baseline and were "fed" a two shot sequence by an assistant (see Figure 1). The first shot was directed down the line (i.e., for a right-handed player, down the right sideline for forehands and left sideline for backhands), after which they moved up to the net. Shots were directed toward targets drawn on the court. The assistants who "fed balls" were highly skilled players and experienced tennis instructors. They were trained for this drill and provided with "feed targets" to direct the hitting of balls to the players. Players came to the practice court in pairs and alternated performing the drill. On each of the 10 practice days, all players hit 40 two-ball sequences (10 forehand approaches followed by 10 forehand volleys, 10 forehand approaches–10 backhand volleys, 10 backhand approaches–10 forehand volleys, and 10 backhand approaches–10 backhand volleys), with the four sequences randomly ordered. For the purpose of analysis, all trials were captured on videotape using 8 mm video cameras positioned at the sides of the court near the net (see Figure 1).

Experimental Design

A single-case, multiple baseline design was selected for this study (Barlow & Hersen, 1984; Hrycaiko & Martin, 1996; Parsonson & Baer, 1992; Seiler, 1992). The players were randomly paired and performed the drill under baseline conditions which included the provision of verbal feedback by the coaches. This feedback centered on two critical elements of the movement pattern identified by the coaching staff: (a) a consistent split-stop, and (b) shoulder turn. The split-stop maneuver involves the player making a brief stop with the feet slightly over shoulder width apart. The purpose is to place the player in balanced position from which movement in any direction is possible. After the fourth practice session under baseline conditions, Player 1 began the intervention phase, while the remaining players continued practicing under baseline conditions. Players 2 and 3 began the intervention after five days of baseline, and Players 4 and 5 began after the sixth baseline day.

Self-Talk Strategy

Upon beginning the intervention phase, the players were introduced to the notion of ST, interviewed about their ST behavior, and taught a two-word ST sequence. The sequence was based on the two volley movement pattern elements which the coaches emphasized to players, and designed using Landin's (1994) recommendations: (a) brief and phonetically simple, (b) logically associated with the referent element of the skill, and (c) conformed to the sequential timing pattern of the task. Consequently, two cues were used in the ST. First, the players were instructed to say "split," after hitting the first ball in the sequence and were moving forward movement to the net. The exact moment of verbalizing "split" was when the feeder struck the second ball of the sequence. Upon saying this simple cue, the player was to make a brief jump-stop with the feet split slightly over shoulder width apart. This action placed the player in a neutral position enabling movement in any direction necessary to intercept the ball.

The second cue "turn" was designed to remind the player to turn the shoulders, which reduces racket head movement and improves visual tracking of the ball. This cue was to be verbalized as the racket was moved back in preparation for the shot, and it followed the sequential timing of the task, for it could not logically be verbalized prior to the first cue and seeing the oncoming ball.

Data Collection

Data on two dependent measures were collected during practice sessions: outcome and movement pattern. Outcome scores reflected the accuracy of the players' volleys. Each trial was scored according to where it landed on the court, and could range from zero to two points. Volleys which landed in the center rectangle of the target (Figure 1) were given two points, those in the larger rectangle received one point, and those falling outside the target scored zero. Outcome scores used in the analyses were each player's average score per session. Trial outcomes were scored during the drill by two observers who had established reliability prior to the start of the study and re-assessed at four points during data collection, using on each occasion 40 trials. Interobserver reliability exceeded .95 on each reliability assessment.

The second performance-related dependent measure was a movement pattern score reflecting the two elements addressed in the cues, split-stop and turn. These scores were obtained from stop-motion analyses of the daily videotapes with each component scored on a zero to one scale. If the player ran through the split stop, or merely slowed down, the element was scored a zero. A full, distinct split stop received one point. For the turn component, if the shoulders remained parallel to the net or turned less than 45° a zero was recorded for that trial. Turning more than 45° (closer to 90° on backhand volleys) resulted in a score of one. Consequently each trial could receive a maximum movement pattern score of two.

Two independent coders, who had achieved an interobserver agreement level using 70 trials, of .93 for the jump stop and .91 for the turn components prior to the scoring of videotapes, scored movement patterns. Interobserver agreement were also calculated at four intervals during the coding process, using 40 trials on each occasion, reaching an agreement of .88 or higher for each component.

Three additional sources of data augmented outcome and movement scores reflecting performance during practice. First, data during match play were collected to supplement the practice data and provide more information regarding the impact of the ST. Due to the limited schedule of the Fall season, competition data were collected on three of the five participants. The initial 10 games of singles matches of the three players were videotaped and coded according to frequencies of net approaches (i.e., number of points during which players moved from the baseline to the net). The rationale for this dependent measure is based on the notion that by increasing players' volley skills, they would exhibit a more attacking style of play and be reflected by more frequent forays to the net. This dependent measure was intended to indicate the players' willingness to go to the net to use their volleying skills during matches, and was perhaps also an indirect measure of their confidence in their volleying ability and potential to win points using this style of play.

Prior to the initiation of the study, and again at its completion, players responded to a brief survey designed to probe beliefs in their volleying during match play. It was composed of three items; each followed by responses on a 5-point scale. The first item, "How confident are you in your ability to win points from the net?" was answered using responses ranging from 1 (*not at all*) to 5 (*very confident*). They selected responses to the second item, "How often do you try to get to the net during matches?" using answers ranging from 1 (*hardly ever*) to 5 (*as much as possible*). The final item, "When at the net, how effective are you?" was answered using responses which ranged from 1 (*very ineffective—I lose more points than I win*) to 5 (*very effective—I win more points than I lose*).

Third, each participant was interviewed at the completion of the study. These followed a semi-structured, interview-guide format and focused on four issues: (a) past experience and use of ST, (b) verification of their use of the two-word ST strategy, (c) perceptions of the strategy's effectiveness, and (d) insights and explanations of the functions of ST.

RESULTS

Practice Performance

Outcome and movement pattern data for each athlete were plotted and visually examined (see Figures 2 and 3). Due to academic and competition schedules, some players were occasionally unable to attend practice. Therefore, these figures depict the data collected during practice sessions each participant attended. Visual analysis followed four established guidelines: (a) stable or descending baseline data, (b) little or no overlap from baseline to intervention, (c) immediacy of change, and (d) magnitude of change (Hrycaiko & Martin, 1996; Parsonson & Baer, 1992). These guidelines provide a basis for determining the effects of the intervention. For example, baseline datapoints that are alternatingly high and low indicate that the target behavior was good one day, poor the next. Such baselines make it difficult to interpret intervention effects. Similarly, application of an intervention hypothesized to raise scores on a selected scale, when baselines are ascending (that is the scores are climbing), may be pointless since the scores are already improving. One other example, the ideal intervention will produce an effect that creates a clear break between the last point in baseline and the first in intervention, and further, that all subsequent points in intervention would be at a level greater than the highest in baseline. Table 1 shows the means and standard deviations for all players across phases and dependent measures.

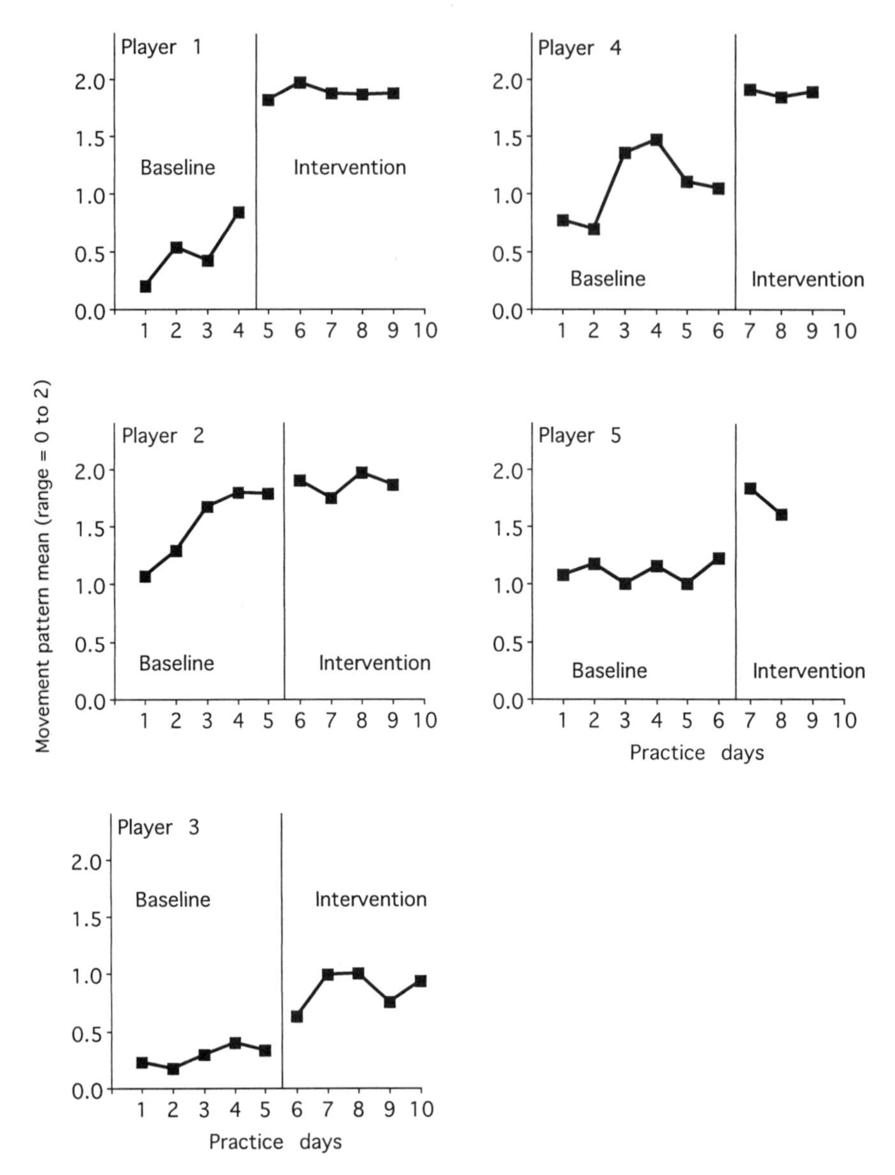

Figure 2. Movement pattern scores.

Visual inspection of movement patterns revealed that four of the five participants had relatively stable or non-ascending baselines (Figure 2). Player 2 showed an ascending baseline and a ceiling effect, which rendered the results of visual inspection suspect. The remaining four players each displayed an immediate change following the start of the ST inter-

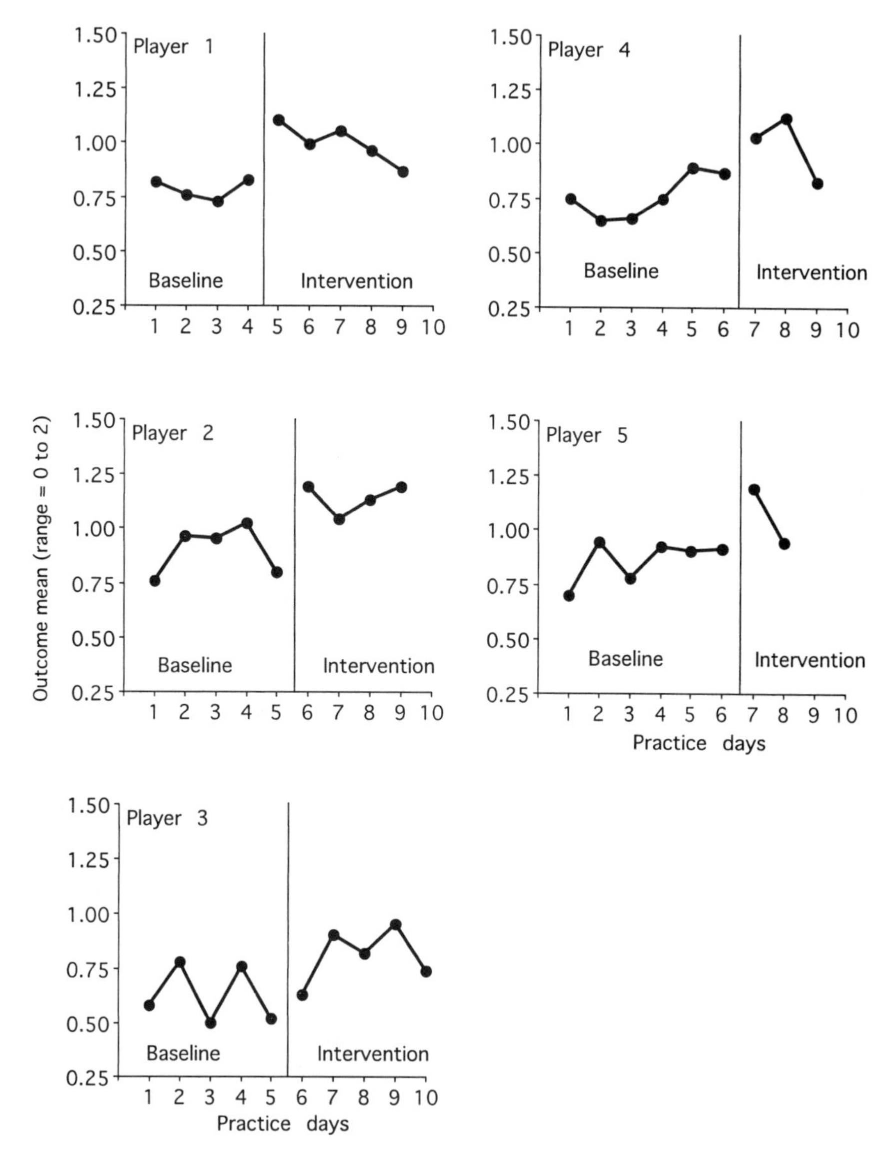

Figure 3. Outcome scores.

vention, with no overlapping datapoints and a magnitude of change ranging from .57 to 1.38 (M = .59, SD = .17). These results indicate that the ST strategy was effective in improving players' performance of the two movement pattern elements on which the cues focused.

Regarding outcome scores (Figure 3), all baselines were fairly stable but only Players 1 and 2 showing immediate effects with no overlapping

Table 1
Mean (SD) outcome and movement pattern scores during baseline and intervention phases

	Outcome scores		Movement pattern scores	
Player	Baseline	Intervention	Baseline	Intervention
Player 1	0.79 (0.05)	0.99 (0.09)	0.50 (0.27)	1.88 (0.06)
Player 2	0.90 (0.11)	1.14 (0.07)	1.52 (0.27)	1.87 (0.09)
Player 3	0.63 (0.13)	0.81 (0.13)	0.29 (0.89)	0.86 (0.16)
Player 4	0.76 (0.10)	0.99 (0.15)	1.08 (0.31)	1.88 (0.03)
Player 5	0.86 (0.10)	1.07 (0.17)	1.11 (0.09)	1.73 (0.16)

Note. Scores could range from 0 to 2.

datapoints. Players 3, 4, and 5 displayed improvements in outcome scores but had one or more datapoints overlap. Visual inspection reveals that the intervention was ineffective for Players 3, 4, and 5 and marginally effective for Players 1 and 2 because their baseline patterns were reasonably stable and there was no overlap in datapoints from baseline to intervention. The magnitude of change in successful trials was also small, ranging from .20 to .24 (M = .21, SD = .02).

Visual inspection of plotted values was supplemented by quantitative analyses using two repeated measures ANOVAs, with outcome and movement pattern scores as the dependent measures. Data used for these analyses consisted of four datapoints for each participant: the two practice sessions just prior to intervention, and the two sessions immediately following intervention.

The ANOVA analyzing movement pattern scores yielded a significant effect for practice session, F (3, 12) = 9.30, $p < .01$. Effect size, calculated using eta squared, indicated 70% of the total variance in movement pattern scores was accounted for by practice session. Due to the small sample size, post-hoc power analysis was conducted to determine the probability that differences of the observed effect size would be detected as significant using the sample size, repeated measures design of the study, and .05 alpha level. The results indicated a power level of .70. These levels of significance, effect sizes, and power estimates reflect Greenhouse-Geisser adjustments. Pairwise contrasts ($p < .01$) among the four datapoints indicated movement pattern scores for the two days immediately prior to intervention were similar (M 1 = .93, SD = .60; M 2 = 1.1, SD = .44), and both significantly lower than the two days following intervention (M 3 = 1.7, SD = .39; M 4 = 1.6, SD = .38).

Analysis of outcome scores yielded similar results: a significant effect for practice sessions, F (3, 12) = 14.11, $p < .01$, with eta squared estimates indicating this factor accounted for 78% of the total variance. Post-hoc power analysis indicated differences of this effect size would be detected as significant at a 99% probability level. Follow-up contrasts indicated significant differences between the pre- and post-intervention sessions (M 1 = .81, SD = .19; M 2 = .81, SD = .11; M 3 = 1.1, SD = .12; M 4 = .98, SD = .11).

Match Performance

Due to the restricted competition schedule during the Fall semester, we were able to collect match performance data for three players on a limited number of occasions. Competition data were collected for Player 1 (one pre-intervention match and two post-intervention matches), Player 3 (two pre-intervention and two post-intervention matches), and Player 4 (one pre-intervention and one post-intervention match). As shown in Table 2, Player 1 showed only a slight alteration improving from 6% to an average of 11% (percent of match play points during which the player approached the net). Player 3 demonstrated an increase in net approaches following intervention, from an average of 7% to 27%. Player 4 displayed a change in net approaches, increasing from 1% to 11% following intervention.

Surveys

The results of the pre- and post-experiment questionnaires indicated that the athletes' perceptions of their volleying ability increased over the course of the investigation (see Figure 4). The frequency at which the athletes reported trying to get to the net increased from a pre-experiment mean of 3.1 (SD = .38) to 4.0 (SD = .63) after the experiment. Similarly, pre to post improvements were also demonstrated in their confidence to win by approaching the net (Pre M = 3.0, SD = .82; Post M = 3.7, SD = .52), and perceptions of effectiveness when at the net (Pre M = 3.3, SD = .49; Post M = 3.8, SD = .41).

Interviews

Audiotapes from the interviews were transcribed and analyzed inductively using the guidelines of Bogdan and Biklen (1992). Analysis followed the constant comparison method and the interview guide was used as a framework to divide transcripts into units. The researchers, working as a team, read responses to each question in a search for patterns. Notes were taken and tentative coding categories developed. Each response was then read individually and sorted into the tentative categories. Each category of responses was then read, discussed, and modified until agreement was reached.

Second, participants responded to questions eliciting validation checks on their use of the two-word ST strategy. All reported saying the cues during practice on most, if not all, trials. Upon probing their answers, two players found the verbal cues fit within the rhythm of the shot and had no difficulty incorporating them into practice. Three players, however, described some initial difficulty with the cues, but became more comfortable using the ST strategy with practice. For example, one player said, "It didn't feel right at the beginning . . . I got better as I went along."

Table 2

Frequency and percent of net approaches during match play in baseline and intervention phases

Player	Matches in baseline phase			Matches in intervention phase		
	Total points	Frequency of net approaches	Percent of points involving net approaches	Total points	Frequency of net approaches	Percent of points involving net approaches
Player 1	70	4	5.71	61	8	13.11
				76	6	7.89
Player 3	71	7	9.86	59	18	30.51
	58	3	5.17	66	15	22.73
Player 4	71	1	1.41	79	9	11.39

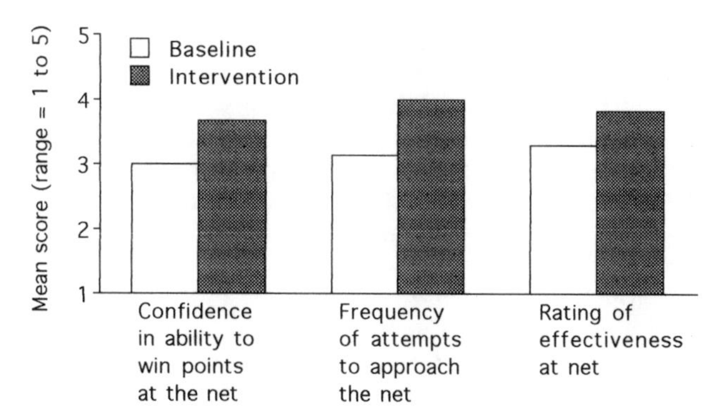

Figure 4. Pre- and post-experiment perceptions of volleying ability.

Similarly, another noted, "It was awkward at first, but got easy with practice."

Third, when asked about their perceptions of the impact of the ST, all players gave positive reports indicating increased confidence (e.g., I'm definitely more confident now than before."), improved volleying performance (e.g., "I think my volleys have gotten a lot better . . . I thought it helped me a lot."), and the adoption of a more assertive style of play reflecting an increased frequency of net approaches (e.g., "Yeah, I think it helped. I came to the net more in my singles."). In addition, four of the five participants indicated using the ST outside of the drill, either using the ST as instructed, or creating their own instructional ST strategy (e.g., "I started saying 'split' when the person was taking practice serves. . ." and "I did them at this tournament, too. Because in my last match, I came to the net a whole lot and I used the cues and I volleyed real well.").

Finally, players were asked their perceptions of how the ST produced the effects they described. The answers centered on two mechanisms. First, the cues helped them gain and maintain an appropriate attentional focus, reflected by comments such as "It got me more mentally into what I was doing," and "It makes you more aware." Second, participants indicated that the cues facilitated the execution of the movement pattern components, which they stressed. "When I said 'split,' I would step into the ball better . . . I remembered to do it." "When you're playing, you can't see yourself. Sometimes when you say it, you don't have to worry about whether you're doing it or not because you say and automatically do it."

DISCUSSION

The present study continued a line of research examining the effects of ST on the performances of skilled athletes. More specifically, the purpose of this study was twofold. First, we were interested in assessing the effectiveness of teaching skilled athletes to use instructional ST. The second purpose was to gain insight into the athletes' perceptions of this ST and how it influenced their performances.

Researchers have established that athletes use ST in a variety of ways and that it can enhance performance in endurance tasks and improve learning by novices (e.g., Mahoney & Avener, 1977; Rotella, Gansneder, Ojala, & Billing, 1980; Ziegler, 1987). However, few studies have examined the impact of ST when used by skilled athletes. Theoretically, the mechanisms through which ST produces its effects are linked to the concepts of attention and information processing, and it is generally believed that ST can help performers remediate movement errors and develop or maintain an appropriate attentional focus (Landin, 1994). In this study, we developed a two-word ST strategy, which focused on two movement pattern components of a target skill, the tennis volley. Players on a collegiate tennis team were taught the ST strategy and used it during practice.

Data were collected through a variety of techniques including questionnaires, interviews, and quantitative assessment of tennis form and accuracy. These data were combined to obtain a more thorough understanding of the ST strategy employed in this study. The analyses, taken together, indicate the effectiveness of teaching athletes ST strategies that focus on critical movement-related elements of skills, and suggest they function through attentional mechanisms. What follows is a discussion of the results from practice, match play including the questionnaires, and interviews.

Performance Scores During Practice. Two sets of performance data were collected. First, visual inspection of movement pattern scores during practice showed that four of the five participants had fairly stable baselines followed by immediate changes, no overlap of datapoints, and a mean magnitude of change of .75. Quantitative analysis of these data supported the conclusion that the onset of ST prompted positive changes in the movement pattern components on which the ST focused. The tennis players in our study used one of the ST cues to "fire" the entire movement pattern and facilitate its performance. This finding supports the theoretical assumptions underlying ST. Recall that one assumption of ST is that it can prompt correct performance of a movement pattern (Landin, 1994; Magill, 1993; Wrisberg, 1993; Zinsser et al., 1998). Verbalizing the cue "split" apparently served as the stimulus to initiate the entire movement sequence for these players, and once started, it "ran off" completely. This is a clear example of the "chunking" ability of expert performers (Wrisberg, 1993) and value of the ST in initiating learned sequences. In regards to facilitating performance, our findings corroborate the results of two earlier reports. Madigan et al. (1992) reported results from a descriptive study showing that ST helped downhill skiers "guide performance" (p. 137). Rushall et al. (1988) presented findings from an experimental study in which ST led to faster times in cross-country skiing. The present findings expand on Rushall et al.'s results in that our ST was designed to remediate a specific movement pattern deficiency and not simply prompt the preferred pattern. Based on our findings, it appears that ST has the potential to not only prompt the correct movement, but also remediate movement pattern errors in skilled athletes.

The second theoretical base of ST emerges from Nideffer's attention work (Nideffer, 1981, 1993; Nideffer & Sagal, 1998). The results of our study, plus the two mentioned above, support the arguments that ST can be used to direct and maintain an athlete's attentional focus, and, thereby, has the potential to influence performance. The elite skiers in Madigan et al. (1992) and Rushall et al. (1988) benefited from ST that focused their attention on critical movement elements whether in short, discrete aspects of the movement, or in long-term, repetitive components. The skilled tennis players in the present study derived a similar benefit. Verbalizing key words help ensure that the proper attentional focus is maintained. This conclusion is supported by interview data (discussed shortly) which indicates that the players thought ST made them "more aware."

The second set of performance data, outcome scores, was expressed as the percent of shots hit into on-court targets. Although the influence on outcomes in the present study was not as pronounced as that on movement patterns, the evidence does suggest that outcome improvements followed movement pattern changes. Visual inspection revealed that three of the five participants had overlapping datapoints indicating that the intervention did not have a consistent effect. However, the quantitative analysis revealed significant differences across the two days just prior to and after intervention. The mean outcome score for the two baseline days just prior to intervention was .81, while the means of the first two days following intervention were 1.08 and .98. Theoretical bases of ST do not address outcomes per se but some researchers have reported that ST can influence outcomes. Van Raalte et al. (1994) examined the relationship between observable ST and performance in tennis matches. Among their findings was that players' negative ST was associated with losing and players who believed in the utility of ST won more points than those who did not. Our results, although corroborating Van Raalte et al.'s findings, are somewhat less definite. The primary distinction is that Van Raalte et al. focused on affective ST, rather than movement patterns as in our study, and this probably accounts for the discrepancies in results.

A long accepted notion among tennis instructors is that developing appropriate movement patterns is foundational to success and that there is generally a delay between movement pattern changes and improvements in outcomes (Bassett & Otta, 1989). Moreover, altering the movement patterns of skilled athletes can produce short-term decrements in outcomes. Our findings clearly indicate that Thornton and Peters' (1982) argument about the potential for ST to interfere with motor activity has merit. Recall that three of the players expressed initial difficulty with the ST, which may have disrupted outcomes in the sessions shortly after intervention. It seems prudent at this point to recommend that ST, particularly as a movement pattern remediator, be used early in the off-season or pre-season, not shortly before the competitive season begins. By doing so, the potential disruption can be overcome. In the present study, although speculative, it is possible that if data collection could have continued outcomes may have shown greater improvement.

Frequency of Net Approaches During Matches. Augmenting the performance data were additional indicators of the impact of ST. These data related to the frequency of net approaches during match play, the players' reports of using an attacking style of play, and their perceptions of the ST's effectiveness. Although only three athletes were able to play pre- and post-intervention sets due to the team's schedule, the data revealed that each adopted a more assertive style of play by attempting to approach the net more frequently. All three displayed increases in net play, but only one showed large changes. The weakness in this data is that we did not evaluate the outcomes of this net play nor did we ask the athletes if they used the ST during their approaches to the net. A definite need in future research is to fully examine the use and effects of ST during actual play for this will provide the most useful information regarding its benefits for skilled players. Nevertheless, the coaches were pleased with these improvements, modest as they were (range = 6 to 27%), due to the general widespread belief that the player who "controls" the net is most likely to win the point (Bassett & Otta, 1989; Holm, 1987). This data, in conjunction with the responses on pre and post questionnaires indicates that ST increased both the players' awareness of the importance reaching the net, and their efforts to do so, during their games.

Exit Interviews. Data from the exit interviews indicated that the athletes believed the ST helped them perform the two essential components of the movement pattern. These findings support one of the hypothesized mechanisms of ST, that is, the notions of chunking and triggering detailed in the introduction and discussed elsewhere in the literature (e.g., Landin, 1994; Magill, 1993; Wrisberg, 1993; Zinsser et al., 1998). The cue "split" appeared to be the most useful to these athletes. Comments obtained in the interviews indicated that the athletes thought this cue led to better performance of subsequent parts of the movement pattern (". . . I would step into the ball better. . ."). This data also corroborates the descriptive reports of skiers using ST during practice and competition to prompt a key facet of the movement pattern such as "weight forward" (Madigan et al., 1992). Further, the exit interview data revealed that the ST led to a greater sense of confidence in the players regarding their ability to be successful at the net, that is, win more points. This cannot be underestimated and the sport psychology literature consistently describes the benefits accruing to confidence in athletics (e.g., Weinberg & Gould, 1995).

While this study does have limitations (e.g., sample size, lack of match play data for all participants) the results have considerable applicability since many sport settings involve small groups of skilled athletes. The value of this study lies in the demonstration that well-constructed ST can remediate movement pattern errors in highly skilled athletes, and that this type of intervention can be successfully implemented in the athletes' normal practice environment.

In summary, the results of this study corroborate findings from earlier

ST research regarding outcomes. We found small, but significant increases in outcomes following the onset of ST. The more important finding is that when the athletes began using the ST procedure, there were significant improvements in movement pattern scores. Typically, movement pattern changes, with a few notable exceptions, have not been evaluated in ST research. While the notion that ST can help beginners develop correct movement patterns is supported by the literature, the idea of skilled athletes benefiting in a similar fashion has been largely speculative. Although further study is needed, the present results suggest ST can help skilled athletes remediate movement pattern problems. Exit interview data supported the empirical findings. The athletes reported using the ST on nearly all trials during the volley drill describing various reasons why they found it effective, reasons which coincide neatly with the theoretical mechanisms of ST. Interestingly, the athletes also reported using this ST protocol with other strokes similar in temporal-spatial requirements. Future research should continue exploring how movement patterns and outcomes are influenced by ST in practice and particularly in competition, a shortcoming in much of the ST research.

REFERENCES

Bassett, G., & Otta, W. (1989). *Tennis Today.* St. Paul, MN: West Publishing Co.

Barlow, D., & Hersen, M. (1984). *Single case experimental designs: Strategiesor studying behavior change.* New York: Pergamon.

Bogdan, R. C., & Biklen, S. K. (1992). *Qualitative research for education: An introduction to theory and methods.* Boston: Allyn and Bacon.

Gallwey, W. T. (1974). *The inner game of tennis.* New York: Random House.

Hrycaiko, D., & Martin, G. L. (1996). Applied research studies with single-subject designs: Why so few? *Journal of Applied Sport Psychology, 8,* 183–199.

Hohm, J. (1987). *Tennis technique, tactics, training: Play to win the Czech Way.* Toronto: Sports Books Publisher.

Johnson, J. D., & Xanthos, P. J. (1997). *Tennis.* Chicago: Brown & Benchmark.

Landin, D. (1994). The role of verbal cues in skill learning. *Quest, 46,* 299–313.

Madigan, R., Frey, R. D., & Matlock, T. S. (1992). Cognitive strategies of university athletes. *Canadian Journal of Applied Sport Sciences, 17,* 135–140.

Magill, R. (1993). *Motor learning: Concepts and applications* (4th ed.). Dubuque, IA: Brown & Benchmark.

Mahoney, M. J., & Avener, M. (1977). Psychology of the elite athlete: An exploratory study. *Cognitive Therapy and Research, 1,* 135–141.

Mallet, C. J., & Hanrahan, S. J. (1997). Race modeling: An effective strategy for the 100m sprinter? *The Sport Psychologist, 11,* 72–85.

Meyers, A. W., Cooke, C. J., Cullen, J., & Liles. L. (1979). Psychological aspects of athletic competitors: A replications across sports. *Cognitive Therapy and Research, 3,* 361–366.

Nideffer, R. M. (1981). *The ethics and practice of applied sport psychology.* Ithaca, NY: Mouvement Publication.

Nideffer, R. N. (1993). Attention control training. In R. N. Singer, M. Murphey, & L. K. Tennant (Eds.), *Handbook of Research on Sport Psychology* (pp. 542–556). New York: Macmillan.

Nideffer, R. N., & Sagal, M. (1998). Concentration and attention control training. In J. M.

Williams (Ed.) *Applied Sport Psychology: Personal Growth to Peak Performance* (pp. 296–315). Mountain View, CA: Mayfield.

Parsonson, B. S., & Baer, D. M. (1992) The visual analysis of data, and current research into the stimuli controlling it. In T. R. Kratochwill & J. R. Levin (Eds.) *Single-Case Research Design and Analysis: New Directions for Psychology and Education* (pp. 15–40), Hillsdale, NJ: Lawrence Erlbaum Associates.

Rushall, B. S. (1984). The content of competition thinking. In W. F. Straub & J. M. Williams (Eds.), *Cognitive Sport Psychology* (pp. 51–62), Lansing, New York: Sport Science Associates.

Rushall, B. S., Hall, M., Roux, L., Sasseville, J., & Rushall, A. C. (1988). Effects of three types of thought content instructions on skiing performance. *The Sport Psychologist, 2,* 28–297.

Rotella, R. J., Gansneder, B., Ojala, D., & Billing, J. (1980). Cognitions and coping strategies of elite skiers: An exploratory study of young developing athletes. *Journal of Sport Psychology, 2,* 350–354.

Seiler, R. (1992). Performance enhancement—a psychological approach. *Sport Science Review, 1,* 29–45.

Thornton, C. D., & Peters, M. (1992). Interference between concurrent speaking and sequential finger tapping: Both hands show a performance decrement under visual and non-visual guidance. *Neuropsychologia, 20,* 163–169.

Van Raalte, J. L., Brewer, B. W., Lewis, B. P., Linder, D. E., Wildman, G., & Kozimor, J. (1995). Cork! The effects of positive and negative self-talk on dart throwing performance. *Journal of Sport Behavior, 18,* 50–56.

Van Raalte, J. L., Brewer, B. W., Rivera, P. M., & Petitpas, A. J. (1994). The relationship between observable self-talk and competitive junior tennis players' match performance. *Journal of Sport & Exercise Psychology, 16,* 400–415.

Weinberg, R. S., & Gould, D. (1995). *Foundations of Sport and Exercise Psychology.* Human Kinetics: Champaign, IL.

Weinberg, R. S., Smith, J., Jackson, A., & Gould, D. (1984). Effect of association, dissociation, and positive self-talk strategies on endurance performance. *Canadian Journal of Applied Sport Sciences, 9,* 25–32.

Wrisberg, C. A. (1993). Levels of performance skill. In R. N. Singer, M. Murphey, & L. K. Tennant (Eds.), *Handbook of Research on Sport Psychology* (pp. 61–72). New York: Macmillan.

Ziegler, S. G. (1987). Effects of stimulus cueing on the acquisition of groundstrokes by beginning tennis players. *Journal of Applied Behavior Analysis, 20,* 405–411.

Zinsser, N., Bunker, L., & Williams, J. M. (1998). Cognitive techniques for building confidence and enhancing performance. In J. M. Williams (Ed.), *Applied Sport Psychology: Personal Growth to Peak Performance* (pp. 270–281). Mountain View, CA: Mayfield.

Manuscript submitted: July 25, 1998
Revision received: December 20, 1998

JOURNAL OF APPLIED SPORT PSYCHOLOGY **11,** 283–297 (1999)

Controlling Competitive Anger among Male Soccer Players

JOHN P. BRUNELLE[1], CHRISTOPHER M. JANELLE, AND L. KEITH TENNANT[2]

University of Florida

This study examined the effectiveness of anger awareness training (i.e., self-monitoring) and role-playing (i.e., modeling and behavioral rehearsal) in reducing participants' angry behavior and angry feelings. Male participants (N = 57) from intact soccer teams were randomly assigned to a role-playing, an anger awareness, or a control group. Pretreatment anger scores indicated that all three groups exhibited similar anger dispositions before the study began. Following pretreatment assessment, angry behavior and self-reported anger were observed and measured during a 15-game round-robin soccer season. Analyses revealed that although angry feelings remained consistent across the duration of the study, the role-playing group was more effective than both the anger awareness and control groups in controlling angry behavior. Findings indicate that although the use of anger awareness and role-playing interventions can reduce angry behavior, the role-playing intervention was a more effective method.

The images of airborne tennis rackets, spit-flying tirades, and amateur fisticuffs have become all too familiar in the world of sport. Anger appears to be an intrinsic product of an environment that locks opposing forces together in athletic competition. Not only has it been accepted as an inherent part of sport, but anger is often encouraged and elicited to improve athletic performance.

---

[1] J. P. Brunelle is now with the Department of Psychology at Virginia Commonwealth University.

[2] L. K. Tennant is now with the Department of Physical Education at the University of West Georgia.

The authors would like to thank two anonymous reviewers, as well as Dr. Robert Weinberg and Dr. Diane Gill, for their helpful comments on an earlier version of this manuscript. Portions of this paper were presented at the meeting of the Association for the Advancement of Applied Sport Psychology in Williamsburg, Virginia.

Correspondence concerning this manuscript should be addressed to Christopher M. Janelle, Ph.D., University of Florida, Department of Exercise and Sport Sciences, 110 Florida Gym, Gainesville, Florida 32611, Phone #: 352-392-0584 (ext. 270), Fax #: 352-392-5262, Email: cjanelle@hhp.ufl.edu

1041-3200/99/0283–0297$1.00/0

On a more universal level, sport participation has historically been promoted as a productive and healthy release of natural human aggression. However, contrary to these popular beliefs, empirical evidence has supported the assertion that anger is an ineffective, noncathartic response to athletic demands (e.g., Jones, 1993). Despite the strong evidence that supports this view, little research has focused on distinguishing effective methods of controlling anger in applied settings. The purpose of this paper is to expound on the need for controlling competitive anger, and to investigate the effectiveness of two popular cognitive-behavioral techniques in reducing angry feelings and behaviors in sport.

Fighting the Myths of Anger

Traditional coaching approaches that exhort athletes to get angry still seem to persist in many sports, continuing to rely on a belief that "firing up" sport participants will increase energy and adrenaline, "producing superhuman efforts in which the athletes hit harder, jump further, run faster" (Kiester, 1984, p. 26). Within the field of sport psychology, both anecdotal and scientific evidence convincingly rejects anger as an effective means of inducing exemplary athletic performance. Rather, experts exalt the controlled and self-regulating athlete (e.g., Loehr, 1983; Orlick, 1990; Ravizza & Hanson, 1995; Suinn, 1986).

Coinciding with this literature, the "Iceberg Profile," identified by Morgan's (1974, 1985) extensive testing with the Profile of Mood States (POMS; McNair, Lorr, & Droppleman, 1971), describes the optimal athlete as one of superior emotional health and control. From his research in sport, Morgan found that successful athletes consistently displayed a "mood profile" of lower-than-normal levels of anger (Morgan, 1974, 1985). Accordingly, it appears that anger interferes with essential concentration, attentional focus, and resulting actions of athletes (Hahn, 1989).

Cultivated by catharsis theory, sport has developed a popular image as a channel for aggressive release, despite a lack of strong empirical evidence (Russell, 1983; Tavris, 1989). In fact, research on aggression and anger has supported sport participation as a perpetuation, not a release, of aggressive tendencies, especially those of a reactive nature (e.g., Bredemeier, 1984; Harrell, 1981; Husman & Silva, 1984; Ostrow, 1974; Patterson, 1974; Ryan, 1970). Evidently, athletes actually display more aggressive tendencies at the end of games and build up more self-reported aggression as the sport season progresses.

Defining Anger

Anger has been described as an emotion that incorporates an individual's perception of a frustrating stimulus, increasingly high levels of arousal, and a subsequent response to the initial frustrating stimulus (Novaco, 1975). Other research has classified anger in terms of two different types of anger expression: "anger-in" and "anger-out" (Spielberger, 1991; Spielberger, Krasner, & Solomon, 1988).

Anger-In. Anger-in describes occasions in which individuals either suppress their anger or direct their anger inward toward the self (Spielberger, 1991). When anger is directed toward the self, feelings of depression and guilt often replace feelings of anger (Spielberger et al., 1988). On the other hand, if individuals suppress anger, they will continue to consciously experience anger as an emotional state. These inner manifestations elevate what Vallerand (1983) termed the *intra*personal consequences of emotion. The potential consequences include destroyed concentration and diminished performance (Hahn, 1989).

Anger-Out. Anger-out involves anger directed toward other people or objects in the environment, with a manifestation of varying modes of aggressive behavior (Spielberger, 1991; Spielberger et al., 1988). Anger may either be expressed with physical attacks such as assaulting other persons, destroying objects, or slamming doors, or expressed verbally with criticism, insults, threats, or extreme uses of profanity (Spielberger et al., 1988). The physical and verbal manifestations of anger can be directed toward the actual source of provocation, or toward persons or objects closely associated with the provoking agent. Vallerand (1983) described these situations as the interpersonal consequences of emotion.

When viewing today's sporting events, it is quite common to see anger that escalates into more external and consequential reactions that affect more than just the athlete's performance. An individual's angry outbursts toward the self, teammates, opponents, coaches, and officials can often escalate into additional aggressive behavior, disruption of team cohesion, and official penalties, ejections, or suspensions.

Controlling Competitive Anger

Although interventions geared toward controlling anger have been virtually ignored in the sport domain, two anger control methods have been used with consistent success in other arenas.

Anger Awareness. A popular method to help cope with distressful emotions is the strategy of enhancing awareness of conditions that surround the typical occurrence of the emotions. Awareness training has routinely been used as a cognitive-behavioral treatment of anger and aggression (Nay, 1995), and has effectively been administered in both individual and group settings (Miller, Eisner, & Allport, 1994). The general goal of the intervention is to increase self-knowledge of critical situations in which the emotions may be experienced, so that the person is better able to identify and cope with the feelings as they present themselves. More specifically, awareness of one's feelings leads to the effective regulation of the expression of those feelings.

In accordance with this line of thought, awareness training has been used effectively in helping people deal with the anger experienced from personality disorders (Miller, Eisner, & Allport, 1994; Robbins, 1993), alcohol and drug dependence (Monti, Abrams, Kadden, & Cooney, 1989), control issues from hospital patients (Eisendrath, 1987), chronic pain

(Braha & Catchlove, 1986), spouse abuse (Taylor, 1984), child abuse (Barth, Blythe, Schinke, & Schilling, 1983), personal responsibility for HIV infection (McDonnell, 1993), and rehabilitation from traumatic brain injury (Marme & Skord, 1993). In addition, those who attempt to reduce the awareness of emotional and cognitive states that are perceived as being threatening or unacceptable (such as anger) are actually more likely to experience maladjustment manifestations of that repression (Waller, Quinton, & Watson, 1995). In spite of the obvious application of the awareness intervention in a wide variety of settings, the application of this intervention to dealing with anger in sports environments has not occurred.

Role-Playing. Another popular method of cognitive-behavioral intervention is through the more interactive process of engaging in role-playing. However, as is the case with anger awareness training, very little attention has been devoted to examining the effectiveness of this intervention in the sport context. In fact, only one study that investigated an anger control treatment program was found in the sport literature. Jones' (1993) case study of an elite racquet player described the successful implementation of an anger control regimen that included role-playing as an essential step in treatment. He found that over a 6-month period of time, the athlete effectively transferred anger control from simulated situations to the actual competitive environment.

As is the case with awareness strategies, research in other realms of human behavior has been much more active in distinguishing effective methods of anger management with role-playing. The behavioral change method has been supported as a highly suitable and productive method of giving participants the opportunity to actively practice and measure their proficiency in anger management (Novaco, 1977). The value of role-playing, according to Novaco, is its ability to sufficiently simulate the activity and intensity of real situations.

The factors involved with an individual's anger range from the immediate perceptions of a provocation to the basic philosophy that guides the person in typical anger-provoking situations (Tavris, 1989). People most often act impulsively without reflecting on alternatives, being solely dependent on their habitual perspective (Radley, 1978). Role-playing offers a chance to adopt other perspectives. In a stress inoculation program for anger control, Novaco (1975, 1977) successfully incorporated role-playing to enlist patients to reinterpret provocations in ways that would avoid angry feelings and reactions. Role enactment slows down a typical anger-provoking situation, allowing an individual to reinterpret the implications and recognize the advantages of alternative responses (Radley, 1978).

Goldstein and Glick (1987, 1994) have reported successful results with role-play training for anger control in their "Anger Replacement Training" of aggressive adolescents. The program allows the youths to role-play emotional situations that have previously led to inappropriate expressions of anger. The trainers use clear descriptions of conflict situations, modeling, and behavioral rehearsal with repetitive demonstrations of appropriate behavior.

Role-playing, with its reliance on rehearsal and repetition in simulated situations, seems highly conducive to the sport model of practicing and scrimmaging to prepare for real game action. The recurring nature of anger in sport certainly offers common and rehearsable anger-provoking situations that justify such an approach. With repeated rehearsal, the athletes can desensitize common provocations in sport, and at the same time strengthen their ability to reinterpret similar situations with less angry feelings and reactions. By relying on the educational doctrine of "learning by doing," role-playing allows an individual to practice and ultimately master appropriate responses to stressful situations (Levenson & Herman, 1991).

In light of these considerations, the purpose of the present study was to understand the relative effectiveness of awareness training and role-playing interventions in controlling competitive anger in soccer. It was hypothesized that although both methods would be effective in reducing both angry feelings and angry behavior, the immersive properties of role-playing would allow a more effective reduction than would anger awareness. The relative effectiveness of the interventions was examined by observing angry behavior and assessing angry feelings during the course of a 15-game soccer season.

METHOD

Participants

Male soccer players (N = 57) enrolled in two Sport and Fitness soccer classes at a large southeastern university were recruited to participate in this study. At the beginning of the semester, players were selected and distributed among four teams in each class based on talent, with the intention of fielding equally competitive teams. Participants from the intact teams were subsequently matched with their teammates and randomly assigned to one of three treatment groups (n = 19 per group): (a) role-playing, (b) anger awareness, or (c) control. The purpose of this procedure was to insure that each team had equal representation among the three treatment groups. In doing so, confounds produced by team performance were controlled.

The players ranged in age from 18 to 28 (M = 20.05, SD = 1.87), with 88% of the players having at least 5 years of competitive soccer experience and 60% having over 10 years experience (M = 9.86, SD = 4.70). In terms of skill level, 61% of the participants played organized high school soccer or higher. Males were chosen as the group of interest due to their extreme overrepresentation among the classes randomly selected for participation in the study.

Treatments

Anger Awareness. The anger awareness treatment included weekly 1-hr sessions during the 5 weeks of treatment. The participants listened to the same educational lecture on anger as the role-playing group. Following the anger education, they engaged in a discussion of their experiences involving both anger instances and anger control. The experimenter suggested alternative reactions to anger-inducing situations without actual modeling or role-playing. The participants were asked to monitor their own anger in game competition over the next 5 weeks of treatment in order to maintain an awareness of their experiences, feelings, and behavior throughout the treatment. Each member of the group was asked to keep a game-by-game journal, recording anger-inducing incidents and his reaction to each incident. During subsequent treatment sessions, the individual participants shared their journal entries, and gave a general evaluation of how their anger control was progressing.

Role-Playing. The role-playing intervention used was similar to that employed in other domains (e.g., Goldstein & Glick, 1994; Jones, 1993). Role-play training included weekly 1-hr sessions over a 5-week period of treatment. The training program began with an educational lecture on the negative effects of competitive anger. Participants were then given live demonstrations of alternative responses to typical anger-inducing situations. They then formed mini-groups of three or four individuals, each assuming the roles of actors or observers. Each mini-group rotated roles in acting out scenarios of common anger-inducing situations in soccer (e.g., a disagreeable referee decision). The first session introduced the participants to role-playing with general instructions and acting exercises. The role-playing exercise in the second and third sessions consisted of scripted scenarios that directed the group to use appropriate responses to typical anger-inducing events in soccer. The last two sessions involved supervised improvisational role-playing exercises during live scrimmages in which participants practiced appropriate responses in "live" action.

Control. The control group participated in activities that demonstrated popular mental strategies to enhance athletic performance (e.g., confidence building, relaxation, flash/trigger words). The subject of anger control was not discussed with the control group. Time spent with this group was equal to the other treatments and organized according to a similar schedule.

Instruments

Angry Behavior Rating Scale. Research assistants, blind to treatment group assignment, observed the participants during each soccer game and recorded the participants' reactions to anger provocations. Observations were then matched with a numerical scoring system adapted from a previous anger control study (see Saylor, Benson, & Einhaus, 1985, for original version) that ranked the severity of both provocations and responses (see Table 1).

Numerical values were assigned to all potential provocations and responses relative to either their anger-provoking potential (for provocations) or their severity (for responses). The less intrusive provocations

Table 1

Angry behavior observation scale showing possible provocations, responses, and respective point values assigned for each incident

Provocation	Point value	Response	Point value
Hard Foul	1 Point	No Anger	1 Point
Verbal Attack	2 Points	Express Frustration	2 Points
Criticism		Raise Voice on Advice	
Self-Error	3 Points	Complaining/Arguing	3 Points
Teammate Error		Physical Frustration	
Poor Team Play		Defensiveness	
Poor Referee Call			
Good Referee Call	4 Points	Swearing	4 Points
No Apparent Provocation		Directed Yelling	
		Physical Retaliation	5 Points
		Overaggressive Play	

were given higher values (e.g., teammate error = 4, verbal attack = 2, physical attack = 1), and the less severe responses were given lower values (e.g., complaining = 2, verbal retaliation = 4, physical retaliation = 5). For each incident, the player provoked was given an "angry behavior score" that equaled the product of the numerical value of the provocation and the numerical value of the response (Provocation Points × Response Points = Anger Points). For example, a player complaining about a teammate's error would receive an anger score of 8 (teammate error [4] × complaining [2]). In general, a more severe response to a less intrusive provocation resulted in a higher anger score for a particular incident. The anger scores of all incidents with which a player was involved were added together and divided by the total number of incidents to calculate an "average anger score" for the participant (Anger Score = Anger Points/Incidents).

Anger Inventory. State anger (angry feelings) was assessed by Spielberger's State-Trait Anger Expression Inventory (STAXI), a 44-item scale that measures the intensity of anger as an emotional state (State Anger), the disposition to experience angry feelings as a personality trait (Trait Anger), and the frequency of anger expression. The Trait Anger dimension includes subscales of angry temperament and angry reaction, while the frequency of anger expression is assessed by three subscales: Anger-out, Anger-in, and Anger Control. Before the first game, participants completed the "trait" and "anger expression" portions of the STAXI. These tests provided control measures for the participants' preexisting anger dispositions.

Procedure

Angry behavior and self-reported anger of each participant was observed and measured, respectively, during a 15-game round-robin season of competitive soccer games. The games were 9-on-9 soccer games between intact teams competing for a soccer class championship. Each game was officiated by a trained referee, and involved two 20-min halves separated by a 5-min halftime break. Teams included 10 to 11 players, with the majority of the players on each team volunteering for the study. Each participant was scheduled to play in 15 soccer games, two games each week, over the duration of the study: (a) six games during the pretreatment phase, (b) six games during the treatment phase, and (c) three games during the retention phase. Because of injuries and other commitments, only 65% of the participants played in all of their team's 15 games ($M = 14.35$ games played). However, all 57 participants played in at least four games during the pretreatment phase, four games during the treatment phase, and all three games during the retention phase.

As mentioned, trained research assistants observed and recorded provocations of angry behavior and responses to the provocations. An observer was assigned to each game, recorded each incident, and cited the player(s) involved, the provocation, and any subsequent responses. For accuracy and efficiency in collecting data, the assistants recorded their observations on-line with electronic tape recorders. Each game was also videotaped to insure accuracy in identifying the correct player and to clarify the behavior cited.

To de-emphasize the true purpose of the study, and to place more significance on the games, participants were told that they were being numerically evaluated by the observers on their physical skills of ball control, passing, shooting, team play, defense, and the win/loss result of each game. The actual purpose of observing the games, unknown to the participant, was to evaluate angry responses to naturally occurring provocations during competition. After each game, the participants completed a disguised version of the State-Trait Anger Expression Inventory (STAXI; Spielberger, 1991) to assess state anger.

As the season progressed through the pretreatment, treatment, and retention phases of the study, participants completed the "state" portion of the STAXI immediately following each game. The "state" portion contained 10 statements of angry feelings that participants rated on a scale ranging from 1 (*not at all*) to 4 (*very much*) about how they felt at the moment. The angry statements of the "state" portion were listed among 20 other statements of different emotions to disguise the anger focus of the testing.

Research Design

The research design for this investigation was a randomized groups design with repeated measures. The independent variables were anger treatment and phase of the study. Three anger treatment conditions were randomly assigned: (a) role-playing, (b) anger awareness, and (c) control. The two dependent variables of angry behavior and state anger were analyzed separately. Both dependent measures were calculated by averaging the anger scores in the games played during particular phases of the study. The pretreatment phase consisted of games 1–6, which took place before the anger control treatment began. The treatment phase included games 7–12 and occurred during the period of anger control treatment. The retention phase of the study included games 13–15 and began 2 weeks after the last session of anger control treatment.

RESULTS

The results of the analyses are presented in the following sequence: (a) pretreatment anger, (b) angry behavior, and (c) state anger. Traditional F tests were computed with conservative degrees of freedom adjustments (Greenhouse & Geisser, 1959) in cases where the sphericity assumption was violated. The predetermined alpha level was set at $p < .05$ for all statistical analyses. Tukey's Honestly Significant Difference (HSD) test was used as a post hoc multiple comparison procedure for significant main effects. For significant interactions, simple effects tests were used to specify differences.

Pretreatment Anger

Pretreatment anger scores calculated from the STAXI were initially analyzed to indicate any preexisting differences among the three groups. One-way analyses of variance (ANOVAs) were used to compare pretreatment scores in stable anger variables among the three groups. The analyses indicated no significant differences between groups for any of the STAXI measures taken at the pretreatment assessment [Trait Anger ($F_{(2,54)} = 2.81$, $p > .05$), Anger-in ($F_{(2,54)} = .31$, $p > .05$), Anger-out ($F_{(2,54)} = 2.14$, $p > .05$), Anger Control ($F_{(2,54)} = 1.15$, $p > .05$), Anger Expression ($F_{(2,54)} = 1.23$, $p > .05$)]. Therefore, it was assumed that the three groups were statistically equivalent in terms of stable anger variables, and subsequently, no covariates were included in the analyses of the dependent variables of angry behavior and state anger.

Angry Behavior

Interrater Reliability. A Pearson product-moment correlational analysis was conducted to assess the interrater reliability between the assistants' observations during a 20-min taped segment of one of the soccer games. The analysis revealed strong interrater reliability coefficients, ranging from $r = .85$ to $r = .96$ ($p < .05$), indicating that the assistants' ratings of angry behavior were sufficiently reliable, and could be included in further analyses.

Observed Angry Behavior. The angry behavior scores were analyzed by a mixed model 3 × 3 (Group × Phase) ANOVA with repeated measures on the second factor, and yielded significant main effects for Group ($F_{(2,108)} = 25.607$, $p < .001$, ($\eta^2 = .32$) and Phase ($F_{(2,54)} = 5.75$, $p < .005$, ($\eta^2 = .18$). The data were described more thoroughly, however, by the significant Group × Phase interaction, ($F_{(4, 108)} = 16.60$, $p < .001$, ($\eta =$

.38). Simple effects follow-up tests indicated that although the angry behavior scores among groups were similar during the pretreatment phase, the role-playing (*M* = 6.19, *SD* = 1.10) and anger awareness (*M* = 7.36, *SD* = 1.92) groups displayed less angry behavior than did the control group (*M* = 9.10, *SD* = 2.37) during the treatment phase. Furthermore, simple effects tests indicated that during the retention phase, the role-playing group (*M* = 5.60, *SD* = 1.24) exhibited less angry behavior than did the anger awareness group (*M* = 7.48, *SD* = 2.52), and that both groups demonstrated less angry behavior than the control group (*M* = 9.17, *SD* = 2.36).

When examining anger score changes within each treatment group, simple effects tests indicated that the role-playing group and the anger awareness group significantly reduced angry behavior as they progressed through the phases of the study. The role-playing participants initially reduced their anger scores significantly from the pretreatment phase (*M* = 9.51, SD = 1.63) to the treatment phase (*M* = 6.19, *SD* = 1.10), and continued this trend with another significant reduction during the retention phase (*M* = 5.60, *SD* = 1.24). The anger awareness group significantly reduced their anger scores from the pretreatment phase (*M* = 8.38, *SD* = 2.07) to the treatment phase (*M* = 7.36, *SD* = 1.92), and maintained this level of angry behavior during the retention phase (*M* = 7.48, *SD* = 2.52). Figure 1 depicts the ratings of angry behavior over the duration of the study.

State Anger

State anger was analyzed by a mixed model 3 × 3 (Group × Phase) ANOVA with repeated measures on the second factor. The analysis failed to indicate any significant main effects for either Group ($F8_{(2, 54)} = 1.47$, $p > .05$) or Phase ($F_{(2, 133)} = 1.85$, $p > .05$). Also, no significant Group × Phase interaction ($F_{(4, 133)} = 0.64$, $p > .05$) was observed.

DISCUSSION

Postulated was that role-playing would be a more effective and enduring method of controlling competitive anger when compared to an anger awareness treatment and a control condition. Pursuant to this hypothesis, the most meaningful finding was the significant Group × Phase interaction for controlling angry behavior, and the implications of this finding for the use of role-playing and anger awareness as interventions to control anger. The anger awareness intervention was effective, leading to a decrease in angry behavior from pretreatment levels. However, role-playing participants continued to reduce angry behavior over the duration of the study, and thereby achieved lower anger scores in comparison to the other groups at the end of the treatment and retention phases.

It appears that by enacting common anger-provoking situations, members of the role-playing group were able to simultaneously act, feel, and think through alternative responses (Shaw, Corsini, Blake, & Mouton,

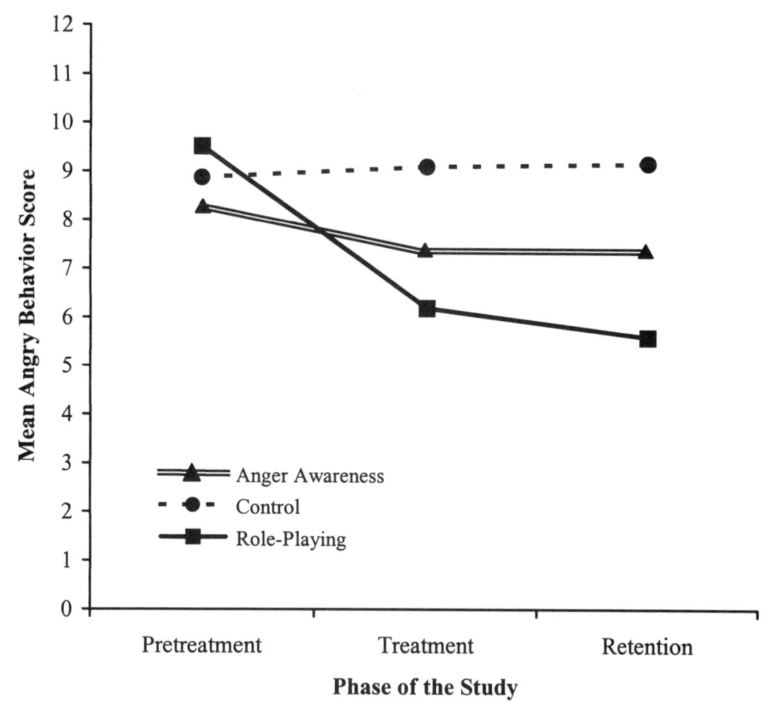

Figure 1. Mean angry behavior scores for the three groups across the pretreatment, treatment, and retention phases.

1980). The direct and active involvement in simulated situations allowed the participants to essentially practice the skill of anger control. The simulated environment encouraged appropriate response strategies that ultimately transferred to the mastery of anger-provoking situations in real soccer action. With enough deliberate attention and active rehearsal of the anger-provoking situations, the appropriate behavior apparently became the dominant response, and subsequently appeared in real game situations.

The fact that the role-playing group continued to display significantly less angry behavior than both of the other groups reflected the enduring nature of role-playing reported by other researchers (Goldstein & Glick, 1987, 1994; Janis & Mann, 1977). With the opportunity to create and engage in alternative behavior, it seems that participants could explore changes that were more compatible to their competitive style, and in turn, adopt these changes for the long-term.

As expected, the anger awareness participants also reduced their angry behavior as the study progressed. They were not only able to reduce their angry behavior scores significantly, but maintained lower anger scores than the control group. However, the anger awareness condition failed to progressively improve anger control as the treatment continued. After matching the role-playing group's initial reduction in anger scores during the treatment phase, the anger awareness group failed to make any additional significant reductions in angry behavior. These results seem to indicate that the self-monitoring procedure of the anger awareness condition had a more modest and leveling effect in controlling anger. As expected, educating athletes about the negative consequences of anger, and directing them toward an organized and objective awareness of their own feelings and behavior was beneficial. However, because the awareness intervention is primarily a passive learning protocol without any rehearsal or practice, a player's ability to control anger during a game appeared to give way to the more natural impulses that were learned by years of previous competitive involvement.

The reports of state anger among the anger awareness and role-playing groups immediately after games did not reflect or follow the reduction in angry behavior. A possible explanation for the lack of a decline in state anger may be attributed to the limited duration of the treatment and measurement of anger control. It appears that it may take more time for players to assume the attitudes and feelings that reflect more controlled behavior. A modest trend toward less state anger was demonstrated by those in the role-playing group from the pretreatment session ($M = 17.31$, $SD = 4.81$) to the retention phase ($M = 15.18$, $SD = 5.68$). With further treatment, and a longer measurement time frame, the role-playing participants may have eventually reported less angry feelings. Alternatively, given that the primary emphasis of both interventions was geared toward the importance of constructively dealing with angry feelings, it is possible that angry feelings would persist, but that the ability to deal with those feelings in a more functional manner would be facilitated.

It is generally understood and expected that the high arousal produced by strenuous sport makes emotion more likely (Tavris, 1989). It should also be understood that sport participants cannot ultimately control the outcome of an event beyond their own individual effort, nor can individual athletes control the actions of the other participants, including opponents and officials. If athletes consistently feel angry and continuously react with overt anger to these external, uncontrollable events, they will eventually reach an arousal level that may hinder performance and create a tense atmosphere of potential aggression. However, if athletes can practice and anticipate the potential anger-inducing stimuli, they can at least control their own thoughts, perceptions, and ultimate responses, to these potentially stressful events. This preparation would seem to allow them more time to concentrate on the performance demands of the sport competition.

Although the implications of maintaining or perhaps even increasing athletic performance through anger control certainly has its appeal, the value of anger control may be found in its influence on the competitive environment as a whole. With the considerable involvement of people in organized sport and the general population's dependency on sport activity for physical and social development, it seems imperative to establish healthy and constructively competitive sport environments. A growing concern for the general public and sport scientists is the amount of psychological stress that athletes, especially young athletes, experience as a consequence of structured competitive involvement (Brustad, 1993). In response to these reasonable concerns, the true significance of this investigation may rely on informing athletes, parents, and coaches of the negative consequences of anger and demonstrating the effectiveness of behavioral rehearsal in advancing psychological and emotional development in sport. By decreasing both covert and overt occurrences of anger, role-play training may not only improve athletic performance but it may increase the health, the enjoyment, and the sportsmanship of competitive sport.

REFERENCES

Barth, R. P., Blythe, B. J., Schinke, S. P., & Schilling, R. F. (1983). Self-control training with maltreating parents. *Child Welfare, 62*(4), 313–324.

Braha, R. E., & Catchlove, R. F. (1986). Pain and anger: Inadequate expression in chronic pain patients. *Pain Clinic, 1*(2), 125–129.

Bredemeier, B. J. (1984). Sport, gender, and moral growth. In J. M. Silva and R. S. Weinberg (Eds.), *Psychological foundations of sport* (p. 400–413). Champaign, IL: Human Kinetics.

Brustad, R. J. (1993). Youth in sport: Psychological considerations. In R. N. Singer, M. Murphey, & L. K. Tennant (Eds.), *Handbook of research on sport psychology* (pp. 695–717). New York: Macmillan.

Eisendrath, S. J. (1987). Issues of control in the general hospital surgical setting. International *Journal of Psychosomatics, 34*(1), 3–5.

Goldstein, A. P., & Glick, B. (1987). *Aggression replacement training: A comprehensive intervention for aggressive youth.* Champaign, IL: Research Press.

Goldstein, A. P., & Glick, B. (1994). Aggression replacement training: Curriculum and evaluation. *Simulation and Gaming, 25,* 9–26.

Greenhouse, S. W., & Geisser, S. (1959). On the methods in the analysis of profile data. *Psychometrika, 24,* 95–112.

Hahn, E. (1989). Emotions in sports. In D. Hackfort & C. D. Spielberger (Eds.), *Anxiety in sports: An international perspective* (pp. 153–162). New York: Hemisphere.

Harrell, W. A. (1981). Verbal aggressiveness in spectators at professional hockey games: The effects of tolerance of violence and amount of exposure to hockey. *Human Relations, 34,* 653–655.

Husman, B. F, & Silva, J. M. (1984). Aggression in sport: definitional and theoretical considerations. In J. M. Silva and R. S. Weinberg (Eds.), *Psychological foundations of sport* (pp. 246–260). Champaign, Ill: Human Kinetics.

Janis. I. L., & Mann, L. (1977). *Decision Making: A psychological analysis of conflict, choice, and commitment.* New York: The Free Press.

Jones, G. (1993). The role of performance profiling in cognitive behavioral interventions in sport. *The Sport Psychologist, 7,* 160–172.

Kiester, E. (1984, July). The uses of anger. *Psychology Today, 18,* 26.

Levenson, R. L., & Herman, J. (1991). The use of role-playing as a technique in the psychotherapy of children. *Psychotherapy, 28,* 660–666.

Loehr, J. E. (1983). *Athletic excellence: Mental toughness training for sports.* Denver, CO: Forum.

Marme, M., & Skord, K. (1993). Counseling strategies to enhance the vocational rehabilitation of persons after traumatic brain injury. *Journal of Applied Rehabilitation Counseling, 24*(1), 19–25.

McDonnell, J. R. (1993). Judgments of personal responsibility for HIV infection: An attributional analysis. *Social Work, 38*(4), 403–410.

McNair, D., Lorr, M., & Droppleman, L. (1971). *Manual for the Profile of Mood States.* San Diego, CA: Educational and Industrial Testing Service.

Miller, C. R., Eisner, W., & Allport, C. (1994). Creative coping: A cognitive-behavioral group for borderline personality disorder. *Archives of Psychiatric Nursing, 8*(4), 280–285.

Monti, P. M., Abrams, D. B., Kadden, R. M., & Cooney, N. L. (1989). *Treating alcohol dependence: A coping skills training guide.* New York: Guilford.

Morgan, W. P. (1974). Selected psychological considerations in sport. *The Research Quarterly, 45,* 374–390.

Morgan, W. P. (1985). Selected psychological factors limiting performance: A mental health model. In D. H. Clarke and H. M. Eckert (Eds.), *Limits of human performance* (pp. 70–80). Champaign, IL: Human Kinetics.

Nay, R. W. (1995). Cognitive behavioral and short-term interventions for anger and aggression. In L. Vandecreek & S. Knapp (Eds.), *Innovations in clinical practice: A source book* (pp. 111–136). Sarasota, FL: Professional Resource Press.

Novaco, R. W. (1975). *Anger control: The development and evaluation of an experimental treatment.* Lexington, MA: Lexington Books.

Novaco, R. W. (1977). A stress-inoculation approach to anger management in the training of law enforcement officers. *American Journal of Community Psychology, 5,* 327–346.

Orlick, T. (1990). *In pursuit of excellence: How to win in sport and life through mental training* (2nd ed.). Champaign, IL: Human Kinetics.

Ostrow, A. (1974). The aggressive tendencies of male intercollegiate tennis team players as measured by selected psychological tests. *New Zealand Journal of Health, Physical Education, and Recreation, 6,* 19–21.

Patterson, A. (1974). Hostility catharsis: A naturalistic quasi-experiment. *Personality and Social Psychology Bulletin, 1,* 195–197.

Radley, A. (1978). Deliberation and awareness in personal conduct. *Journal of Phenomenological Psychology, 8,* 181–202.

Ravizza, K., & Hanson, T. (1995). *Heads-up baseball: Playing the game one pitch at a time.* Indianapolis, IN: Masters Press.

Robbins, M. (1993). Disturbances of affect representation in primitive personalities. In A. Wilson and J. Gedo (Eds.), *Hierarchical concepts in psychoanalysis: Theory, research, and clinical practice* (pp. 235–262). New York: Guilford Press.

Ryan, E. D. (1970). The cathartic effect of vigorous motor activity on aggressive behavior. *Research Quarterly, 41,* 542–551.

Russell, G. W. (1983). Psychological issues in sports aggression. In J. H. Goldstein (Ed.), *Sports violence* (pp. 157–181). New York: Springer-Verlag.

Saylor, C. F., Benson, B., & Einhaus, L. (1985). Evaluation of an anger management program for aggressive boys in inpatient treatment. *Journal of Child and Adolescent Psychotherapy, 2,* 5–15.

Shaw, M. E., Corsini, R. J., Blake, R. R., & Mouton, J. S. (1980). *Role playing: A practical manual for group facilitators.* San Diego, CA: University Associates.

Spielberger, C. D. (1991). *Manual for the State-Trait Anger Expression Inventory.* Odessa, FL: Psychological Assessment Resources, Inc.

Spielberger, C. D., Krasner, S. S., & Solomon, E. P. (1988). In M. P. Janisse (Ed.), *Health psychology: Individual differences and stress* (pp. 89–108). New York: Springer Verlag.

Suinn, R. M. (1986). *Seven steps to peak performance.* Toronto: Hans Huber Publishers.

Tavris, C. (1989). *Anger: The misunderstood emotion* (Rev. ed.). New York: Simon & Schuster.

Taylor, J. W. (1984). Structured conjoint therapy for spouse abuse cases. *Social Casework, 65*(1), 11–18.

Vallerand, R. (1983). On emotion in sport: Theoretical and social psychological perspectives. *Journal of Sport Psychology, 5,* 197–215.

Waller, G., Quinton, S., & Watson, D. (1995). Processing of threat related information by women with bulimic eating attitudes. *International Journal of Eating Disorders, 18(2),* 189–193.

Manuscript submitted: November 1, 1997
Revision received: August 1, 1998

JOURNAL OF APPLIED SPORT PSYCHOLOGY **11**, 298–320 (1999)

Critical Issues Confronting the Advancement of Applied Sport Psychology

JOHN M. SILVA III

University of North Carolina at Chapel Hill

DAVID E. CONROY

University of Utah

SAMUEL J. ZIZZI

West Virgina University

Despite considerable progress over the last 10 years, applied sport psychology confronts several persistent issues that continue to limit the growth and development of the field. Specifically, issues requiring more comprehensive and proactive attention and initiatives include: the training of graduate students, the accreditation of graduate programs, the job market, and the establishment of systematic educational outreach programs. Suggestions are offered regarding how enhancements in each of the aforementioned issues can be initiated, and potential benefits gained by students, faculty, and the general public are identified and discussed. Given the climate in many academic institutions emphasizing program downsizing, sport psychology may be approaching and confronting one of the most crucial crossroads in its existence. Without direct efforts to assure academic credibility and public confidence in the standards of training and practice, sport psychology may fail to actualize a meaningful future role in the competitive field of allied health service provision.

John M. Silva, Department of Physical Education, Exercise and Sport Science; David E. Conroy, Department of Exercise and Sport Science; Samuel J. Zizzi, School of Physical Education.

Correspondence concerning this article should be addressed to John M. Silva at the Department of Physical Education, Exercise and Sport Science, CB#8700, The University of North Carolina, Chapel Hill, NC 27599-8700. Electronic mail may be sent via the Internet to silva@unc.edu

1041-3200/99/0298–0320$1.00/0

Since its inception in 1985, the Association for the Advancement of Applied Sport Psychology (AAASP) has accomplished a tremendous amount to advance the field of sport psychology. Applied sport psychology has evolved academically and professionally, and a science-practice approach to graduate training is very popular with many professionals and prospective students. The adoption of certification criteria (AAASP, 1990) and the establishment of ethical principles (AAASP, 1995) have been landmark events for applied sport psychology. Although educational and public interest have promoted greater attention to the field, very little energy has been directed toward a number of professional development issues which influence the current quality of training and practice and how the field will progress in the future.

A decade ago Silva (1989) identified four defining issues confronting sport psychology: accreditation, information dissemination, interorganizational collaboration, and use of title. With the establishment of the Sport Psychology Council (SPC) the challenge of interorganizational collaboration has been acted upon, however to date the SPC remains a relatively untapped resource. AAASP certification has the potential for alleviating some concerns about title, however, issues of title will persist until awareness of certification standards reaches beyond the AAASP membership and into relevant professional groups involving athletic directors, administrators in professional sports, coaches, the Association of State and Provincial Psychology Boards, and the American Board of Professional Psychology. The persistence of debate regarding title has continued to retard the growth of the field and this debate has caused considerable confusion for prospective students interested in becoming sport psychologists. From direct correspondence with students interested in applying to a graduate program in sport psychology, it is obvious that many students are often misinformed and are initially under the impression that what department they receive their degree from is more important in the development of their professional future than the specific type and depth of training they will receive as a student interested in specializing in sport psychology! Professionals and students alike must realize that receiving a degree in psychology or even being liscensed in psychology does not in and of itself permit one to label themself as a sport psychologist and engage in practice outside of their area(s) of competence. Similarly, repeated delays in initiatives designed to disseminate information have inhibited the growth and professionalization of sport psychology (Alford, 1997). The authors maintain that the lack of organizational movement toward training enhancement and accreditation has slowed economic and employment developments in the field. This is evidenced by the current lack of recruitment initiatives by professional sport teams of certified sport psychology consultants.

A number of students and professionals have expressed concerns at AAASP meetings (Murphy, 1996; Silva, 1996a, 1996b, 1997a, 1997b, 1997c; Students', 1997), and via the internet, that the organizational leadership of AAASP must facilitate meaningful initiatives in a timely manner that enhance training programs and the practice of sport psychology. Whether the current leaders in sport psychology choose to address professional training issues now, or in the immediate future, these are the issues that will impact how sport psychology presents itself to the academic and athletic communities and the public consumer. The major critical issues presented in this paper require not only reflection but a course of systematic action.

Training in Applied Sport Psychology

Sport psychology has its roots as an applied science! Since Coleman Griffiths' early science-practice efforts in his work with the Chicago Cubs, sport psychology has been positioned to apply knowledge to participants (Wiggins, 1984). Similar to other helping professions, sport psychologists face an ever-present social mandate to demonstrate the efficacy of their methods and techniques. In response to this demand, the contemporary job market for sport psychologists supports the science-practice training model. Students without skills in both the research and application of sport psychology will continue to be challenged to find full-time employment in sport psychology. Since the majority of career opportunities in applied sport psychology are academic positions, mentoring in research skills and grantsmanship will be required for career advancement (Andersen, Williams, Aldridge, & Taylor, 1997). Formal training in the application of sport psychology principles will also be necessary to address inquiries from athletes and coaches who inevitably bring forward questions, concerns, and requests for services from professionals familiar with sport psychology. Unfortunately, while research training has been and continues to be accessible in sport psychology graduate programs, applied training and supervised applied experiences are underdeveloped in contemporary programs (Andersen et al., 1997; Silva, 1996b, 1997a, 1997b).

Existing deficits in applied sport psychology graduate training must be eliminated if science and practice are to be integrated in training programs. Three challenges stand out as primary tasks for applied sport psychology program directors and faculty. These challenges are: (a) establishing a formal and recognizable program identity, (b) establishing a graduate program composed of a critical mass of faculty specifically trained in sport psychology, and (c) developing and establishing supervised practicum experiences.

A primary source of frustration for students has been the discrepancy between the experiences expected upon application and enrollment and the experiences actually received while participating in the program. Programs should consider constructing specific, formal written profiles that clarify their training goals and methods for prospective students. Equally concerning is the fact that many sport psychology graduate programs are represented by a single faculty member specifically trained in sport psychology. A master's or doctoral program in a specialty area simply cannot provide students with comprehensive graduate training experiences or a context of perspectives on the field with only one faculty member. Student-to-faculty ratios and faculty numbers need to be considered more closely to ascertain the minimum number of graduate faculty required to establish a critical mass and provide adequate breadth and depth of training. Mass and diversity in faculty is needed to further nurture the interdisciplinary interaction of sport psychology graduate students with faculty in psychology, counseling, and allied health professions.

Contemporary applied sport psychology training programs can also benefit from the establishment and enhancement of formal supervised practicum experiences available for graduate students that involve consulting with athletes, teams, and exercise participants under the direct supervision of an AAASP certified sport psychology consultant. More programs must offer formal supervised practica or internships in order to enhance graduate student training in the practice of sport psychology. It is unfortunate than many students continue to learn through trial and error just as previous generations of sport psychologists have learned how to practice. This training model is inefficient and outdated and no longer reflects the current evolution of the profession. Graduate programs must be reviewed carefully by faculty and a decision must be made regarding the identity of the program and the ability of a program to properly educate and train future generations of sport psychologists.

Evaluating Program Identities

An interesting phenomenon has occurred in recent years whereby the term "applied sport psychology" has taken on two very different meanings. One interpretation focuses on training students to conduct applied research while the second interpretation describes training in the application of sport psychology principles with clients. The majority of graduate programs do not specify their interpretation of "applied sport psychology" for prospective students. Too often students discover these divergent interpretations only after entering a program and subsequently experience dissatisfaction with the type and level of training received. To alleviate this concern, each program should form a clear program identity and delineate how that identity translates into a specific training model with specific training experiences for students. For example, if the training in a program is primarily centered around science (research), the orientation should be clearly conveyed in writing to students interested in the program before they apply to the program. If a program is based on a science-practice model, students should understand the nature of research and applied training experiences offered before applying to that program. The 5th edition of the Directory of Graduate Programs in Applied Sport Psychology (Sachs, Burke, & Gomer, 1998) has provided an opportunity for programs to self-rate their orientation on a research to practice continum. This may provide prospective students with some general information, however, the actual research/practice orientation of any program should be carefully investigated by a prospective student. Clarifying program identities, training goals, and training procedures will enable students to select programs which address their emerging professional interests.

Unfortunately, requests to clarify a program's identity can be mistaken for a threat to a program's uniqueness and the faculty's academic freedom. Some faculty may fear that establishing formal program identities and training models will lead to a loss of program diversity or a loss of academic freedom in constructing a program. The primary goal of a comprehensive graduate program review should not be to create a "standardized" identity to which each program must conform. Rather, a review of graduate programs would be desirable to stimulate the development of a host of unique programs, each of which is designed to provide the minimal experiences necessary for competency in the science and/or practice of applied sport psychology. Beyond minimum training criteria, programs would be free to form their own unique identities within sport psychology by providing specialized experiences in areas such as rehabilitation counseling, group or team dynamics, and individual-athlete performance enhancement. A comprehensive program review or self-study will help clarify existing program identities and establish a basis for organized program development across the field.

Core Faculty and Course of Study

Once a program identity has been established, the composition of the program should be carefully examined. Faculty that compose programs at each university should evaluate the diversity and depth of perspectives feasible given their specializations and training. This self-evaluation will allow each program to realize how narrow or broad its focus should be (e.g., research only or research and practice). This decision will of course significantly influence the course of study offered to students. A quality program should involve faculty members with expertise in complementary areas of sport psychology such as health psychology, social psychology of sport, and intervention/performance enhancement. Having a critical mass of sport psychology faculty with complementary interests and training allows students to be educated and trained beyond the fundamentals of sport psychology and thus receive knowledge and adequate mentoring once a specialized focus is selected during training in the graduate program.

The responsibility for offering breadth and depth in training perspective requires both intra- and inter-departmental cooperation. Intra-departmental coursework should include a core of courses in sport psychology, performance enhancement interventions, exercise and health psychology, and social psychology of sport. In order to properly prepare the student for AAASP certification, coursework in motor learning, motor control, information processing, exercise physiology, psychophysiology, clinical psychology, counseling psychology, social psychology, and developmental psychology must be available to the student.

The need for inter-disciplinary cooperation in a sport psychology training program has been addressed by many authors (Lutz, 1990; Petrie & Watkins, 1994; Silva, 1989; Taylor, 1991). Of particular importance for students interested in the practice of applied sport psychology are courses on counseling theories and skills, individual and group dynamics, psychopathology, the psychological requirements of sport performance, psychometrics, and psychological assessment.

Without a balance of interdisciplinary coursework and specific training experiences in applied sport psychology, students will be limited in their approaches to both research and practice. Applied sport psychology consultants (with clinical, counseling, or exercise science backgrounds) who do not possess the necessary background and experiences in exercise science, counseling, and behavior change issues may rely on a "cookbook" approach dependent on "psychological skills training." Reliance on technique-driven approaches to service provision will be inherently limiting for the consultant and the client (Corlett, 1996). Behavior change is a very difficult process that requires an ability to identify and conceptualize complex dynamics and contingencies that generally result in overt behavior. The student who receives interdisciplinary training will be more likely to achieve a level of knowledge and training that will facilitate effective intervention and promote desirable behavior change. The complexity of meaningful behavior change will be reinforced for the student through supervised practicum and internship experiences. Thus, balanced intra- and inter-disciplinary training in sport psychology has the potential to prepare students to provide valuable consultation services and to produce scholarly inquiry to support the further development of professional practice. Although many student graduate programs appear to acknowledge the importance of balanced training, very few appear to have formal mechanisms in place to facilitate this type of training for their students.

Supervised Practicum Experiences

It is unfortunate that student interest in applied sport psychology has not been matched by the development of appropriate applied training models. Several professionals have discussed the need for specialized applied experiences in sport psychology as a necessary component of training if a student is interested in developing a consultative practice (e.g., Murphy, 1988; Silva, 1984, 1996a, 1996b, 1997a, 1997b, 1997c; Simons & Andersen, 1995; Taylor, 1991). Not suprisingly, the AAASP Graduate Tracking Committee found that an unacceptably high number of advanced degree recipients whose course of study focused primarily on sport performance enhancement consulting did not have any practicum or internship experiences in their graduate programs (Andersen et al., 1997). In addition to experience working with sport groups and individual athletes on typical performance enhancement concerns, it may also be worthwhile to provide opportunities for students in the form of rotations in relevant areas such as academic advising, career transition, injury rehabilitation, and substance abuse education. Faculty and students have publically addressed the fact that supervised training opportunities are very limited in most contemporary applied sport psychology graduate programs (Cogan, Petrie, Richardson, & Martin, 1998; Conroy, 1997; Murphy, 1996; Silva, 1997b, 1998; Students', 1997; Wiechman, 1998; Yukelson, 1998; Zaichowski, 1997). To develop a standard for applied training in sport psychology, it will be necessary to develop a more formal model through which students may obtain supervised experiences. Faculty resources will be required to accommodate the supervised practicum experiences that are crucial to quality applied training. This type of one-on-one supervised experience is the cornerstone of counselor training and should have already become an integral part of the standard training model for programs in applied sport psychology. The supervised intervention experience provides an excellent learning environment in which trainees can develop their general counseling skills and learn to apply specific sport psychology knowledge and techniques in a "safe environment" for both the client and the trainee.

Few graduate programs at either the masters or doctoral levels appear to be meeting students' needs for training in the application of sport psychology principles through formal supervised practicum and internship experiences (Andersen & Williams-Rice, 1996). Student experience has indicated that, when questioned about the absence of supervised practica and structured internships in "applied" sport psychology training programs, graduate program directors and faculty have provided many explanations, ranging from a maze of perceived bureaucratic and ethical obstacles to a lack of resources and even a lack of interest (Conroy, 1996). It should be noted that none of these explanations have been compelling enough to prevent other helping professions from advancing the training models provided to their students. Students will continue to be unduly challenged to develop competencies in applied sport psychology without the development of training programs which are designed and supervised by trained and experienced sport psychology consultants. The limited applied experiences which most students acquire are often the products of their own efforts to assemble "an experience" to fill that void in their training and to develop a "competency" in applied sport psychology. Unfortunately, these experiences are usually unorganized and inadequately-supervised experiences for students. Consequently, learning is not systematic and the benefits for students are unpredictable at best. Andersen et al. (1997) found that the average graduate with a doctorate in sport psychology has not acquired enough applied experience to meet the AAASP certification guidelines. Andersen et al. (1994) documented that most sport psychology students received fewer than 200 contact hours of *supervised* applied experiences during their graduate training. This total does not represent half of the contact time required for AAASP certification! Obviously, many students are not receiving sufficient supervised experiences. Rather than passively waiting for a legal procedure (fraud, negligence, malpractice) to stimulate advancement in applied sport psychology training, students and professionals alike would be prudent to assume a proactive orientation toward enhancing quality supervision in applied sport psychology training. Such an approach in any profession increases the likelihood of competent practice being offered to consumers of services.

The casualties of the deficits in contemporary applied training programs are widespread and significant. The students who receive incomplete training leave graduate programs with a superficial understanding of the complexities involved in establishing consulting relationships in sport. These young professionals often do not know how to design and implement an intervention program with an athlete or a team or may grossly underestimate the challenge involved in facilitating *meaningful* behavior and performance enhancement. Coaches and athletes who obtain the services of a poorly-trained sport psychology consultant place themselves, and the quality of their personal and team performance at risk. Institutions and agencies which employ improperly trained consultants assume liability for mistakes. The probability of making such mistakes is greater in the professional who has received limited supervised experiences in applied sport psychology training. Finally, the reputation of sport psychology as a practicing profession is at risk when untrained individuals (young or established professionals) are allowed to represent themselves to the public as competent sport psychology consultants. This is of particular concern from an ethical perspective given that many sport psychology consultants are very aware of the lack of adequately supervised sport psychology consulting experiences either in their retooling process or in their original graduate training. The consequences of deficits in the applied area of training programs are significant and worthy of collective reflection, attention and action by the leaders of the field.

One of the most effective means of enhancing applied sport psychology training is graduate program accreditation. Accreditation is defined as a "voluntary self-regulatory process of quality assessment and enhancement among institutions and professional programs of higher education and training" (APA, 1986, p. 1). It is worthwhile to examine how the American Psychological Association used program accreditation to respond to a similar crisis of unregulated training which faced the field of clinical psychology in the 1940s.

The Issue of Accreditation

At the end of World War II, there was a tremendous demand for trained clinicians to treat soldiers who incurred psychological complications as a result of their experience in the war. Concern was high about the availability of properly trained and competent clinicians. This situation led to a rapid expansion in the number of psychology programs that were "training" clinical psychologists. Subsequent inconsistencies in both the content and methods of training (similar to the situation in contemporary sport psychology) became readily apparent. In 1945, a concerned Veteran's Administration requested that the American Psychological Association (APA) identify the graduate programs which were indeed training individuals properly in the science and practice of psychology (Routh, 1994).

In 1945, APA President Carl Rogers recognized that a failure to regulate training in clinical psychology would have been an abuse of public trust in the profession and he called for a committee to *establish* accreditation criteria for graduate programs in clinical psychology (Routh, 1994). The very next year, 1946, a tentative list of approved graduate training facilities was published in the first volume of the *American Psychologist* (Sears, 1946). The following year, APA published a description of the model training program and a list of *18 programs* which met these criteria (Sears, 1947). A related report published by the APA Committee on Graduate Training in Clinical Psychology (Report, 1947) in the same volume of the *American Psychologist* provided a more detailed description of the components of the recommended model for graduate preparation; this report came to be known as the Shakow report and it provided the basis for the science-practice model.

In 1949, the APA convened a conference on training in clinical psychology with 71 representatives from "universities, mental health agencies, and allied professions" (Raimy, 1950, p. 3) and formally endorsed the Shakow report. This meeting took place in Boulder, Colorado and the resulting science-practice model is often referred to as the Boulder training model. Contemporary interpretations of the Boulder model have emphasized the dual-relationship between science and practice in advancing psychology (Belar & Perry, 1992; Hoshmand & Polkinghorne, 1992). Although the relationship between science and practice has been strained at times, it continues to be a worthy ideal for applied psychological professions which must demonstrate the efficacy of their work.

A Cost-Benefit Analysis of Accreditation in Sport Psychology

Despite the tremendous success of the APA accreditation process in regulating and enhancing standards of graduate training, the initiation of accreditation in the specialty of sport psychology has been slow to develop. Many arguments used against accreditation are outdated and/or unfounded and appear to be grounded in fundamental misunderstandings of the accreditation process. Common concerns voiced in opposition to accreditation in sport psychology will be reviewed and contrasted against benefits documented by other fields which have implemented formal training standards via program accreditation.

Perceived Obstacles to Accreditation in Sport Psychology. Commonly cited arguments against accreditation in sport psychology relate to the cost of accreditation for the institution, the effects of accreditation on the smaller graduate programs in sport psychology, the larger impact of accreditation on the growth of the field, especially in academic settings, and the impact of accreditation on the academic freedom of faculty. Concerns about the cost of accreditation are largely overstated. Graduate programs which are interested in seeking accreditation are generally held responsible for an application fee to cover administrative costs, a two-day site visit from a group of two to three visitors, the cost of any program enhancements which the accreditation committee and site visit team recommend, and an annual fee to cover administrative costs in reviewing annual reports. The application fee for APA accreditation as of January 1998 for new doctoral programs is $2,000. Most organizations also establish an annual fee for maintaining accredited status. While APA charges $4,500 for a site visit, a two-day site visit by two individuals can be liberally estimated at $2,000 for all travel and lodging expenses. Given the cost of program enhancements not withstanding, the total cost of accreditation over a five-year cycle could be set by AAASP at approximately $5,000 or an average of $1,000 per year. Obviously, the greatest cost in the implementation phase for any profesional organization moving in this direction is in the human resource investment required.

Despite the financial costs and other university resources required for accreditation, outcome studies have indicated that faculty and administrators generally perceive accreditation to be a "cost-effective" measure in view of the consequential benefits and program enhancements (Zellman, Johansen, & Van Winkle, 1994). Interestingly, a separate study of the effects of accreditation on athletic training graduate programs indicated that accredited programs actually increased their resources following accreditation (Roth, 1989). Specific increases in resources included the addition of new faculty lines, an increased ration of full- to part-time employees, a decreased supervision ratio, the reallocation of departmental funding to support the accredited program, more computers, more support personnel, an increase in library holdings, and the establishment of a departmental professional library (Roth, 1989). In view of these facts, it becomes difficult to understand how programs committed to training sport psychology students could not find a way to afford the cost of accreditation!

Opponents of accreditation also fear that financial crises will force universities to eliminate graduate programs which fail to earn accredited status. Rather than lose faculty positions and jobs, these opponents argue that the field would be better off postponing training regulation and enhancement until the field becomes more well-established. In reality, inadequate graduate programs are likely to be terminated by cost-conscious administrators regardless of whether accreditation procedures are enacted. Programs which fear unfavorable evaluations by an accreditation committee and are not able or willing to upgrade their programs to develop needed competencies in their students should reflect upon the question of whether they should be in the business of training future professionals. Programs with one faculty member or lacking in critical training experiences may find that Deans eliminate their programs prior to the initiation of any accreditation process by the field of sport psychology. On the other hand, the accreditation process can serve as an objective index of program quality for administrators. Thus, accredited programs should be better able to protect themselves from administrative elimination or down sizing than unaccredited programs.

Unfortunately, some professionals seem to fear that program accreditation will stifle individual creativity in structuring a graduate training program. In reality, accreditation facilitates greater program diversity. Accredited programs would cover the core training areas and students and faculty would have the freedom to further specialize their program of study with the security that they have met the minimum requirements for training sport psychologists. Accreditation and academic freedom are interdependent forces which complement and protect rather than oppose each other (Elman, 1994). The fact remains that not every existing applied sport psychology program will be accredited and enhancements will be necessary in many existing programs. This process of self-enhancement will require the critical and creative efforts of faculty as well as institutional support. Fortunately, accreditation procedures in other fields have demonstrated a history of short- and long-term benefits which greatly outweigh the costs of the process.

Consequences of Accreditation in Sport Psychology. The consequences of accreditation are far-reaching and seem fairly consistent regardless of the setting being accredited. Selden and Porter (1977) have identified internal, external, professional, and societal benefits of accreditation. With regard to documented internal benefits, accredited programs have gained prestige (Zellman et al., 1994) and "stature on campus" (Roth, 1989, p. 35). Additionally, the faculty's involvement in and awareness of the program increased in the process of evaluation and planning (Roth, 1989). Program goals became clarified (Roth, 1989; Zellman et al., 1994) and faculty morale (Zellman et al., 1994) and program cohesion (Roth, 1989) have been shown to increase as a consequence of the accreditation process. Selden and Porter (1977) also identify the benefit of a general raising of standards among educational institutions (p. 8). Zellman et al. (1994) documented student-oriented innovations in curricula, enhanced cultural diversity in curricula, and enhanced student performance in accredited programs. Notably, Roth (1989) found that accreditation in athletic training programs led to an increased applied training component and better integration of research into the program.

Selden and Porter (1977) identified external benefits of accreditation as a useful reference for students researching programs in a specialization as well as a measure of quality for external granting agencies. Professionally, accreditation can be linked to and thus strengthen certification and licensure criteria. Accredited specialty programs are also able to gain increased support (Selden & Porter, 1977) and add resources (such as faculty) to their programs (Roth, 1989). Roth (1989) also found that accredited programs were able to increase their interdisciplinary involvement and collaboration. Finally, Selden and Porter (1977) argue that accreditation is valuable protection "against harmful external and internal pressures" (p. 14–15), such as politically-motivated influences from legislators and administrators. Thus, accreditation will help to secure the academic freedom of graduate programs and the faculty contributing to those programs.

There are a number of specific consequences of accreditation which would be probable in applied sport psychology. First, accreditation is likely to stimulate greater inter-disciplinary interaction in training programs. As a result, applied sport psychology will gain greater recognition "across campus." A public commitment to enhancement and self-regulation should afford the field an increased degree of respect in academia. By raising the standard of training for future professionals, the field will also be better able to articulate its social relevance both to service populations and funding agencies. Subsequent impressions of applied sport psychology should contribute to professional growth and within a few years, the impact of well-trained young professionals may be actualized as additional markets open for individuals trained in applied sport psychology because of increased recognition of competency by professional sport teams and the general public.

The job market should become more fertile as programs desiring accredited status seek to add faculty. It is true that adding faculty to sport psychology programs will be a challenge for many programs and not all programs will be successful in adding new faculty. Fortunately, accreditation will provide programs with some leverage in requesting additional faculty, especially for establishing a critical mass to meet minimum training standards. Faculty and administrators will nevertheless need to be creative and resourceful as they broach the issue of adding faculty. It may be worthwhile to examine the potential for dual or adjunct appointments between exercise science, psychology, and athletic departments. The utilization of dual appointments should also facilitate the development of formal, supervised applied experiences for students. Several Exercise and Sport Science (ESS) departments may have to make some difficult decisions regarding the focus of the department. Currently, many Exercise and Sport Science departments attempt to offer several specialization degrees without the faculty to support these so-called "Ph.D.'s" in sport psychology, exercise physiology, motor learning, etc. Exercise and Sport Science departments may need to streamline to one or two Ph.D. specializations and different universities will become known for their exceptional programs in one or two areas. This approach will be a significant improvement over having 4 or 5 mediocre "Ph.D." specializations in one academic department. Despite the short-term challenges inherent in adding faculty positions, conscientious and resourceful efforts to add faculty will ultimately contribute to a larger job market for well-trained applied sport psychologists which should last beyond the initial stage of program growth.

Voluntary accreditation would be likely to stimulate much-needed graduate training advancements by enhancing the diversity of program offerings, especially as they relate to supervised, applied training experiences. At the same time, programs would have to formulate identities and thus acquire a greater clarity of focus. This enhanced program focus will help prospective students to identify training programs suited to their interests. Consequently, students who are interested in learning how to practice will be less likely to find themselves in research-only sport psychology programs and vice-versa. Furthermore, by endorsing an integrative science-practice model, programs will be more likely to prepare students with the skills which are required in the contemporary job market.

Administrative Responses to Accreditation. From the perspective of graduate program directors, Skinner, Berry, and Jackson (1994) reported that over 80% of the training directors who went through the APA accreditation process perceived the accreditation standards in a favorable light and at least 75% of the training directors valued the accreditation committees input as "educational" (p. 297). Based on the athletic training accreditation process, Roth (1989) advised that the accreditation process was best approached from a "vision of excellence" (p. 38) perspective. This comment is important because accreditation is often misconceptualized as a concrete standard for curriculum design to which programs are bound. On the contrary, accreditation is actually a *voluntary,* dynamic process of self-enhancement among educational programs. Earning accredited status demonstrates an ongoing commitment to self-regulation and enhancement (Bender, 1983). This commitment to the future of the field is desperately needed in contemporary applied sport psychology.

An Action Proposal for Accreditation in Sport Psychology

Despite the lag in organizational attention to an obvious training need, there have been no definitive arguments put forth to oppose the development and implementation of a voluntary accreditation procedure for applied sport psychology graduate programs. Similar to Rogers' insightful perception over fifty years ago (Report, 1947), a failure to regulate training in applied sport psychology today will be an abuse of whatever public trust currently exists in the profession. It is no longer possible to dodge accreditation under the pretense that "the field isn't ready for it." Students are asking for a more advanced training model. At the 1997 AAASP Conference in San Diego, CA, a vote was taken in the student meeting on the need for accreditation of graduate programs in sport psychology. Of the over 80 students present for the vote, fewer than 5 students voted in opposition with the remainder voting in support for program accreditation (Students', 1997). Accreditation can both stimulate and guide much needed enhancements in sport psychology graduate programs. The job market is demanding a more advanced training model and it is time to embrace the issue and establish training standards and accreditation criteria in applied sport psychology. Faculty must allay their personal fears and objectively assess the benefits of program development that will be initiated and sustained by the accreditation process. Furthermore, sport psychology must remember that psychology, a much larger field even in the 1940s, started with only 18 accredited programs (Sears, 1947).

The Role of AAASP

AAASP can address the accreditation issue by advocating the benefits of accreditation for the field of sport psychology. This process will require the formation of an AAASP Graduate Training Standards and Accreditation Committee. A recommended committee composition of two student members, one Past President, the current President, and three at-large members would provide diversity, experience, and perspective. This committee would be charged with developing a model and process to systematically advance the state of graduate training in applied sport psychology. It may be helpful to initiate this process in two stages thus making the process more accessible to the programs which are upgrading to meet the accreditation standards. The first step in the review process would involve the formation of a committee to develop the specific accreditation standards, a review protocol, and a registry of programs. The second step in the process would involve a transition from a registry of programs into the formal accreditation of programs in applied sport psychology. While this process would require some organizational resources, its culmination would indeed mark a historical advancement in the field. Furthermore, as a non-profit organization, AAASP is chartered to return its resources to the membership. Investing AAASP funds in a process that has the potential to advance the field as a whole is an investment that will pay professional dividends that can not be quantified by dollars and cents.

Step I: A Graduate Program Registry

The first step in the process of voluntary program accreditation would begin with the systematic development of criteria proposed for admission into the registry. Programs would engage in a comprehensive self-study to determine how effectively they meet the registry criteria. To create a Sport Psychology Graduate Program Registry, AAASP would need to develop a Sport Psychology Standards and Review Protocol for Master's and Doctoral programs that would allow for an initial, informational review of three areas within each program: (a) the core academic content should be reviewed for evidence that the available interdisciplinary coursework develops the competencies required for certification, (b) a critical faculty mass and faculty-to-student ratios should be established so that doctoral programs in particular are able to manage the advising and supervised practicum experiences essential to comprehensive training in applied sport psychology, and (c) because it is recommended that the field first pursue the accreditation of a science-practice model, a review of both the research training and practicum experiences provided within the course of a program will be essential. A balance of research and applied experiences would increase the probability of producing competent professionals, who are then adequately qualified for certification *and* available faculty positions in sport psychology.

Once the criteria for review are established and interested programs have completed a self-study, program folios would be submitted to

AAASP for review. An AAASP committee would either initially approve these programs for the registry or provide the programs with specific recommendations for program enhancement. After this first stage, those programs which were unable to demonstrate their ability to develop the defined competencies in students would notify AAASP of their intent (or lack thereof) to meet the registry standards, and project the year in which they realistically expected to meet those standards. Concurrently, AAASP would establish the Graduate Program Registry and publish the universities which meet the standards in the *Directory of Graduate Programs in Applied Sport Psychology* (Sachs, Burke & Gomer, 1998) and in the *Journal of Applied Sport Psychology*. The programs which are listed on the Registry would also be the first programs eligible for accreditation since they should be the most prepared for full accreditation. The compilation of a Graduate Program Registry would mark the completion of the first step in graduate program accreditation for applied sport psychology.

Step II: Graduate Program Accreditation

As graduate schools submit their programs for review, approval of the accreditation standards by the AAASP Fellows will merge with the registration process. A committee coordinated with the Standards committee would be charged with the task of developing a procedure for program accreditation. The procedures used by APA for program accreditation are well-established and may be worth considering as a model for applied sport psychology accreditation. The APA requires that programs seeking accreditation declare the specific training model being used to train students and then demonstrate the program's fit with the declared model. Since accreditation is a voluntary process, it is the programs responsibility to establish the burden of proof that it meets or exceeds the accreditation criteria. Science-practice training programs often demonstrate their compliance with the model by providing outcome measures related to research productivity, teaching involvement, service delivery, professional service, degree completion rates, and job placement success (Gaddy, Charlot-Swilley, Nelson, & Reich, 1995). The presentation of this evidence in the form of a comprehensive self-study is followed by a site visit from a team representing the accreditation committee. The APA allows programs to have some input in selecting the site visitors. This site visit is usually funded by the department seeking accreditation. Shortly after the site visit, the site visit team files its report with both the department seeking accreditation and the accreditation committee. The department then has an opportunity to review the team's findings and address how they will respond to the perceived weaknesses in their program. Based on the information gathered through the self-study, the site visit, and the program's response to the site visit team's report, the accreditation committee makes a decision regarding the status of the program's application. Programs may be granted either full or provisional accreditation status. Fully accredited programs must file an annual report in subsequent years detailing any modifications in the training program and the program's continued compliance with the training model. Assuming that the program is relatively stable and does not provide the committee with any reason for premature reevaluation, future self-studies and site visits would be scheduled to take place at five years intervals following the initial accreditation. Provisionally accredited programs must file annual reports and also document their efforts to address program weaknesses.

Programs which are not satisfied with the committee's decision regarding their status are entitled to appeal that decision. In any case, the committee reserves the right to place fully- or provisionally-accredited programs on probationary status for significant changes that impair the program's ability to provide the minimal educational experiences for students. It is recommended that the AAASP committee charged with developing procedures for sport psychology base their approach on the APA model since it has been met with favorable reviews from the programs involved in the process (Skinner et al., 1994). This general model would be tailored to match the determined criteria for the field of sport psychology. Psychology and other disciplines in ESS (e.g., athletic training, sport management) have embraced such standards. What makes applied sport psychology so different that movement toward program enhancement has not been embraced and enacted?

The accreditation of graduate programs in applied sport psychology can take many forms and one such proposal has been advanced in this paper. It is a sad but accurate reflection of the level of training in contemporary applied sport psychology that when the accreditation process is initially implemented, few programs will likely meet the proposed guidelines. However, this position is not an acceptable rationale for failing to pursue accreditation at the present time. If only a few programs meet the preliminary guidelines, at least there will be a few programs in which students can be confident that they will get quality, comprehensive training in applied sport psychology. A few high quality programs are better than none, and far better than many not properly training future professionals. These accredited schools will become the prototypes for a developing network of accredited programs in the near future. As noted, psychology started out with only 18 accredited programs; sport psychology should be realistic and place quality before quantity.

The Job Market

Persistent misconceptions continue to exist regarding employment in the field of applied sport psychology. Students interested in pursuing the specialization of applied sport psychology are often misinformed concerning the nature of job availability, and continually discouraged by the myth that there are no jobs in sport psychology. The reality of the situation indicates the ratio of jobs to new Ph.D.s graduating with specialized training in sport psychology compares favorably with other academic disciplines in the social sciences. Students need only read *On the Market* (Boufis & Olsen, 1997) to understand the extraordinary level of competition for jobs in other fields and how the competition for jobs in sport psychology pales in comparison to many of these fields. As an example, consider the number of students coming out of doctoral programs in sport psychology to those graduating from clinical psychology programs. Clinical psychologists flood the field each year with new Ph.D.s searching for positions, whereas the production of young professionals in applied sport psychology is very limited. Thus, the number of available sport psychology jobs is quite small in comparison to the number of clinical psychology jobs offered each year, however, the relative placement rate for sport psychologists is favorable. Recently, the AAASP Graduate Tracking Committee indicated that for the last five years, approximately 30 new Ph.D.s have entered the market each year (Andersen et al., 1997). Consider that in 1996, over 20 sport psychology-related jobs were available at universities in North America (Stevens, 1996). A fairly fertile employment situation appears to exist for recent graduates seeking sport psychology positions in academia. Additionally, this example assumes each new graduate plans on pursuing a career in academia and excludes the possibility of independent employment in the consulting market or employment in another related area (e.g., athletic academic advising, university counseling centers). Results of the AAASP Graduate Tracking Committee (Andersen et al., 1997) support this claim since the vast majority of sport psychology doctoral graduates who were interested in academic careers were placed in academic jobs with an emphasis on sport psychology. Thus, it appears that jobs do exist in sport psychology and students must become more informed regarding the type of training that will best prepare and position the young professional for academic sport psychology.

A major source of the confusion over the viability of the sport psychology job market may be the type of training received by job applicants. As the field exists today, individuals seeking to become sport psychologists are best served by getting a broad-based, science-practice training within the interdisciplinary specialization of sport psychology. Consider, for example, the persistent myth that a doctoral degree from a general clinical or counseling psychology program will prepare an individual for a career in sport psychology. The reality of the job market is that if a student seeks a university position in sport psychology in the United States, well over 90 percent of these positions are in ESS departments. Further, these departments have traditionally hired Ph.D.s from ESS programs with specializations in sport psychology and interdisciplinary training in clinical or counseling psychology. Individuals with pure clinical or counseling training are naturally at a competitive disadvantage for these position searches and this situation will continue until either psychology departments demonstrate an interest in hiring sport psychologists or a standard training model is developed for sport psychologists that makes it possible for students trained in either psychology or ESS to be able to compete for these academic positions. Critically examining the reality of the sport psychology job market provides a more optimistic employment outlook than is currently portrayed, especially for graduates of exercise and sport science programs. Several recommendations are offered below to promote more accurate representations of the field with respect to employment opportunities.

AAASP's Role In Promoting Job Opportunities

AAASP should create a job database that can be updated by sending out a form or e-mail notice twice a year to universities requesting information on sport psychology related jobs that are available. This information would allow AAASP to stay abreast of employment opportunities within the field. AAASP could then promote these sport psychology job openings in the AAASP Newsletter and on the AAASP homepage on the World Wide Web. These advertisements would centralize information for those attempting to locate employment opportunities and, in addition, send the implicit message that there is a strong desire from the organization for *competent* professionals to fill the available positions. While AAASP is seeking information on, and promoting available sport psychology jobs, administrators at North American universities should be formally contacted by e-mail or a mailing that informs them of AAASP certification and encourages the requirement of certification or application for certification as a basic component of job announcements for sport psychology faculty positions. As a part of this outreach, AAASP should annually contact ESS and Psychology department chairs with a mailing to update them on relevant training issues such as accreditation and certification. This last effort should contribute to enhancing public awareness of the minimum level of training necessary for an individual to be considered competent in sport psychology.

After encouraging students to develop broader skills within the specialization of sport psychology and communicating certification standards to the academic community, other branches of the university and relevant non-academic organizations will need to be contacted and informed about the potential role of sport psychology professionals in their work. Communicating openly with university counseling centers, academic advising units, and independent sport organizations/leagues will assist in clarifying the nature of the job market in sport psychology. Such initiatives increase the overall awareness of the profession of applied sport psychology in the public domain, and enhance the field's professional reputation. Educating professionals about sport psychology will help tap into more new and existing job markets for sport psychology than ever before, a necessary step in the fields ongoing development.

Educational Outreach

The logical extension of communicating with academic units regarding the nature of applied sport psychology would involve a systematic marketing and outreach effort toward private individuals and groups who may desire contact with sport psychology practitioners. To effectively facilitate the education of individuals and sport organizations regarding the current status of applied sport psychology, however, would demand a very efficient use of AAASP's resources. This educational outreach process would have the benefit of informing national organizations regarding the qualifications of sport psychologists and stimulating the development of greater career opportunities for sport psychologists. Ultimately, such contact will be influential in increasing student placement in diverse fields related to sport psychology.

The primary outreach issue challenging the field's growth is a general lack of communication with external sources regarding the nature of applied sport psychology and the qualifications necessary for the proper preparation of a sport psychologist. Andersen et al. (1997) note that consulting opportunities have not increased for sport psychology graduates in recent years. Potential outreach efforts should be directed at, but not limited to, athletes, coaches, athletic directors, NCAA, professional organizations, and the public. The educational process for these groups would involve both promoting AAASP Certification standards as the minimum criteria for practice and addressing general misconceptions surrounding sport psychology. By clarifying the nature of sport psychology and the minimum training requirements for sport psychology service provision, AAASP may contribute to expanding the opportunities available for work in applied sport psychology.

Certification should be promoted and used more as a tool to educate those in positions to hire sport psychologists. Many individuals in administrative positions continue to hire practitioners who are not specifically trained in sport psychology, preferring to base their decisions on personal networks and referrals from associates. Too often this practice results in the hiring of former athletes with no formal training in sport psychology or clinical psychologists with no specific training in sport psychology. Knowledge of AAASP certification would provide administrators, coaches, and organizations with a basis on which to judge candidates for employment, ideally leading to an increased number of competent professionals working with athletes. To affect change on a national level, AAASP must commit to educating coaches, sport administrators, National Governing Bodies (NGBs) and other sport organizations on the current status of certification. Enhancing awareness of the minimum standards for sport psychology service provision will also enhance understanding of the nature of applied sport psychology. When individual and organizational levels of sport become aware of the necessary qualifications of an applied sport psychologist, increased employment opportunities for competent sport psychologists may be enhanced. Misconceptions about sport psychology are sufficiently wide-spread to suggest that significant time and energy will be required for comprehensive outreach efforts to be successful.

AAASP Outreach Consultant Proposal. One possible means for directing organizational attention and effort to outreach without placing an undue demand on individual AAASP members would involve creating the new position of AAASP Outreach Consultant. This position could be a two-year paid internship, and the individual would be responsible for formally and informally educating athletic organizations at all levels. The minimum qualifications should include a Master's Degree with a specialization in sport psychology. This position would provide a unique opportunity for a student in the field to gain experience within the organization and to develop a vast network of sport psychology connections nationwide. The outreach consultant would be the impetus for the educational process and, after some time in the position, be able to return to AAASP with tremendous feedback regarding the experience. This individual could present her/his realistic assessment of the state of the field at each AAASP conference. Creating a position for an AAASP Outreach Consultant would be an excellent step toward reducing practice outside of one's competencies and increasing awareness in the public domain regarding the qualifications of applied sport psychologists.

AAASP must adopt a more proactive role in disseminating information and creating a public awareness of applied sport psychology. The existing financial resources of the organization can be used to generate and distribute informational materials on the profession of applied sport psychology and to fund an internship to advocate applied sport psychology at the national level. These educational efforts should subsequently increase employment opportunities for qualified professionals, improve understanding of applied sport psychology on a national level, and stimulate a more efficient entry process for students interested in careers in applied sport psychology. The AAASP Outreach Consultants position would be one of the most progressive uses of AAASP funds imaginable!

Sport Psychology: Advancement is the Goal

A central purpose of AAASP has been to develop and promote the professional and scientific aspects of applied sport psychology. The authors have provided a description of several issues which confront the advancement of the field. Specific action plans for progress on these issues have been proposed (Silva, 1996b, 1997a, 1997b) and it is anticipated that colleagues will recognize the urgency of these issues in determining the future existence and quality of the field of sport psychology. As the field moves toward the 21st century, AAASP must continue to adopt a proactive role in facilitating advancement. The AAASP leadership and professional membership must mobilize together to place meaningful issues at the forefront of the Association's agenda. Students and young professionals, the future of the field, must also assume a more proactive role in the advancement of the field and thus facilitate the emergence of sport psychology as a worthy and notable discipline *and* profession in the 21st century.

REFERENCES

AAASP passes certification criteria. (1990, Winter). *AAASP Newsletter, 5,* 3, 8.

AAASP (1995, Winter). Ethical principles of AAASP. *AAASP Newsletter, 10,* 15, 21.

Alford, L. (1997, Winter). Organization and Outreach and Education Committee Report. *AAASP Newsletter, 12,* 9, 25.

American Psychological Association (1986). *Accreditation handbook.* Washington, DC: APA.

Andersen, M. B., Van Raalte, J. L., & Brewer, B. W. (1994). Assessing the skills of sport psychology supervisors. *The Sport Psychologist, 8,* 238–247.

Andersen, M. B., Williams, J. M., Aldridge, T., & Taylor, J. (1997). Tracking the training and careers of advanced degree programs in sport psychology, 1989 to 1994. *The Sport Psychologist, 11,* 326–344.

Andersen, M. B., & Williams-Rice, B. T. (1996). Supervision in the education and training of sport psychology service providers. *The Sport Psychologist, 10,* 278–290.

Belar, C. D., & Perry, N. W. (1992). National conference on scientist-practitioner education and training for the professional practice of psychology. *American Psychologist, 47,* 71–75.

Bender, L. W. (1983). Accreditation: Its misuses and misconceptions. In K. E. Young, C. M. Chambers, H. R. Kells, & Associates (Eds.), *Understanding accreditation: Contemporary perspectives on issues and practices in evaluating educational quality.* San Francisco, CA: Jossey-Bass Publishers.

Boufis, C., & Olsen, V. C. (1997). *On the market: Surviving the academic job search.* New York: Riverhead Books.

Cogan, K. D., Petrie, T., Richardson, P., & Martin, S. (1998, September). Applied sport psychology training at the University of North Texas Center for Sport Psychology. In K. D. Cogan (Chair), *Interdisciplinary approaches to applied sport psychology training.* Symposium conducted at the Annual Conference of the Association for the Advancement of Applied Sport Psychology.

Conroy, D. E. (1996). Science-practice and accreditation in applied sport psychology. *Journal of Applied Sport Psychology, 8,* S51.

Conroy, D. E. (1997, September). A cost-benefit analysis of graduate program accreditation in sport psychology. In J. M. Silva (Chair), *Initiating program accreditation in sport psychology.* Symposium conducted at the Annual Conference of the Association for the Advancement of Applied Sport Psychology.

Corlett, J. (1996). Sophistry, Socrates, and sport psychology. *The Sport Psychologist, 10,* 84–94.

Elman, S. E. (1994). Academic freedom and regional accreditation: Guarantors of quality in the academy. *New Directions for Higher Education, 88,* 89–100.

Gaddy, C. D., Charlot-Swilley, D., Nelson, P. D., & Reich, J. N. (1995). Selected outcomes of accredited programs. *Professional Psychology: Research and Practice, 26,* 507–513.

Hoshmand, L. T., & Polkinghorne, D. E. (1992). Redefining the science-practice relationship and professional training. *American Psychologist, 47,* 55–66.

Lutz, D. J. (1990). An overview of training models in sport psychology. *The Sport Psychologist, 4,* 63–71.

Murphy, S. M. (1988). The on-site provision of sport psychology services at the 1987 U.S. Olympic Festival. *The Sport Psychologist, 2,* 337–350.

Murphy, S. M. (1996, September). Wither certification? In J. M. Silva (Chair), *Current issues confronting the advancement of applied sport psychology.* Symposium conducted at the Annual Conference of the Association for the Advancement of Applied Sport Psychology.

Petrie, T. A., & Watkins, C. E. (1994). A survey of counseling psychology programs and exercise/sport science departments: Sport psychology issues and training. *The Sport Psychologist, 8,* 28–36.

Raimy, V. C. (1950). *Training in clinical psychology.* New York: Prentice-Hall.

Report of the Committee on Training in Clinical Psychology of the American Psychological Association submitted at Detroit meeting of the American Psychological Association, September 9–13, 1947 (1947). Recommended training program in clinical psychology. *American Psychologist, 2,* 539–558.

Roth, R. A. (1989). NCATE: Institutional perspectives from the pilot studies. *Action in Teacher Education, 11,* 33–38.

Routh, D. K. (1994). *Clinical psychology since 1917: Science, practice and organization.* New York: Plenum.

Sachs, M., Burke, K., & Gomer, S. (1998). *Directory of graduate programs in applied sport psychology.* Morgantown, WV: Fitness Information Technology, Inc.

Sears, R. R. (1946). Graduate training facilities: I. General information, II. Clinical psychology. *The American Psychologist, 1,* 135–150.

Sears, R. R. (1947). Clinical training facilities: 1947: A report from the committee on graduate and professional training. *The American Psychologist, 2,* 199–205.

Selden, W. K., & Porter, H. V. (1977). *Accreditation: Its purposes and uses.* Washington, DC: Council on Postsecondary Accreditation.

Silva, J. M. (1984). The emergence of applied sport psychology: Contemporary trends—Future issues. *International Journal of Sport Psychology, 15,* 40–51.

Silva, J. M. (1989). Establishing professional standards and advancing applied sport psychology research. *Journal of Applied Sport Psychology, 1,* 160–165.

Silva, J. M. (1996a). Current issues confronting the advancement of applied sport psychology. *Journal of Applied Sport Psychology, 8,* S50–S52.

Silva, J. M. (1996b). A second move: Confronting persistent issues that challenge the advancement of applied sport psychology. *Journal of Applied Sport Psychology, 8,* S52.

Silva, J. M. (1997a). Initiating program accreditation in sport psychology. *Journal of Applied Sport Psychology, 9,* S47–S49.

Silva, J. M. (1997b, August). Advancing progressive training models in applied sport psychology. In C. M. Janelle (Chair), *Training, employment, and accreditation issues in sport psychology—Student perspectives.* Symposium conducted at the meeting of the American Psychological Association, Chicago, IL.

Silva, J. M. (1997c, September). Accreditation: A process designed to enhance preparatory and professional standards. In J. M. Silva (Chair), *Initiating program accreditation in sport psychology.* Symposium conducted at the Annual Conference of the Association for the Advancement of Applied Sport Psychology.

Silva, J. M. (1998, September). Interdisciplinary approaches to training in applied sport psychology at the University of North Carolina at Chapel Hill. In K. D. Cogan (Chair), *Interdisciplinary approaches to applied sport psychology training.* Symposium conducted at the Annual Conference of the Association for the Advancement of Applied Sport Psychology.

Simons, J. P., & Andersen, M. B. (1995). The development of consulting practice in applied sport psychology: Some personal perspectives. *The Sport Psychologist, 9,* 449–468.

Skinner, L. J., Berry, K. K., & Jackson, T. L. (1994). Accreditation of doctoral psychology training programs: Results of a nationwide survey. *Professional Psychology: Research and Practice, 25,* 296–299.

Stevens, D. E. (1996) Personal Communication with J. M. Silva, September 1996.

Students' Vote on Graduate Training Accreditation Issue. (1997, September 25). The Annual Conference of the Association for the Advancement of Applied Sport Psychology.

Taylor, J. (1991). Career direction, development, and opportunities in applied sport psychology. *The Sport Psychologist, 5,* 266–280.

Wiechman, S. (1998, September). Applied sport psychology training at the University of Washington. In K. D. Cogan (Chair), *Interdisciplinary approaches to applied sport psychology training.* Symposium conducted at the Annual Conference of the Association for the Advancement of Applied Sport Psychology.

Wiggins, D. K. (1984). The history of sport psychology in North America. In J. M. Silva and R. S. Weinberg (Eds.), *Psychological foundations of sport.* Champaign, IL: Human Kinetics.

Yukelson, D. (1998, September). Applied sport psychology training at Penn State University. In K. D. Cogan (Chair), *Interdisciplinary approaches to applied sport psychology training.* Symposium conducted at the Annual Conference of the Association for the Advancement of Applied Sport Psychology.

Zaichkowsky, L. D. (1997, September). *Initiating program accreditation in sport psychology: A reaction.* Symposium conducted at the Annual Conference of the Association for the Advancement of Applied Sport Psychology.

Zellman, G. L., Johansen, A. S., & Van Winkle, J. (1994). *Examining the effects of accreditation on military child development center operations and outcomes.* Santa Monica, CA: RAND.

Manuscript submitted: February 19, 1998
Revision received: November 10, 1998

JOURNAL OF APPLIED SPORT PSYCHOLOGY **11**, 321–328 (1999)

Putting the Accreditation Cart Before the AAASP Horse: A Reply to Silva, Conroy and Zizzi

BRUCE D. HALE

University of Maine

STEVEN J. DANISH

Virginia Commonwealth University

While Silva et al. (1999) must be congratulated for leading a discussion of accreditation of graduate programs in applied sport psychology, the authors appear to have "put the cart before the horse." They have adopted an extreme one-sided position that suggests that accreditation of programs is the only viable solution for some of the training and employment problems that currently exist in the applied sport psychology profession. This response questions some of their assumptions and conclusions and offers several alternative solutions to these problems in a more balanced analysis of the current situation. It is hoped that these articles will stimulate further discussion at AAASP meetings and among practicing professionals.

Almost 20 years ago (Danish & Hale, 1981), we suggested a possible model for the development of the applied sport psychology profession. We expected and received both opposition and praise. In the interim, AAASP was formed, as was a certification program for sport psychology consultants. This certification program has helped move the organization and its members toward professionalization as it focuses on the competence of the individual seeking certification. Unfortunately, recognition by the public of sport psychology as a unique profession, separate from psychology, has not been forthcoming.

If sport psychology is to continue its efforts to become a unique profession, additional steps must be taken. We applaud the efforts of Silva

---

Bruce D. Hale, Academic Support Services for Student-Athletes; Steven J. Danish, Director, Life Skills Center, Department of Psychology.

Correspondence concerning this article should be addressed to Bruce D. Hale, 109 Memorial Gymnasium, University of Maine, Orono, ME 04469. Electronic mail may be sent via Internet to Bruce.Hale@umit.maine.edu.

1041-3200/99/0321–0328$1.00/0

et al. (1999) to take the next step, although we do not agree with the direction they recommend. As part of their discussion about program accreditation, they raise a number of important issues including the ownership of sport psychology programs and how they differ from exercise science programs, the lack of adequate resources and specialist staffing, and foremost, the inadequate training of recent graduates in sport psychology. It is ironic that many of the issues they raise are identical to some of the questions we raised in earlier papers (Danish & Hale, 1981, 1982).

The suggestions they make about the importance of the marketing of sport psychology, the creation of outreach opportunities, a graduate student consultant position, and the improvement of the supervised practicum, should be heeded. However, we adamantly disagree that accreditation is the needed solution. In our initial article, we took the role of active proselytizers for a new model, this time we take the role of vociferous skeptics. We question the rationale of their conclusions, the relevancy of their historical analogies, and the accuracy of their assumptions about the state of sport psychology. In this reply, we will discuss our concerns as well as propose possible alternatives.

Putting the "Accreditation Cart" in Front of the "Needs Horse"

While we share many of the authors' concerns about such issues as the over-recruitment of graduate students, the lack of clarity in many of the training programs, the lack of expert supervisors, and the inadequate training in applied interventions, we cannot agree that "lack of organizational movement toward training enhancement and accreditation has slowed economic and employment developments in the field" (Silva et al., 1999, p. 5).

Like many of their conclusions, we think the authors have misinterpreted the history of applied psychology and ignored recent developments. Most of all, however, they have side-stepped the most critical issue–does the need for applied sport psychologists really exist? Before implementing widespread accreditation of graduate programs, the profession must first determine whether the public actually needs applied sport psychology services. The authors incorrectly cite the history of APA-accreditation of clinical psychology programs as an analogous situation to what currently exists in applied sport psychology. As they rightly note, the impetus for accreditation of APA programs was the tremendous demand for trained clinicians to treat soldiers who incurred psychological complications as a result of World War II. Where is the analogous situation in sport psychology? Whenever we make a decision to intervene in a situation (in this case, initiating program accreditation), regardless of how well our intentions, if it is directed at a solution that is irrelevant to the problem, the solution itself can become the problem. In other words, the unintended consequences of our decision may be greater than the intended ones. We fear that is the case with accreditation. As Luke Patrick (personal communication, December 8, 1998, via SPORTPSY on the Internet) has argued:

> The history of certification, accreditation and licensure across the professions shows that three factors need to be in place for the proverbial ball to get rolling: (a) an appreciable segment of society that needs a particular services; (b) evidence that the lay public cannot adequately provide the service to itself; and (c) reason to believe that there is a cost to inadequate service provision (i.e., people get hurt, or even more significant, lose money as a result of unqualified individuals providing services). It is this need that drives accreditation, and not vice versa. If despite all our enthusiasm and hard work, this need for sport psychology has not been recognized on a large scale for thirty some years, we need to regroup, folks.

Since the need for the service has not yet been established, the push for accreditation is "putting the cart before the horse." The authors identify three critical training challenges for our profession: (a) establishing a recognizable program identity, (b) establishing a program composed of a critical mass of sport psychology faculty, and (c) developing and establishing supervised practicum experiences. None of these challenges requires prior accreditation of graduate programs to become a reality. Why not enhance the quality of the horse first (increase the public need for sport psychology), and determine whether accreditation is the best way to meet these challenges, before we spend a lot of time and money redesigning the cart?

Silva et al. also overestimate the status of applied sport psychology training within the structure of most current exercise science- or psychology-based graduate programs. One can conclude from a cursory examination of listed programs in sport psychology that about 90% of all graduate programs in sport psychology are still offered within physical education or exercise science departments, and most programs still emphasize research and teaching, not applied interventions. In the fourth edition of the Directory of Graduate Programs in Applied Sport Psychology (Sachs, Burke, & Butcher, 1995), only about 45 graduate programs in North America offer some sort of doctoral degree in sport psychology, and none list "applied sport psychology" as their major specialization. Although the fifth edition of the Directory encourages program directors to estimate the extent of an applied emphasis in their programs, the percentage has not changed significantly in four years. Applied sport psychology remains a minor area.

Some psychology departments offer sub-specializations in sport psychology as a part of their counseling or clinical psychology programs, but the numbers are few and do not seem to be expanding. Finally, within most exercise science departments, training in applied sport psychology is still a small part of the program, and the usual focus is on a research and teaching emphasis. We may want applied sport psychology to be a strong emphasis in graduate training, but it is not yet, and there seems to be no movement toward a greater emphasis. The authors seem to ignore this reality.

The Dangers of Investing in Designing a Fancy Accreditation Cart

A. Will Universities Pay for Accreditation?

Silva et al. suggest that accreditation will bring financial benefits and resources to sport psychology programs. Until very recently, accreditation teams used to be able to lobby university administrators for more resources. However, as their budgets have tightened and the concept of accreditation has lost some of its clout, universities have become less willing to provide more resources. Comparisons with twenty-year old accreditation efforts in other professions, such as NATA and APA, may be historically interesting, but have limited relevancy to today. Unless a program has been identified as critical to the mission of the university, administrators are unlikely to be bullied into adding more resources. To the best of our knowledge, no sport psychology program has received this designation. As Department Chair David Dzewaltowski (personal communication, December 7, 1998, via SPORTPSY on the Internet) noted:

> Does any institution offer a degree program in sport psychology? From an administrative perspective, funding a degree program is very different than having an emphasis area. If there is a degree program in the United States, how was it justified? In other words, what rationale was provided? Would any sport psychology degree program (as defined by AAASP at the Ph.D. level) be able to justify itself due to college mission, credit hour production, extramural funding, and/or job availability? Why would an institution of higher learning be concerned with spending money on accreditation or responding to the recommendations of an evaluating agency of an emphasis area with one or two faculty and a few students?

B. The Politics of Accreditation

Justifying accreditation to universities from a resource perspective is just one of the problems we face. There are political and legal realities of accreditation as well. For an accreditation process to be recognized by university administrators, AAASP would have to become a recognized accrediting entity by the division within the U.S. Department of Education (DOE) that is responsible for recognizing accrediting bodies, the Accreditation and Eligibility Determination Division of the Office of Postsecondary Education. It is difficult to imagine that this group would not be concerned that we would be seeking to accredit a part of a profession that another organization controls. One needs only to look at the definition of a psychologist developed by APA to see that "applied sport psychologist" can easily be subsumed under this title. DOE would likely recommend that AAASP work this out with APA, and this would be impossible. For if APA acceded to our request, their control of the licensing of psychologists would be in serious jeopardy and that would impact psychological practitioners' third party payments. Therefore, AAASP would need to take legal action and the battle that would ensue would truly parallel the one between David and Goliath. Our "legal slingshots" would be far too weak. It is important to remember that the battle would not be just between APA and AAASP, although that would be overwhelming enough. It would be between APA and the state licensing boards, which are regulatory commissions, on the one side, and AAASP on the other. AAASP has neither the money, power, nor will to challenge either the licensing boards or APA.

C. The Financial and Psychological Costs to AAASP

The largest, and potentially, most damaging problems are internal. Accreditation is expensive. Standards have to be promulgated. There are some members who feel that the present certification standards do not adequately assess the candidate's applied skills. What will happen when we try to develop accreditation standards? The process to develop these standards is likely to be intensive, expensive, and fraught with conflict. In case anyone has forgotten, talk to someone who was on the AAASP committee to determine certification standards or review the minutes of those meetings. And remember those standards pertained just to individuals, not a whole institution or program. Accreditation has much more to do with an individual's career since to date certification has not provided additional opportunities for those awarded certification. The benefits of developing standards that the organization can accept may not be worth the costs of organizational disunity.

If standards are developed, site visitors will have to be selected and trained; higher education institutions will need to prepare the reports that serve as the information that is evaluated (these reports are often several hundred pages long); each site visitor will have to receive a copy of the report, review the report and visit the site; the visitors will be required to write evaluative reports and send them to a central place; the Accreditation Committee will need to meet and review materials, and if a program is not approved, the Committee will need to provide due process which involves the ability to appeal. The appeal will come from a university with all its legal capabilities. Someone will need to pay for the appeal procedures, hearings, attorneys, and hearing officers. If these costs are billed in their entirety back to the applicant, it will make accreditation less attractive. If a program is denied accreditation, it has the option of suing AAASP in civil court. If a suit is filed, AAASP must be prepared to pay legal expenses, hearings, and any penalties that may accrue. The insurance costs for initiating such a program will be extremely high, and with the first appeal will become higher. Finally, all of these procedures have to be worked out and put in place as a part of the development of standards. It will take several years to do all this and require considerable organizational support, staff, and equipment. Dues will need to be raised significantly.

Furthermore, one of the issues DOE considers in the recognition process is a requirement that the relationship between the sponsoring association and the accreditation function must be sufficiently separate to assure that accreditation cannot be influenced by political interests within the association. Given that the Executive Board of AAASP has fiduciary responsibility for our activities, and this would include accreditation, a complete system would need to be developed so the Board could exercise this responsibility without interfering in the process. Considerable clarification of the bylaws and statements of relationships to insure an independent office with independent staff would be necessary.

D. The Impact of Accreditation on Training

Silva et al. also seem to infer that creating standards and establishing formal programs will not have a deleterious effect on program content. The effect of APA accreditation has drastically reduced program flexibility and continues to do so. Danish and Smyer (1981) have described some of these restrictions, and the list of "shoulds" developed by Silva et al. that are included in their recommended program also provide a glimpse of the narrowing of educational choice.

Moreover, the accreditation standards become a set of guidelines that replace an assessment of an individual's competence. This is true for APA. Candidates from accredited programs who have completed all the coursework are automatically seated for the licensing exam which has little or nothing to do with applied competencies. Once they pass the test and have the necessary applied experiences (mostly unevaluated), they are licensed. Our certification program may not be all we want it to be, but it is as least as rigorous in assessing applied competencies. Because of the lack of adequate assessment of competence, it is possible that practitioners from accredited applied sport psychology programs who are sued for malpractice could sue their program and university for inadequate preparation, as could the plaintiff.

Alternatives for Enhancing Applied Training and Our Image

Silva et al. offer some very useful improvements to enhance training, marketing, and delivery of applied sport psychology services. The initial step of hiring a graduate marketing consultant to staff an AAASP office in order to enhance the image of applied sport psychology and to explain the nature of services makes good sense. Why not have this individual undertake a market needs assessment survey to see how well the public understands our profession and practices and how much they would be willing to use our services? Once we know what their needs are, we can move programs forward to target these needs. As part of this assessment we should consider expanding our reach and work with youth (Danish, Green, & Brunelle, 1997).

Recently AAASP, under the leadership of President Robin Vealey, established a Committee of Graduate Training to survey the general population's needs, offer proposals to enhance graduate training, undertake market planning, self evaluate graduate training models, assess levels of consultants' competencies, and examine the need for future accreditation. This committee should be allowed to formulate proposals before any move toward accreditation occurs.

The first step toward accreditation could be tried with little cost to anyone. This would involve the development of criteria or proposed accreditation standards by the committee. Then current programs could engage in self study to see how closely they meet these criteria and what obstacles would have to be overcome to meet them. Or why not have one or several current programs, like the University of North Carolina at Chapel Hill for instance, begin a trial program where they bring in external reviewers to assess whether they meet the proposed criteria or not and have the university pay the evaluators to write a report? Then see if the university would be willing to fund such improvements and actually make them. After several years, examine whether the strengthened program increases enrollments, job opportunities, and evaluations of graduates. These small experiments at several schools would be more cost effective than forcing all programs to accept accreditation with no guarantee of positive results.

As an unlicensed exercise scientist and a licensed psychologist, we both agree that the current AAASP applied graduate training is inadequate. If the major problem of professional acceptance by the public is created by a poor training process that produces poorly prepared professionals, which then causes a poor impression where the market does not respond to these "amateurs," then the immediate solution is to make the training process more rigorous. Perhaps AAASP could take a lesson from the British Association of Sport and Exercise Sciences (BASES), which requires a planned three-year supervised experience including greater contact hours with clients, closer professional supervision, and even payment to supervisors. This simple step could enhance consultants' competencies without heading down the long, expensive road toward accreditation. Furthermore, AAASP, like BASES, might then consider rewarding some kind of certification to Master's graduates who complete this closely monitored practicum during their program.

Certainly it will benefit the public, AAASP, and individual practitioners if more applied consultants are certified by AAASP. It may be easier to find new ways to offer incentives to become certified rather than close the door on young professionals who do not graduate from accredited programs. Perhaps we can convince all NGBs for Olympic sports to only hire certified consultants to work with elite teams. If the financial benefits of consulting could be improved, more individuals would become certified and the overall quality of practitioners would increase, leading to a greater need for services in the future.

These are but a few suggestions that we hope the Graduate Training Committee will contemplate. It makes sense to try small steps first to see if the market for services can be enhanced.

Let the Discussion Continue

In our response (Danish & Hale, 1982) to others' criticism of the sport psychology delivery model that we presented 18 years ago, we realized that not all professionals would jump on our "cart" and embrace our model. Over the years some of our ideas have been vindicated (e.g., the NCAA CHAMPS Life Skills model), others have been reworked. We call on the profession and AAASP to enthusiastically debate the proposals made by Silva et al. and closely evaluate the potential long-term consequences of adopting accreditation requirements. It is our position that currently accreditation is an unnecessary bureaucratic exercise that will not solve the basic problems that exist in the applied sport psychology profession, and may, in fact, hurt us. Smaller steps taken to create a national market for applied professionals, internal movements in AAASP to enhance the quality of graduate programs and supervised experience, and the education of general public will result in many of the same goals identified by Silva et al. without the unwarranted costs and dangers of accreditation.

Let the discussion continue.

REFERENCES

Danish, S., Green, S. & Brunelle, J. (1997) Expanding sport psychology's reach. *AAASP Newsletter, 12 (3),* 14–15.

Danish, S. J., & Hale, B. D. (1981). Toward an understanding of the practice of sport psychology. *Journal of Sport Psychology, 3,* 90–99.

Danish, S. J., & Hale, B. D. (1982). Let the discussions continue: Further considerations on the practice of sport psychology. *Journal of Sport Psychology, 4,* 10–12.

Danish, S. J. & Smyer, M. A. (1981). The unintended consequences of requiring a license to help. *American Psychologist, 36,* 13–21.

Sachs, M., Burke, K., & Butcher, L. (eds.) (1995). *Directory of graduate programs in applied sport psychology*. Morgantown, WV: Fitness Information Technology, Inc.

Silva, J., Conroy, D., & Zizzi, S. (in press). Critical issues confronting the advancement of applied sport psychology. *Journal of Applied Sport Psychology.*

Manuscript submitted: March 22, 1999
Revision received: May 25, 1999